ON THE TRAIL OF MERLIN

The authors at Merlin's Stone, Carmarthen.

ON THE TRAIL
OF MERLIN

A Guide to the
Celtic Mystery Tradition

Ean Begg & Deike Rich

The Aquarian Press
An Imprint of HarperCollins*Publishers*

The Aquarian Press
An Imprint of GraftonBooks
A Division of HarperCollins*Publishers*
77–85 Fulham Palace Road,
Hammersmith, London W6 8JB

Published by
The Aquarian Press 1991

10 9 8 7 6 5 4 3 2 1

A CIP catalogue record for this book
is available from the British Library

ISBN 0-85030-939-5

Typeset by Harper Phototypesetters
Limited, Northampton, England
Printed in Hong Kong

Contents

Acknowledgements 8

Introduction 9

England 39

Wales and the Marches 73

Isle of Man 95

Ireland 115

Scotland 143

Brittany 159

Spain 189

Glossary 196

Bibliography 202

Index 206

Acknowledgements

So many people have helped us in so many ways in the writing of this book that a complete list of them would run into pages. It also seems invidious to single any out for special acknowledgement, but without Jacqueline Modé and her two fellow 'druidesses', Martine and Claudine, we would have been hard put to it to penetrate the mysteries of **Brocéliande**. In Wales, Robin Holtom was an invaluable and tireless guide, a fine photographer and a kindly host. Our thanks are also due to Tom MacIntyre, poet and playwright, author of *Rise Up Fair Sweeney,* for the invaluable light he shone on our trail through Ireland. As for the great debt we owe to earlier writers, we ask them to accept our gratitude through the pages of our bibliography which, although not comprehensive, is one in which all the books have been carefully consulted and have played their part in ours.

We would have got nowhere without our maps and are grateful to their compilers and publishers. The maps we have used in this book, unless otherwise indicated, are as follows:

England, Wales, Scotland and the Isle of Man: Ordnance Survey 1986 *Motoring Atlas of Great Britain* and Ordnance Survey *Landranger* series.
Northern Ireland: Michelin and Ordnance Survey of Northern Ireland
Irish Republic: Michelin and Ordnance Survey of Ireland
France and **Spain**: Michelin

All photographs by the authors except the following:

The authors at Merlin's Stone by Robin Holtom
Glastonbury Tor and Cadbury Castle by Simon McBride, courtesy of Susan Griggs Agency, London
Loe Pool by Phyllis Smith
Afon Pib by Robin Holtom
Merlin's Bridge at Navahermosa by Jennifer Begg
The Cave of Montesinos by Connie Burchell-Rich

Introduction

The Zen of Pilgrimage

There are many good reasons for not writing a guidebook to Merlin. If he ever existed, it was almost 1500 years ago and, from the strictly historical viewpoint, cannot be linked plausibly to more than one or two sites on the borders of what is now England and Scotland; yet he has half a dozen tombs dotted round the Celtic lands of the West. So, on the one hand, the whole project is too fey and fanciful, while on the other, it is too pedantically literal and concretistic in its obsession with map references and directions. Every people has its own sacred mountains, springs, rocks, trees – its own Merlin – which symbolize inner states and psychic experiences, so to hunt them all down with the Ordnance Survey is surely missing the point. Furthermore, the essence of these places is their elusive seclusion and mysterious solitude, so to encourage people to go there is to risk the destruction of something precious and fragile, the very object of this quest. Merlin and the Celtic spirit, whose representative he is, are indeed fragile, but enduring. His subterranean cry is still audible and still uncomprehended, but, with the circling of the years, it may be that this is the right time to seek once more the Holy Grail, the vital question concerning the meaning of existence, that needs to be answered anew. This is an inner quest, but it needs to be incarnated in a matter, and for the errant one on the way, this matter is the Zen of pilgrimage, in which inner and outer reflect each other. Such few pilgrims and fellow wayfarers as actually find any of the stages of the treasure hunt will know they are on holy ground, and pass through it as unobtrusively and courteously as a stag or wolf.

Pilgrimage – travel to a sacred site for the good of the soul – died in Britain with the Reformation. In the United States it never existed. Tourism is something different – travel to broaden the mind, satisfy curiosity, or simply to seek pleasure and relaxation in a more favourable climate – and is largely an Anglo-American invention that has now become a world-wide phenomenon and a major industry. True pilgrimage has never ceased to play an important part in the lives of almost all peoples other than Protestant Christians. Whereas Mecca exists solely for salvation, and all Moslems yearn to make the Haj at least once in a lifetime, Rome and Chartres, not being forbidden cities, have suffered some contamination of their sacredness by the demands of mass tourism. Of course, from the very earliest days, trips to Jerusalem, Rome, Canterbury and **Santiago de Compostela**, were expected to provide sightseeing and fun as part of the trip, and restaurants, souvenir shops and guides flourished as a result. Nevertheless, the pilgrims were all part of the living cultural and spiritual tradition, at one with the shrines they were visiting. The Bible stories and lives of the saints that they saw depicted all around them in the great cathedrals were like the air they breathed, as familiar and interesting to them as the characters and dramas of popular television series to people today. Some holy places, like Delphi and Assisi, still possess the alchemical power to transform tourists into pilgrims, but mostly the coach-loads gaze, alienated, as the pageant of the past unfolds, at a story of which they are no longer a part.

One aim of this book is to rekindle the embers of the pilgrim instinct that lies deep in the heart of each of us and has been considered good for the soul at all times and in all places. For the aim is not an antiquarian quest for things past, but a journey to another world that is both inner and outer. However far-fetched such an aim might seem, it is fully in keeping with the traditions of the Celts, in which myth and history are often indistinguishable and the Otherworld no further away than the fairy mound at the end of the lane. Of the great figures in the Celtic tales one is never quite sure what world they belong to, whether they are heroes and heroines, gods and goddesses, or both. Although they are our ancestors and spirits of the land, we know them less well than the deities of Olympus, organized for us and filtered through centuries of classical scholarship. In our faerie lands forlorn there is no Parthenon, no Paestum; we have no Homer or Virgil to sing of gods and men; the names of the characters are confusing, constantly interchangeable and difficult to pronounce. In spite of these apparent disadvantages, we believe that the Celtic world particularly lends itself to the sort of pilgrimage we have in mind.

If it is true that the gods never return to temples once profaned, then a religion without temples made with hands provides a lasting point of contact with the spirits of its sacred places, as long as technology, with its noise and business, does not impinge too far. The sites we shall be visiting are for the most part off the beaten track of mass tourism, far from cities and motorways, tepid seas and beach umbrellas. They are hard to find and may entail walking through bogs and briars in those mists with which Celtic magicians know only too well how to enshroud the land and hide its hallows. On such journeys it is often not until you lose yourself that you stand any chance of finding yourself, which is the true goal of pilgrimage.

The literary sources

What the old French poets called the *Matière de Bretagne*, stories from the Celtic West, began to percolate into the consciousness of the rest of Europe around the beginning of the twelfth century, the same period that witnessed the building of the great cathedrals to Our Lady, the foundation of the Templars, the rise of the Troubadours and the flowering of the alternative Christianity known as Catharism. The phenomenal success of this Celtic material spread with great speed through France, England, Germany, Spain and Italy, where as early as 1125 King Arthur and his knights were carved on the portal of Modena Cathedral. This was the Grail that the wasteland of Europe in the Dark Ages had been thirsting for. Through the centuries the tales became ever more tangled and involved in the telling, until all lands, from Iceland to Sicily, had found their places at the Round Table. What an odyssey we should have had if we had attempted a guidebook to all those places which now by extension can claim some connection to Merlin's legend – one lifetime would scarcely suffice. So we had to be content with the imprint of his enchantment on the ancient Celtic realms of Britain, Ireland, Brittany and Galicia.

Historia Regum Britanniae

The first question many will want to ask is: 'Was there ever a real person called Merlin?' The answer has to be that we don't know. The first clear written reference to him by name occurs in *The History of the Kings of Britain* by Geoffrey of Monmouth, which appeared in 1136, incorporating a somewhat earlier work, *The Prophecies of Merlin*, which gives no biographical details. Geoffrey situates Merlin in the period when Vortigern was King of the British about the middle of the fifth century. Vortigern almost certainly did exist since he is mentioned by the Welsh historian Nennius who wrote at the beginning of the ninth century and gives this name to the *pre-eminent ruler* or *proud tyrant* referred to by an earlier writer, Gildas, who was born in about AD500. Vortigern is execrated as a murderer, usurper and traitor who invited the Saxons to settle in Briton as mercenaries.

According to Geoffrey's account, Vortigern tried to build a strong-hold in Snowdonia whose foundations daily collapsed. His magicians advised him to sacrifice a fatherless child and mix his blood with the mortar. His spies discovered in **Carmarthen** a boy whose mother was a nun and the daughter of the King of Demetia and whose father was an incubus. This was Merlin, surnamed Ambrosius or Emrys. Taken before Vortigern, he confounded the magicians by telling them of two dragons in a pool beneath the foundations that were the cause of the instability. Merlin then makes a number of prophecies about the future of Britain and the continued struggles of the white dragon and the red dragon, culminating in the prediction that the true rulers, Aurelius and Uther are on their way from Brittany with an army, to overthrow Vortigern. This comes to pass and Aurelius assumes the throne, defeats the Saxons and restores order in the land. He wishes to erect a memorial to the scores of British Chieftains whom Hengist and his men treacherously massacred at a banquet. Merlin is suggested as architect and proposes bringing the stones of the Giants' Ring from **Mount Killaraus** in Ireland and setting them up at **Stonehenge**. This he does with the help of an army led by Uther Pendragon. When they return with the stones Merlin correctly interprets the appearance of a comet as announcing the death of Aurelius and the succession of Uther to the kingship.

Their next meeting is when Uther, crazed with lust for Ygraine, wife of Gorlois, Duke of Cornwall, sends for Merlin to help him win her. By his art, Merlin transforms Uther into the exact likeness of Gorlois and accompanies him with another escort, both of them disguised as trusted friends of Gorlois, into the impregnable castle of **Tintagel**. There Uther spends the night with Ygraine, and Arthur is conceived while Gorlois dies in a sortie from Dimilioc. This is Merlin's last appearance in Geoffrey's *History* except for one reference at the very end to a prophecy he makes to Arthur concerning the right time for the Britons to regain the sovereignty of their land.

Vita Merlini

In his later Latin poem of 1530 lines, the *Vita Merlini*, Geoffrey of Monmouth gives quite a different account of Merlin's life. Here he is King of Demetia (Dyfed) as well as a bard and prophet. He takes up arms in support of his friend Peredur (Perceval), King of Venedotia (Gwynnedd), along with Rodarcus, King of the Cambrians (Rhydderch of Strathclyde) in a war against Guennolous, King of Scocia. After a great battle, in which the three brothers of Peredur are killed, Merlin goes mad with grief and retires to the forest of Calidon. Here he lives as a wild man of the woods among the animals, feeding on roots, herbs and wild fruits. In winter he falls on hard times and bewails his lot and that of his dear companion, a wolf, now aged and starving.

His sister, Ganieda, the wife of King Rodarcus, sends a messenger to persuade him to join them at court, but, once there, Merlin soon grows restless and pines for the wilds of Calidon with its oaks, hills, glens and meadows. No coaxing, not even the gift of cups wrought by Wayland the Smith, can persuade him to remain, so the King puts him in protective custody. He languishes, silent and sad, until one day the King, when caressing Ganieda's hair, dislodges a leaf from it. All are amazed when Merlin bursts out laughing and, after some discussion, Rodarcus agrees to set him free if he will explain why. Merlin tells him that Ganieda picked up the leaf while dallying with her lover in the greenwood.

In an attempt to discredit Merlin as a seer, Ganieda introduces one of her pages in three different guises and asks her brother to foretell the death these apparently different individuals will suffer. He predicts three different fates, and thus in the eyes of the King fails the test. He still yearns, however, to return to the forest. Ganieda asks what would then become of his wife, who up till now has played no part in the story, and Merlin responds that she is free to remarry on condition that he never sees the new husband.

Merlin is released, and the youth, who was used to test him, dies the triple death – falling from a rock, hanging on a tree and drowning – that had been prophesied. Happy in his forest, Merlin one night observes the planet Venus emitting a double ray and knows that his wife Guendoloena is about to remarry. He sets off the next day, riding a great stag and leading a herd of deer as her wedding present. The bridegroom, watching from an upstairs window, laughs to see the prophet so strangely mounted. At this Merlin tears off an antler, hurls it at him and kills him instantly. While escaping, he falls into a river, is recaptured and taken back to court.

Once again he pines for the natural life and Rodarcus, to distract him, takes him for a walk round the town. Merlin twice emits his famous laugh, on seeing a door-keeper begging and a young man buying a new pair of shoes. He later explains to his brother-in-law that the beggar was seated on a treasure and the youth has already drowned. Rodarcus is now prepared to bow to the prophet's will, but Ganieda still begs him to stay.

Merlin persuades her to let him go by allowing her to build him as a forest home an observatory with 70 doors and 70 windows, where she may install servants to look after him and where she may visit him as often as she wishes.

During one of her stays, after a number of prophecies concerning future disasters, Merlin tells her to return to court as Rodarcus is dying. He also says she will find the great poet Taliesin there, newly returned from consulting with St Gildas the Wise in Brittany, and asks her to invite him to the forest. This Ganieda does, and, after burying Rodarcus, determines to join Merlin and Taliesin and devote her life to the service of God in the wilderness.

Meantime the two sages have been enjoying a wonderful conversation, with Taliesin discoursing on the creation of the four-tiered universe, and the nature of earth, moon, sun and stars and the beings that inhabit the different cosmic levels. Finally, Taliesin gives a long description of Avalon, the Isle of Apple Trees and abode of Morgan, to which he and Merlin, piloted by Barinthus, had conducted the wounded Arthur. He wonders if the King is now healed and ready to return, but Merlin replies that the calamities are not yet at an end, and will not be so until all Britons unite to evict their foes and redeem the fallen sceptre. He then recounts the whole history of their times from the flight of Ambrosius and Uther to the treachery of Mordred and Arthur's depature for Avalon.

At this point the dialogue is interrupted by the arrival of a messenger announcing the emergence of a new spring on the mountain-

Fountain of Barenton. Here Merlin, disguised as a student, met Vivian, fell in love with her and performed his magic for her.

side. As soon as Merlin drinks of it and washes his face he comes fully to himself once more. Taliesin provides a commentary by describing all the famous healing fountains of the world, including **Barenton**. The notables of the land flock to the spot and beg Merlin to be King, but he declines, revealing to them his great age, older than the oldest tree in the forest, where he is determined to remain.

A flock of cranes flies overhead, prompting Merlin to give a disquisition on the nature of various species of birds. As he is speaking, a madman rushes up, whom Merlin recognizes as a former friend of his, Maeldin. Once, when they had been hunting with others, they had stopped by a spring to refresh themselves and had eaten the sweet-smelling apples that lay strewn on the grass, all, that is, except Merlin, as there were not quite enough to go round. Those who ate of the apples ran off wild and mad into the forest – the apples having been poisoned by a woman who had loved Merlin and lived long years with him despite his scorn, and was now seeking revenge.

Maeldin drinks from the spring and returns to his right mind. He decides to join Merlin in his retreat, Taliesin follows suit and Ganieda makes the fourth, soon to assume Merlin's mantle of prophecy, which he gladly surrenders to her.

Medieval Welsh Texts

It was long academic fashion to accuse the much maligned Geoffrey of Monmouth of having completely invented Merlin and all his works. Such a view is no longer tenable. In the Welsh literature there are various references to a character called Myrddin, whose history is similar to Geoffrey's Merlin, and a number of poems ascribed to him which also provide source material for the *Vita*. In their present form all these writings belong to the century after Geoffrey or later, but the core of some of them dates back as far as the sixth century. It is generally accepted that Myrddin's name was latinized into Merlinus to avoid unpleasant associations with French *merde* and Latin *merda*. One should not forget, however, that the twelfth century was the time of the earliest troubadours to whom play on words was an important part of their hidden, green poetic language of birds. It would not have been lost on poets that the word Merlin meant fish and bird, weapon and battlement, among various other possibilities. Myrddin itself signifies sea-fortress in Welsh, more specifically that of **Carmarthen**.

For a full account of Geoffrey's possible sources in Welsh literature we refer the reader to Tolstoy's *Quest for Merlin* or *Merlin in the Earliest Records* with which Geoffrey Ashe introduces *The Book of Merlin* where he demonstrates the development of Geoffrey's researches in the course of writing the *Prophecies*, the *Histories* and the *Vita Merlini*.

In the *Black Book of Carmarthen* there is a dialogue of Myrddin and Taliesin where the two bards describe and discuss the Battle of **Arderydd**. Myrddin reveals that 140 men of rank suffered battle-madness and perished in the forest of Celyddon. Of the poems attributed to Myrddin himself from the *Black Book of Carmarthen*, the *Apple-trees* tells of a love-affair with Gwenddydd (Ganieda), problems with Rhydderch, the torque of gold which he wore at **Arderydd**, his guilt at the death there of Gwenddydd's son and his grief at the loss of his lord, Gwenddolau. He suggests that the apple-tree, at whose foot he had dallied amorously and which stood on a hill (cf. **Broad Law** near **Drumelzier**), was a place of supernatural refuge for himself and his little pig. In his poem *Greetings* he apostrophizes the pig at some length, bewailing the indifference of Gwenddydd, the persecutions of Rhydderch and the thinness of his cloak in the bitter cold. From the *Red Book of Hergest* comes the dialogue between Myrddin and his sister Gwenddydd in which she comforts him in his grief and forgives him for the death of her son at **Arderydd** as well as encouraging him to receive Communion before his death. A stranger reference, in the *White Book of Rhydderch*, seems to make Merlin the primordial deity of Britain, which bore the name *Clas Merdin, Merlin's Precinct*, before the first settlers came here. The mysterious, very small book in the British tongue, lent to Geoffrey by the Archdeacon of Oxford, and which Markale surmises came from Brittany, must have provided Geoffrey's main source for material not found in the Welsh texts mentioned above.

So much for the major sources of Geoffrey's work. As for the extra-ordinary proliferation of Merlin literature from the period of Geoffrey of Monmouth to the present day, it is clearly beyond the scope of this guidebook even to attempt a summary and we therefore refer the reader to the bibliography. Four texts, however – *L'Estoire de Merlin*, *Huth Merlin*, *Didot Perceval* and *Buile Suibhne* – are of exceptional importance.

L'Estoire de Merlin

L'Estoire de Merlin is one of a five-volume series dating from the early thirteenth century known as the *Vulgate Cycle* and sometimes as the *Prose Lancelot*, one of the volumes.

The book opens with a prologue in hell in which Satan decides to arrange the incarnation of an *Antichrist*. The conception and birth of Merlin then proceed much as in Geoffrey of Monmouth:

The infant Merlin, exceptionally hairy, saves his mother from execution by drawing attention to the judge's own irregular paternity. After the overthrow of Vortigern and Uther Pendragon's succession to the throne, he summons Merlin to court, but Merlin, in the guise of wood-cutter, a shepherd and a boy, makes the King come to him in the forest before helping him against the Saxons and bringing back the stones of Ireland to **Stonehenge**.

The Tintagel episode does not differ much from Geoffrey's account but after the birth of Arthur, we are told, Merlin entrusts him to a wise knight, Antor, who already has a son called Kay.

Merlin returns to the forest until the death of Uther sixteen years later. Consulted by the barons about the future of the monarchy, he places a stone with an anvil, in which a sword is inserted, outside the cathedral at Christmas. Whoever succeeded in drawing the sword would be the new King. The familiar story then unfolds in which Arthur gains *Excalibur* and the kingdom, though not without difficulty. The barons rebel and are only defeated through the magic of Merlin and the courage of Arthur. Merlin then urges Arthur to assist King Leodagan in Brittany who is at war with King Claudas, the vassal of Julius Caesar. Merlin at this point retires to the forest of Romania, near Rome, where he resolves Julius Caesar's marital problems. Caesar's wife has twelve lovers disguised as ladies-in-waiting. The Emperor's seneschal is a beautiful young woman who is also in travesty. In his confusion, Caesar has a dream which he cannot understand. A stag (Merlin) appears the next day, kneels before the Emperor and tells him that the only person who can explain his vision is the wild man. Caesar finds the wild man who, with a great meaningful laugh, interprets the dream, after which the Empress is executed and Grisandole, the seneschal, takes her place.

Meantime Arthur has fallen in love with Leodagan's daughter Guinevere. Merlin, on his return, advises the King to pursue the war in Britain against the Saxons while he himself visits the **Forest of Brocéliande** where he falls in love with Vivian (see **Barenton**).

He then visits Arthur in disguise and urges him to establish the Round Table. The seat to the right of the King should always remain empty in memory of Christ until the arrival of the best knight in the world, destined to achieve the Holy Grail. Having fulfilled his mission, Merlin turns his attention increasingly to Vivian in **Brocéliande**. He intervenes in a battle on Salisbury Plain between Arthur and one of his nephews, after which he attends the marriage of Arthur and Guinevere. He returns once more to Brittany in the company of King Ban and King Bohort and stage-manages the conceptions of Sir Lionel and Sir Lancelot, prior to his return to Vivian, to whom he imparts all but one of his magic secrets. After one final visit to Britain, where he helps Arthur to defeat the giants, Merlin tells the King and Queen that he is leaving them forever and that the Holy Grail is now in Brittany. Arthur then sends forth all the Knights of the Round Table in quest of Merlin and it is Gawain who finally hears his voice and talks to him in his enchanted castle of air where Vivian, having learnt his final spell, keeps him happily imprisoned:

> **I am madder than ever**
> **for I love my mistress Vivian**
> **more than my freedom.**

Huth Merlin

In about 1200 Robert de Boron wrote a vernacular French verse romance, *Merlin*, as a continuation of his *Joseph d'Arimathie*. Only a fragment of that poem remains, but the *Suite de Merlin* or *Huth Merlin*, a prose version, also of the thirteenth century, is believed to draw heavily on it as well as on other sources.

Two fourteenth-century manuscripts of this text, both incomplete, are still extant. One was lent by Alfred J. Huth (BLAWD 38117) to Gaston Paris and Jacob Ulrich, who published it in 1886. The other (Cambridge University Library ADD 7071), discovered in 1945 by Eugene Vinaver, still remains unpublished.

What distinguishes the *Huth Merlin* from other accounts is first of all the naming of Blaise. He was the confessor of Merlin's mother and became Merlin's companion and chronicler. Next we have the story of Arthur's incest with his half-sister, the wife of King Lot of Orkney, already the mother of Gawain. Merlin predicts the destruction of the kingdom, which the birth of Mordred, the fruit of this illicit union, will bring about. Arthur, out-heroding Herod, arranges a massacre of the innocents born around the fated time, but in the end they, and Mordred himself, are saved.

There then ensues a very different version of the *Excalibur* episode. A maiden, sent by Morgan from Avalon – possibly Morgan herself – arrives at court with a sword at her waist. Only a knight with a pure heart can undo its belt. Balin succeeds in this task but, against Merlin's advice, keeps the sword for himself. The consequences, Merlin prophesies, will be the casting of three kingdoms into mourning, thirty years of misery and the wounding of the holiest man in the world. Balin beheads the maiden and sets out on various adventures. Eventually, in a wonderful castle, he finds a lance in a golden basin. He wounds King Pellehan, the castle crumbles, Merlin appears – to announce that henceforth the kingdom will be known as the wasteland – and Balin dies.

The remainder of the story concerns Merlin's relationship with Nivienne (Vivian). She appears at Arthur's court hunting a white hart, and Merlin immediately falls in love with her. Eventually he accompanies her to Brittany where he builds a magical castle for her near the lake of Diana. Merlin predicts to King Ban and Queen Helen that their son Galahad/Lancelot, much beloved by Vivian, the Lady of the Lake, will become the best knight in the world. Vivian succeeds in enclosing Merlin in a tomb whose stone can never be raised. Merlin explains to King Bagdemagus that his efforts to free him are in vain. His cry, however, which continues to be heard throughout the kingdom, never ceases to be the source of wonders.

Didot-Perceval

This is a prose adaptation of *Perceval* by de Boron and quite possibly his own work with additions by other hands. It deals with Perceval's quest for the Holy Grail and the role Merlin plays in it.

The rich Fisher King, Brons, lies gravely ill in his castle in Ireland where the Grail is kept, but he cannot die until the best knight in the world comes and asks the vital Grail question. Perceval comes to King Arthur's court, having been sent there by his father, Alain le Gros, to become the greatest of all knights. Against Merlin's advice Arthur lets Perceval sit in the Siege Perilous, the stone splits and a cry issues from the dark, reproaching Arthur. Perceval promises to seek the Grail Castle without rest. He has various adventures, slaying knights and enjoying the hospitality of a damsel. He ends up in his father's house, where he was born, and there meets his sister who tells him that his mother has died of grief and of the Holy Grail and its properties. He promises that this time he will be successful. They go to the hermit (Merlin) who advises him not to kill any knights nor to be distracted by damsels, and to ask the Grail question. He sets out with his sister and is helped by two seven-year-old naked children in a tree who tell him about the Grail and where to find it. He finally reaches the castle where his grandfather, the Fisher King, entertains him richly. He is shown a bloodstained lance and a vessel containing blood, but he forgets to ask what they are for. The castle disappears, Perceval sets out again in search for it and wanders about for seven years, capturing many knights whom he sends to Arthur's court. Eventually Merlin comes to him and tells him to seek the Grail within a year. This time Perceval heeds the advice and when shown the Grail by the Fisher King asks: 'Whom does the Grail serve?' At this the old King is healed, transformed and then dies. Perceval becomes guardian of the Grail and the world is released from a spell. The Siege

Perilous is restored to wholeness and Merlin tells Arthur and the Knights of the Round Table that his task is completed and disappears.

Buile Suibhne

The text of this book is extensively described and quoted from in the introduction to and itineraries of Ireland. The original text of *Buile Suibhne* in the Royal Irish Academy was composed some time between 1200 and 1500, though, as with the Myrddin material, much of it dates back to the ninth century and probably much earlier. We have used the 1913 edition by J.G. O'Keeffe and the modern translation by Seamus Heaney, *Sweeney Astray*, first published in 1983.

Tolstoy, referring to the four distinct versions of Merlin's career that have survived, states: 'That they all ultimately represent the same saga (though obviously with accretions and distortions acquired along the way) is abundantly clear and is accepted by the best authorities.' Markale considers it an open question whether the legend of Sweeney derives from that of Merlin or vice versa.

Merlin and religion

The Old Gods

Janus-like in so many ways, Merlin faces both the old Celtic pagan religion and the new Celtic Christianity. He undoubtedly continued and embodied the spirit of druidism, and may even have been the last great druid of the Strathclyde Britons. He also, in his various forms, had close and ambiguous relations with a number of contemporary Christian saints, with some of whom he has even been identified. The last stand of the British druids against the might of Rome, so graphically described by Tacitus, was in about AD60 on the beaches of **Anglesey**, but in Ireland and the Scottish Highlands, druidism continued to thrive. We know this from the encounters of St Patrick, and other representatives of Christianity, with the druids. in AD570, when St Columba converted Nechtan, King of the Picts, to Christianity, near Inverness, he also chivalrously sent a healing stone to his adversary, Nechtan's chief druid Broichan.

The Romans had always tolerated the Celtic religion of the buffer states between the walls of Hadrian and Antoninus. So Merlin's position as chief druid to King Gwenddolau at the time of the battle of **Arderydd**, AD573, need occasion no surprise. Druidism and Christianity coexisted at the time to an extent that St Gildas found thoroughly reprehensible. The great early Celtic saints and Culdees were themselves Christianized druids, not the alien pedlars of a totally strange cult like the Levantine missionaries who spread the Gospel to the rest of Europe. Significantly, the early Irish Church is unique in having no martyrs.

What do we know of druidism and the druids? Nothing from any pre-Christian Celtic pen, for the only writings that have survived, in the form of Ogham inscriptions, do not tell us of religious belief or practice. Greek and Roman writers are our major source of information, and since the Celts, whose name, *Keltoi*, means the hidden ones, were their northern neighbours, their testimony should be taken seriously. They saw the Celts as a highly religious people, and their priests, the druids, as wise philosophers and magicians. The main element of Celtic religion was belief in the survival of the soul at death, followed by reincarnation. The druids, an aristocratic caste, celebrated religious rituals, acted as judges and instructors of youth, were prophets and diviners, knowledgeable in the lore of the stars and the healing properties of herbs. They lived in the depths of distant forests and held an annual convention near Chartres. They were comparable to the Magi, Brahmins and Chaldeans of the East, and, in terms of Greek philosophy, came closest to Pythagoras with whom they may have had some contact.

Among the classical writers who showed respect to the druids was Julius Caesar, who, however, had no hesitation in exterminating them wherever he could find them. His real reason was that they were the power behind the throne, the spirit of Celtic separateness and independence. The excuse given for their suppression was a familiar one: they were the instigators of the barbarian practice of human sacrifice, abandoned by the Romans some two centuries earlier. In fact, however, the Roman and Celtic religions had much in common. Both venerated the personified powers of nature, though the functions of the Mediterranean deities were much more clearly defined than those of the Celts who, in their individualistic way, had at least 400 different known names for their gods and goddesses. This is because the Celtic world was never unified and each tribe expressed its experience of the archetypes in its own idiosyncratic forms of worship. With such a variety, the Roman attempt to place an Olympian grid over the Celtic pantheon never quite worked. As will be evident, all the Celtic gods overlap, are linked by family ties and have many functions in common.

When they sacked Delphi the Celts laughed at the Greeks for worshipping gods in human form since *they* did not make their offerings to idols, preferring to cast them into lakes, wells, springs and rivers, to propitiate the life-giving force of Mother Nature.

Cernunnos

The male figure corresponding to Mother Nature is the Horned God, the stag-headed Cernunnos, Lord of Wild Things and closest in spirit to Merlin in his forest mode (see **Sherwood Forest**). This is the pre-Celtic shamanistic god of hunters, the magician whose likeness was painted on the cave-walls of Lascaux some 30,000 years ago. He also has a bull form, linking him to the age of Taurus (*c.*4000–2000BC), when the great megaliths were erected in what became the Celtic lands. The druids took over **Carnac** and **Stonehenge**, cut mistletoe, the panacea, from oak-trees in sacred groves, and sacrificed two white bulls to increase the fertility of their flocks and herds, which probably included deer. Up to 300 years ago Scottish Highlanders were still risking the wrath of the Kirk by sacrificing bulls at Loch Maree and other parts of the far north. Cernunnos has obvious affinities with Pan and Dionysos, but we only know them through classical art and literature from a distance of two thousand years. The stag's head still lives on in our culture as the title of the chief of Clan McKenzie and the badge of regiments, colleges, inns and families, as well as in the tales of Robin Hood and a number of extant pagan rituals such as the Abbots Bromley horn-dance. Shakespeare knew him as Herne the Hunter whose oak stands in Windsor Great Park. That he is not always horned is shown by the priapic colossi of Cerne and Wilmington. In Brittany he became canonized as those Christian druids Edern, Herbot, Ronan and Cornély. He had, however, already undergone a transformation in Roman times into Faunus, Dianus and Janus, the consort of the Lady of Wild Things, latinized as Diana. The aspects of Cernunnos that were unsuitable for canonization provided the major ingredients for the Christian iconography of the Devil, while the Tarot trump preserves something of his essential nature.

Belen

Another Celtic god related to both Cernunnos and Merlin is Bel/Belen/Bile. He is the lord of life and death, associated with the solar power in whose honour the Beltaine fires were lit on the eve of May Day and from which all household fires were kindled. One of Belen's sacred hills was Mont St Michel and another was the highest point in **Brocéliande** just above **Barenton**. From **Barenton** he rules the weather through his stone, now *le perron de Merlin*. As Hyperborean Apollo his temple was **Stonehenge**, where once again his path crosses Merlin's. His feast, Beltaine, 1st May, was when cattle were driven, between two fires, to the summer pastures, and when Venus and Maid Marian were licentiously celebrated round the Maypole as a preliminary to maying in the greenwood.

Lugh

The god with whom Tolstoy most closely associated Merlin is a pan-Celtic deity known variously as Lug, Lugh, Lugos and Llew. Important cities named after him range from Lugo in the west to Leignitz in the east and from Lucca in the south to Carlisle in the north, including Lyons, the bull-town of Laon (cf. **Carmarthen**), Leiden and probably London *en route*. He is the many-skilled one, god of all arts and crafts, with a long and sure hand wielding a magical spear. He is a bright, white, luminous, solar god like Belen, but his bird is the raven. Of the classical gods he much resembles Hermes/Mercury, but his most precise analogue is Wotan/Odin, a resemblance which Tolstoy makes much of in *The Coming of the King*. He suffers a threefold death, like Merlin, and has been associated by Hubert Butler in his *Ten Thousand Saints* with Moling, the saint who befriended Sweeney, the Irish Merlin, at the time of his triple death (see **St Molings**). His feast, Lughnasadh, 1st August, celebrated the feast of the first fruits of the harvest and was a time when trial marriages were entered into, farmhands were hired, animals were sold and annual games were held, lasting a fortnight (see **Teltown**), his last recorded appearance having been in AD177 when, in a mist, he introduced Conn of the Hundred Battles to the sovereignty of Eire, though he lingers on in much diminished form as the *Leprechaun* (little stooping Lugh). For links between Merlin and Lugh in his divinely youthful form of Mabon see **Lydney** and **Lochmaben**. Like other pagan gods, Lugh went underground with the advent of Christianity.

Bran

One other major Celtic deity merits attention for the close parallels he offers to elements in the Merlin myth. His name means *raven* and he was the son of Lir and brother of Manannan (see **Isle of Man**), both marine deities. He possessed a life-restoring cauldron, one of the prototypes of the Holy Grail, and may be the origin of Brons, the Fisher King, who was also wounded in the leg. The castle named for him at Llangollen, **Dinas Bran**, has good claims to be considered the British home of the Grail King. After being wounded in Ireland, Bran urges his seven remaining followers, one of whom is Taliesin, to decapitate him, after which his head accompanied, entertained and encouraged them for ninety years on its way to Tower Hill in **London**. There it protected the island of Britain from foreign invasion until Arthur dug it up. Today Bran's ravens continue to fulfil this function. It is probable that the legend of Bran influenced the Greek belief that the Titan Kronos (Saturn), having been dethroned by Zeus, sleeps in the western Isles of the Blest, where he dreams the deeds that his mighty son performs. Bran has many points in common with the Dagda, the Irish druid god, possessor of a magic cauldron. He appears in the Arthurian legends as Ogma, the wild man of the woods with a mighty staff, the lord of the animals, inventor of the Ogham script and dispenser of knowledge.

Merlin shares many features with Bran and the Dagda above all as the archetype of natural wisdom. All three are renowned for martial prowess; Merlin and Bran are both tutelary deities of the island of Britain and continue to watch over it from the tomb and teach its people. All three are associated with druidic magic.

There is another Bran, son of Febal, who was lured by a fairy woman, bearing a branch of apple-blossom, to undertake the sea voyage to the Irish Avalon, Emain, the Land of Women. When Bran returned to Ireland he found centuries had elapsed and to land would mean death and disintegration, so he sailed away once more and his further wanderings are unknown until he re-emerges in Christian form as St Brendan.

In the oldest text referring to an Irish sea voyage to the Otherworld, the hero is not Bran but Maeldun, almost the same name as Maeldin, Geoffrey of Monmouth's healed madman of the *Vita Merlini*, who joins Merlin and Taliesin in the Forest of Celyddon. When he appears, Taliesin has just given a long description of the Isle of Avalon where he and Merlin brought the wounded Arthur with the help of the skilful pilot Barinthus. Is it too far-fetched to see in the arrival of the famous navigator, Maeldin/Maeldun, Merlin's former companion, the re-assembly of the complement of that barque of death? Maeldun was also, like Merlin and a number of saints, the son of a nun, reputedly the victim of rape. These speculations lead us naturally to the Christianization of the odysseys of Bran and Maeldun in the voyage of St Brendan and to the general problem of Merlin's role as a link between the old Celtic gods and the new Celtic saints.

Merlin and the Saints

Lochmaben. Site of the major shrine of Mabon, the Celtic Apollo, and traditional birthplace of Robert the Bruce.

That Merlin, or a religio-political movement under his name, should have sought to restore the old order in Britain after the departure of the legions is hardly surprising. This tendency was, indeed, already in progress in the mid-fourth-century, when the power of the Christian Church was temporarily weakened by the policies of the Emperor Julian the Apostate, who tried to restore a paganism enlightened by the Gnosis of the mystery schools. The excavations at **Lydney** not only illustrate this counter-revolutionary process at work, they show its methods. Prime among these was a tendency towards a monotheism that mirrored Christianity, just as Julian promoted the cult of the Unconquered Sun to set against the youthful

god, the Christ child. This is why Merlin combines the attributes of so many of the gods. Mabon (cf. **Lochmaben**), liberated from imprisonment in Gloucester by Kay and Bedivere, not far up the silver arm of the Severn from **Lydney**, was the British answer to Christ and Sol Invictus – and Merlin was his prophet and avatar. From his shrine at **Lochmaben** we know that healing and dream-interpretation played a major part in this cult, as they did at **Lydney**.

The movement was doomed to failure. The surprising durability of the vestigial Christian Church, combined with the irresistible onward march of the Teutonic invaders from the east, who had broken Rome, and the endless internecine feuding of the Celtic peoples, strangled it at birth. The old gods never return to their temples – at least not in the old familiar form. A new solution was required to meet the desperate situation – a solution in the alchemical sense of the word, too, *solve et coagula*, dissolve the existing structures and re-establish them in a new way. The history of eastern Europe in 1989–90 shows how quickly such transformation can occur. What was required was something to unite the Celtic world and enlist the help of the Christian Church – the old enemy – which had succeeded in showing itself to be the only structure in western Europe capable of maintaining some semblance of order and civilization, as well as treating in an organized way with the new Germanic overlords. The solution lay in pan-Celtic druidic Christianity, apparently part of the Great Church, but in reality very different. Rome rumbled it and superficially imposed its will at the Synod of Whitby in AD664, but its influence was to remain strong, not only in its Celtic fastnesses, but, thanks to its missionary endeavours, throughout Europe, for another five centuries.

The extraordinary phenomenon of Merlin's involvement, and even identification, with so many Christian saints, as well as his am-biguous position within the spectrum of Christian history, can best be explained by the adaptation of druidism to the church. If this occurred it was probably not through conscious conspiracy, but by a gradual consensus, including radicals and hardliners alike, that there was no alternative. No wonder there was no need for martyrs in Ireland with Christian super-druids like Patrick and Columba to ease the transition. Two famous druidic tricks, shape-changing and hiding things in a mist, were to prove their worth metaphorically in the sixth century, as an examination of the Celtic saints of the period shows. Almost all of them are closely linked, like the old deities, not only with each other, but with all the branches of the independent Celtic nation – Ireland, Wales, Scotland, Man, Cumbria, Strathclyde, Cornwall and Brittany.

Columba and Cadoc

Three saints sought out Merlin in his self-imposed exile in the forest to calm his troubled mind with words of consolation. One was

Columba, apostle of the Scots and Picts and founder of Iona, an Irishman of royal blood. Another was Cadoc, contemporary of David and master of Finnian who taught Columba and founded Llancarfan, the school of Gildas, Brendan and Malo. There are two other Saint Cadocs, one from Scotland, one from Brittany, unless, as seems likely with ancient saints of the same name, they are one person claimed by three different regions. The Cadoc who visited Merlin is, traditionally, the Breton one, son of a Welsh king, who settled on a small island in the wide estuary of the Etel in Morbihan, near **Carnac** (see **St Cado**). His skill as a musician and poet would have drawn him to Merlin, who at once burst into song when he first encountered the saint after his long journey to Celyddon to see him. Of the Scots Cadoc nothing is known.

Kentigern

Merlin's third saintly visitor, Kentigern or Mungo (*dearest*) is the patron of **Glasgow**, whose cathedral he founded on a burial-ground consecrated by St Ninian. He was visited there by St Columba, and they exchanged staffs as a token of love. He was consecrated by an Irish bishop, spent some time in Wales with St David at whose death he was present, and, at the request of King Maelgwn, founded a large monastery at Llanelwy. It is now called St Asaph's, after the monk Kentigern left in charge on his return to Scotland. Kentigern was accustomed to recite his psalter standing in the Clyde and would spend long periods, including the whole of Lent, in the wilderness. This is where his story leads us to parallels with that of Merlin. He was born of Thenew, a virgin abused by a daemonic spirit, or by a young man of noble birth. As he was the grandson of King Urien, patron of Taliesin, his grandmother would have been Morgan/Modron and his uncle Owain, also the most likely candidate to have been his father. When his mother's pregnancy was discovered, she was thrown off a cliff in a wagon and set adrift in a coracle, where she gave birth to the saint. They can be seen together in their boat on the walls of **Caerlaverock Castle**. St Serf or Servan saved him from the sea at Culross, as Elphin saved Taliesin, and brought him up as his dear disciple. In later life Kentigern, like Merlin, spent much time with King Rhydderch, whose capital was **Dumbarton**. Another side to the story of Merlin, Gwenddydd and the leaf is told of him: Rhydderch's queen gave her lover a ring which the king saw on the sleeping knight's finger and threw into the Clyde, threatening his wife with death unless she produced it. She asked Kentigern to help her, and he, remembering, perhaps, his mother's problems, retrieved the ring from the belly of a salmon, saving the Queen's life and providing **Glasgow** with its coat of arms.

   The Life of St Kentigern is one of the major confirmatory sources for the existence of Merlin–Lailoken. During his frequent spells in the wilderness, Kentigern met Merlin, for whom he felt great compassion, calling him his brother, although the wild man would interrupt his services with ecstatic prophecies (see **Hoddom**). Merlin received absolution and Holy Communion at the hands of the saint, as depicted in **Stobo Kirk**, and prophesied his own death that very day. This came to pass when, stoned and beaten by the shepherds of the local kinglet, Meldred, he fell off a steep bank into the Tweed at **Drumelzier** and was impaled on a fisherman's post. St Kentigern died the same year.

Dubricius

The similarities between the careers of Merlin and the Welsh saint, Dyfrig or Dubricius, are so remarkable that they led Goodrich to speculate that they might have been the same person. For a full outline of the parallels between them see **Madley**. Dyfrig, according to tradition, handed over the primatial see of Wales to St David, and was also the spiritual father of St Samson, the apostle of Brittany and first Bishop of **Dol**, whose parents went on pilgrimage to the temple of **Lochmaben** in the hope of conceiving a child. In Ireland he acquired a caravan in which to carry all his books and priestly equipment needed on his missionary journey. Passing with it through Cornwall to catch a ferry to Brittany at Fowey, he came across some pagans celebrating Lugnasadh, and left us an eyewitness account of it. St Méen or Mewan, who founded the monastery and town that still bears his name in **Brocéliande**, and caused the water of **Gaël** – famous for the healing of rabies – to flow, was a native of Archenfield, where Dyfrig's father was the minor king.

Martin

For some of the parallels between Merlin and St Martin, whose names become one in the Chronicle of William of Newburgh, see **Galicia**, **Lake District** and **Land's End**. Martinmas coincides with the period of Samhain and was traditionally a time of fairs, feasting and fine weather. In 1918 his feast, 11th November, became the Day of the Dead for the West.

Brendan

So much for some of the well-attested historical saints whose biographies have by some alchemy become mythically commixed with the tincture of Merlin. We must now consider a second category of saints who are best described in the title of Saintyves' magisterial book of 1907 as *Les Saints Successeurs des Dieux*. Just as there are two Brans there are two Brendans. The St Brendan whom we left a few pages back with his companion Barinthus was a historical character, born near Tralee, with a hermitage on Mt Brandon. He is the Christianization of Bran, son of Febal, the famous voyager.

After his famous voyage to the earthly paradise, *the land of the promise of the saints*, St Brendan visited Brittany with St Malo and probably Barinthus. St Malo founded the great port that bears his name as well as that of St Servan. Its diocese included the parish of Concoret, and hence **Barenton**. St Brendan gave his name to a village and church in the **Forest of Quintin**, a part of the ancient **Brocéliande**, which also claims the tomb of Merlin. And what of Barinthus? It was he who had first visited the *Isle of Delights* and inspired Brendan to undertake the voyage. Bellamy is convinced that he penetrated to the very heart of the mystery of **Brocéliande** to become the Saint Barenton under whose patronage the magic spring was placed. This brings him very close to Merlin, and **Barenton** very close to the earthly paradise where the enchanter conjured up a garden of delights for Vivian. But Barinthus is also the archetypal pilot and ferryman. In Geoffrey of Monmouth's fine Latin:

Illuc post bellum Camblani, vulnere laesum
Duximus Arcturum nos conducente Baryntho . . .

(Thither, after the battle of Camlann, we took the wounded Arthur, piloted by Barinthus.)

Brittany is the land of Ankou, skeletal, scythe-bearing captain of a phantom ship, ferryman of wandering souls to the Otherworld from the **Baie des Trépassés** or Tréménac. According to Henri Martin, in his *Histoire de France*, one of his names is Barinte. This probably derives from a Celtic word meaning fair-haired, a title of the Irish sea-god Manannan, whose closest Welsh equivalent is Bran the Blessed, who could wade across the Celtic Sea, towing the British fleet behind him.

Merlin Saints in Brittany

Some Merlinesque saints show him in his Cernunnos form. At **Lannédern** in Brittany, St Edern is to be seen in three images riding a stag, exactly like Merlin when he took a wedding present to his wife. He is an interesting example of a figure who was originally the semi-divine son of Nudd, who then emerges as one of Arthur's original companions and lover of Guinevere, before Lancelot, to crown his career as a Christian saint. He has colleagues, like Herbot and Ronan in West Brittany and Cornély of **Carnac**, who also have a special affinity with horned beasts. His father, Nudd, Nuada of the Silver Hand to the Irish, is even more closely involved in Merlin's career as a Christian saint.

Mylor

St Mylor or Mellor, a name close to the Scots form of Merlin, Meller, when a prince of seven years, was threatened with death by a usurping uncle who cut off his right hand. It was replaced by a silver one, which, by the time he was fourteen, worked as though it was natural. This Christian legend neatly unites two traditions: that of Nuada, King of the Tuatha de Danaan and surpreme leader of the gods, who lost a hand in battle, replaced it with a silver one and was unable to resume the kingship for seven years, and that of the divine child, such as Mabon/Merlin. Both are forms of Lugh, Merlin's tutelary deity in Tolstoy's *The Coming of the King*. St Mylor's relics were placed in Amesbury Abbey of which he is the patron. Amesbury is the site of **Stonehenge**, named traditionally for King Ambrosius/ Emrys.

Merlin and the magicians

Melkin

Of western magicians who offer particularly strong associations with Merlin, the first, Melkin, lived 'before Merlin', but since he was also the 'uncle of David', the circumstances of whose birth are in the Merlin mould and who was a contemporary of Merlin-Lailoken, presumably it was not very much before. His name in Welsh, Maelgwn, he shares with another sixth-century figure, greatest of the kings of Gwynedd and patron of Taliesin, who had spent some time as a monk, before a partial apostasy to the old religion of the druids. The prophecy attributed to Melkin, although discounted by scholars as a serious historical document of the Dark Ages, is interesting for a number of reasons. It links **Glastonbury** with an important entombment of paganism, perhaps that of Gwynn ap Nudd, as well as with astrology and, possibly, crystal-gazing. He tells of the burial of Joseph of Arimathea there, with two cruets containing the sweat and blood of Jesus. One day 'open shall these things be and declared to living men'.

Eon de L'Etoile

The next of our magicians in chronological order is Eon de l'Etoile, a heretical Robin Hood, who flourished in the Forest of **Brocéliande** in the first half of the twelfth century. This was the time when numerous heresies, especially Catharism, were flourishing, when Merlin and Arthur entered mainstream literature, along with the Grail and its guardians, the historical Knights Templar, and when the Plantagenets began their conquest of the Celtic world (Henry II actually stayed at Paimpont). Eon was a native of Loudéac in the western part of what was then greater **Brocéliande**, and evidently of noble birth. He may have spent some time as an Augustinian hermit in the vicinity of **Barenton** before discovering, through a revelation by the spirit of Merlin, his true vocation as the Aeon who shared the rulership of the world with God. With his power of high-speed mobility, his ability to summon up magnificent banquets, like Albertus Magnus or the Grail, and the glorious nimbus of light that surrounded him, he soon attracted an enthusiastic and faithful following on whom he bestowed names such as Wisdom, Knowledge and Judgement, like those of the Gnostic Aeons a millennium before. With his band he raided monasteries and castles, using some of the loot to help the poor survive the terrible winters of the 1140s, as well as keeping good cheer in the new priory of le Moinet. His staff of office was a forked wand, traditionally used for dowsing and for warding off Korrigans, the fairies particularly prevalent in the parish of Concoret, named for them. Eon, with his magical, man-carrying sparrowhawk and the lore gleaned from an age-old oral tradition in the forest, last refuge of the druids in Brittany, had surely no fear of the powers of the night. No doubt the properties of hallucinogenic plants would have been well known to him. In 1148 Pope Eugenius III was holding a council at Reims to examine and condemn certain heresies, and had Eon brought before him. His followers, in their orders of Cherubims, Apostles and Saints, all went to their deaths bravely, in defence of his claim to be the son of God, and Eon himself was committed on grounds of insanity to the prison of Suger of St Denis, where he soon died, having, it was said, regained his reason. His strange history did nothing to weaken the Merlin traditions in **Brocéliande**, above all at **Barenton**, and may, in Markale's view, have influenced the further development of Merlin as a literary figure after Geoffrey of Monmouth. The stones of le Moinet were used to build the village of Folle Pensée and the church of St Léry, while the fountain of **Barenton** was eventually placed under the protection of St Mathurin, a third-century Gaul from Sens (sens = sense, way!), invoked for the healing of madness.

Melerius

Not long after the death of Eon, Giraldus in his *Itinerary Through Wales* tells, in the neighbourhood of **Caerleon**, of 'a Welshman named Melerius, who . . . acquired the knowledge of the future and occult events'. He had the experience, reversing many Celtic legends, of the beautiful girl he loved turning into a loathly damsel, after which he was mad for many years. After his recovery at **St David's**, he discovered he had the faculty of foretelling the future with the aid of spirits in the guise of hunters. Whenever the spirits became oppressive he was relieved by contact with the Gospel of John, beloved of the Cathars. Giraldus cattily remarks that when the *History of the Britons (sic)* by Geoffrey Arthur (of Monmouth) was placed on his chest, the spirits returned in greater numbers than usual and remained for a longer time, indicating the book's falsity. Melerius was familiar with an incubus in Lower Gwent, who was in the habit of visiting the woman he loved and would reveal to him hidden things and future events. These included matters of importance, such as his accurate prediction to the local ruler, Howel, that he need not fear the vengeance of Henry II since he would have to take an army to France and raise the siege of an important city, which turned out to be Rouen. In the entry for **Eildon Hills** we refer to a contemporary Celtic magician who achieved greater international fame than Melerius, as astrologer to the Emperor Frederick II, Michael Scot. Both he and Thomas the Rhymer, from the same breeding-ground of magic, have strong connections to the Merlin myth and the magician archetype.

John Dee

One last magus, this time from the sixteenth century, merits our attention as Merlin redivivus, and that is Dr John Dee. Son of a Welsh official at the Tudor court, he was born in London in 1527 and lived the second half of his life in Mortlake. A brilliant scholar of Cambridge and Louvain, he taught at Paris and Reims before receiving a pension from Edward VI, casting the horoscope of Queen Mary and becoming court astrologer to Elizabeth I, for whose coronation he elected a favourable day. He also advised the Queen on naval and intelligence matters and became deeply involved in alchemy and scrying, or crystal-gazing, by means of which he was in constant communication with angels and archangels, especially Uriel. He was almost certainly one of the models of Prospero in *The Tempest* and for Merlin in Spenser's *The Faerie Queene*, unsurprisingly since, in Tolstoy's words, he 'regarded himself, and was widely regarded as, a sixteenth-century counterpart of Merlin'. He lived, beyond his time, into the reign of magic-fearing James I and VI, predicted by Thomas the Rhymer to coincide with the flooding of Merlin's tomb. Many of the witches and wizards persecuted by King James had, unlike John Dee, animal familiars, harking back perhaps to an older tradition of nature magic with which Merlin would certainly have been in sympathy.

Merlin's Beasts

The Wolf

Wolves suffer from a sinister reputation. The spectre of lycanthropy continues to haunt our imaginations and cinema screens. The devil is a wolf, when he appears as a teacher of heresy to lead astray the Christian sheep; wolves in general symbolize avarice, greed, rapacity and lust, whilst the she-wolf denotes specifically the voracious whore in what the French call her *lupanar* (brothel); and at the Last Battle, Ragnarok, the Fenris Wolf will swallow the sun. As well as being a devourer, the wolf can also nourish, as Romulus, Remus and Mowgli would testify. According to medieval bestiaries, they copulate on only twelve days of the year and whelp during the first thunderstorm of the month of May, which emphasizes their affinity to Belen, as to Apollo. So they are bright as well as dark animals, and their eyes penetrate the night. St Francis of Assisi made a friend of the wolf of Gubbio, and Wotan delights in feeding Geri and Freki from his own dish at table in Valhalla. In Spain the wolf is one of the favourite mounts of sorcerers. A number of Celtic gods and saints have wolf familiars and St Ronan (see **Locronan**), who has strong Merlin associations, was even accused by a local druidess of being a werewolf.

Merlin's wolf is his companion who shares his miseries in the wintry forest, suffering apparently even more than Merlin from cold and hunger, to whom he sings in the *Vita Merlini*: 'Tu lupe, care comes . . . You wolf, dear companion, who were wont to wander through the byways and glades of the forest with me . . . cruel hunger has brought both you and me to the end of our tether.' It is while he is lamenting thus that a passer-by hears him and brings news of him to his sister Gwenddydd, who sends messengers to him. That Merlin has as a totem animal an old, grey wolf, an image of himself as guide of souls, connected with various Celtic gods and saints, is quite natural, but the situation is complicated by the homonymous play on words that exists between *bleiz*, the Brythonic Celtic for *wolf* and Blaise, the mentor, chronicler and close companion of Merlin, who often visited him in Northumberland. St Blaise, whose cult became extremely popular in the west from the eighth century, protects cattle and cures afflictions of the throat. His feast, 3rd February, coincides with Oimelc/Imbolc, when the ewes' milk begins to flow with the lambing season and the victory of Brigit, the spirit of rebirth, over the hag of winter. In Christian times these feasts were replaced by Candlemas and by the festival of St Brigit, daughter of a Druid, Mary of the Gael and foster-mother of Jesus, who kept the flame of Celtic tradition burning at Kildare.

One of the miracles attributed to the wolf-saint, Blaise, was to force a wolf to disgorge a pig belonging to a poor old woman, while St Serf, Kentigern's mentor, restored a pig to life after it had been eaten.

The Pig

The pig is a loathsome and unclean animal according to Mosaic and Islamic law, symbolizing greed and lust, and was a great problem to ascetic anchorites such as St Antony. In Tibet it represents ignorance, an idea not far removed from the injunction not to cast one's pearls before swine. In the Celtic world, on the other hand, it is viewed more positively. It is, first of all, the preferred dish for the banquets that take place both here and in the Otherworld. The wild boar, *le solitaire* or solitary one, is the animal symbol of the druid, adept in magic and prophecy, protector of heroes, bringer of abundance and good fortune. The position of swineherd was one of the most honoured among the Celts (see **Tristan** (Glossary), **Bath**, **St Mullins**, **Madley**).

It is difficult not to see Merlin's little pig from the **Black Book of Carmarthen** as a tender little pink creature from a Valentine's card, sitting under his apple-tree, but from the text it would seem to be as wild and feral as the wizard himself:

> O little pig, a happy pig,
> Do not burrow thy lair on the top of a mountain,
> Burrow in a hidden place in the woodlands
> For fear of the hunting-dogs of Rhydderch Hael,
> defender of the Faith . . .

So the little pig, whom he described later as lively and lustful, is not approved of by the Church. Perhaps she is Vivian/Gwenddydd, representing all the women who hid the sacred knowledge when the druids were gone and maintained the traditions of Diana, however much they were hunted down by the hounds of God to be burnt as witches.

The Stag

In contrast to the wolf and the pig, the stag receives almost universally good notices from the Christian writers. In other words, Cernunnos, the stag-god, the oldest and most powerful deity among the Celts, was the most important target for assimilation into the Church. We have referred in the text and introduction to a number of saints with stag associations of whom the most important, as an analogue of Merlin, is Edern. Saints Eustace and Hubert, both converted by an encounter with Christ (cf. **Pont du Secret**), who appeared to them between the antlers of a stag, have their feast days on the 2nd and 3rd November, precisely at the time of Samhain, when the church celebrates Hallowe'en, All Saints and All Souls. This is when the living and the dead come closest together, time is abolished and the fairy world is open to mortals. For the stag to appear at this unpropitious time gives assurance of rebirth once the rigours of winter are passed.

The feast of another stag-saint, who has no known date, country or tomb, Julian the Hospitaller, 29th January, two days before Imbolc, emphasizes the two sides of the symbolism – death and rebirth. According to Emma Jung and von Franz, the stag carries the 'archetype of the Self and the principle of individuation' as well as being Christ's shadow. This natural guide of souls causes springs to flow and shows the hunter the way to them and to his true love. The stag-man depicted on the cave-wall at Lascaux is probably the oldest representation of a magician in existence, linking Merlin to the spirit of the ancestors hunting in the primeval forests. (The Horned God is continually cuckolded and betrayed by man's growing intellectual pride and when Merlin kills Guendoloena's new husband with an antler for laughing at him from an upstairs window, he is striking a blow for natural religion against the spirit of superiority based on book-learning and the trappings of civilization.)

Merlin and Woman

Merlin, unlike most wizards, finds that it *is* love that makes the world go round. The women associated with him are powerful figures. Whilst on one level they are all representatives of the Celtic triple goddess in her various guises, they are also of flesh and blood, fiercely opposing the gradual erosion, under Christianity, of their traditional rights and prerogatives as independent beings, free to bestow the friendship of their thighs on the man of their choice and, at a higher level, the sovereignty of the land on him who had earned the right to it. Sovereignty in Scotland was inherited through the female line until the twelfth century.

Consider Macbeth

Carmelide

The first woman and teacher in Merlin's life is his mother, Carmelide, and, in the absence of a father, her presence and influence would have been of paramount importance. Educated by her, a nun of royal descent, he demonstrates his wisdom as an infant, when he saves her from capital punishment by his uncanny ability to discern the true from the false. Later, at the age of seven, before Vortigern and his druids, he saves his own life at **Dinas Emrys**. Here his mother disappears from the story and Merlin enters a lengthy process of preparation for his future mission as magician–adviser to kings.

Dinas Emrys, the hill in Snowdonia where the seven-year-old Merlin confronted Vortigern and his magicians, revealing the existence of the two warring dragons in a subterranean pool.

The origin of the name Carmelide is unknown, but Mount Carmel, from which the Carmelite order takes its name, contains the cavern where their mystical founder, the prophet Elijah, who has a number of points in common with Merlin, has his tomb, and he, too, lives for ever. Carmelide is also the name of the kingdom ruled by King Leodagan, father of Guinevere, sometimes located at **Carhaix** in Brittany or at **Carmel Head** in Anglesey where Merlin helps Arthur win a battle.

Ygraine

Ygraine, wife of Gorlois, is of Otherworld ancestry and enters into this world with great treasures. The paths of Merlin and Ygraine cross when Merlin stage-manages the conception of King Arthur (see **Tintagel**) and ensures that the royal line of Britain shall continue through her daughters.

Mélusine

A Celtic serpent goddess of the Otherworld, mistress of the magic arts, builder of monasteries, castles and cathedrals, she marries Raimondin, a mortal, who finds her by a spring. She is abundantly productive and gives birth to many sons who marry into all the royal houses of Europe and Jerusalem and are linked with the quest for the Holy Grail. She is the French equivalent of Ygraine – Mother of the Lineage. In one tradition she is the daughter of Merlin and Morgan and in another the niece of Morgan Le Fay and granddaughter of Ygraine.

Guinevere

According to Heinrich von dem Türlin, Guinevere was of Otherworld origin and a bestower of sovereignty. She is the daughter of King Leodagan of Carmelide. Arthur falls in love with her and, against Merlin's advice, marries her. As part of her dowry she introduces the Round Table – originally designed by Merlin – to the court of Arthur. Without the Table and her 'betrayal' of Arthur with Lancelot – comprehensible to pagan Celts, but reprehensible to Christian writers – together with her failure to present the King with an heir, there would have been no new spiritual order – manifested in the Quest for the Holy Grail.

Morgan, Morgan Le Fay

This great goddess is an ambiguous character with a long history who appears under various names and forms. Originally she was Morrigan, the 'Great Queen' of the Otherworld, part of a female trinity whose specialities were war, death and fertility. Her bird is the sea-crow or raven. In Brittany she assumes a Venus-like, sea-borne personality and is represented in a multitude of carvings as a mermaid or wouivre. It is Geoffrey of Monmouth who first names her as Arthur's half-sister, daughter of Gorlois and Ygraine. The sworn foe of Guinevere, she plots against Arthur and the Order of the Round Table and throws away the scabbard that protected him from mortal wounds. In **Brocéliande** she creates the **Val-sans-Retour** where she imprisons unfaithful lovers and, in Ariosto, she has a castle at the bottom of a lake whose surrounding waters seem like walls of solid crystal (cf. **Caer Arianrhod** and **Comper**). She is the High Priestess of magic and healing as well as of intrigue and deception. She rules, with her college of priestesses, over Avalon, where the dead are ferried to their Otherworldly existence. Morgan is often portrayed as evil and frightening, like all Otherworldly figures who bring knowledge from the realm beyond, yet it is also she who accompanies the fatally wounded Arthur, after the battle of Camlann, on his final journey to her realm, where she tends him until the day when, healed, he will return to rule Britain once more.

Morgan is Merlin's equal in every way and is sometimes portrayed as his wife. Whilst it is Merlin's task to advise and guide the King in his rulership over the land of mortals, it is her fate to rule over the Otherworld and from there to ensure that the goddess is honoured and her laws are not transgressed. Like Guinevere, Morgan plays a decisive role in bringing about the end of the age of Arthur.

Guendoloena and Eorann
In Geoffrey of Monmouth's *Vita Merlini* Guendoloena is Merlin's wife. She stands in the same relationship to Merlin as Eorann to Sweeney. Their husbands go mad at a great battle and begin a life as wild men. Guendoloena, with Merlin's permission, remarries, but her new husband is killed by him. Eorann takes a new lover, but Sweeney himself is killed by a jealous swineherd. The relationship that Merlin and Sweeney have with their wives is ambiguous, compounded of nostalgia, self-pity and the desire to be free in the wilderness.

Ganieda, Gwenddydd (Welsh for the planet Venus)
After the death of her husband, King Rhydderch, Merlin's sister, Ganieda, takes over the organizing of his life and builds for him an observatory with seventy doors and seventy windows in his beloved forest. Here a healing spring restores Merlin's senses, and his friends, Taliesin and the mad Maeldin, come to live with him. He devotes the remainder of his life to the study of the heavens and the uttering of prophecies, finally passing on his knowledge and skills to Ganieda. The *Vita Merlini* closes with her prophecies.

Vivian, Nimuë, Lady of the Lake
The final female character in the story of Merlin is Vivian, probably based on the earlier figure of Gwenddydd. When old, tired and no longer given to making prophecies, Merlin meets Vivian, according to different accounts, by a spring, at the court of Arthur or at the

college by the fountain in **Brocéliande**. They fall in love, become inseparable and journey together. Merlin teaches her all he knows except for one spell: how to imprison a man, purely by enchantment, unbeknownst to him, without walls or bars. Eventually, to prove his love to her, he gives away his final secret, and whilst he is asleep she enchants him into a castle of air to which only she has access. Merlin is happy with this arrangement and continues to make prophetic utterances to those who can hear him. As far as we know, Vivian, like Ganieda, carries on Merlin's work.

There are other versions of this story where Vivian is portrayed as calculating and designing, only interested in Merlin's power and knowledge or where Merlin appears as a lecherous fool, pursuing the innocent Vivian who, finally, in order to save herself from his sexual advances, elicits the fatal spell from him.

The return of the dragon

For four hundred years Merlin was a central figure in the literature and popular mythology of western Europe. Then, from the middle of the sixteenth century, fashions changed. The condemnation of his prophecies by the Council of Trent, on the one hand, and the new wind of humanism on the other, signalled the advent of a different taste in the marvellous. Chivalry and magic fell into suspended animation with *Don Quixote*, to await for almost two centuries the resuscitating kiss of the Romantics in Germany, Britain and France. Since then, Merlin, Arthur and their knights and ladies have never been far from the forefront of western imagination. In the last decade the myth has achieved a new prominence. But what does Merlin, in particular, have to offer us at the close of the twentieth century which has witnessed so many changes?

Over the past thirty years we have seen a striking development of depth psychology, particularly that of C.G. Jung, who had so much in common with Merlin that one esoteric group in the Channel Islands even sees him as his reincarnation and, like Merlin, a prophet of the Aquarian age. The purpose of true depth psychology is the quest for the Self and it was Merlin who first made the world fall in love with this inward journey towards what he called the Holy Grail. The knights set out hopefully, one by one, on this quest, but only the one who asked the right question would achieve it. Thus the search for collective unity, the creation of a United Kingdom, symbolized by the Round Table, had become an individual quest.

When Merlin disappears from this world Arthur sends his knights in search of him, thereby indicating that Merlin himself is intimately associated with the object of the quest. Only from achieving the Grail could the Waste Land be healed; thus individual and collective aims converged. It is now, however, no longer just Merlin that the seeker will find, but also Vivian. In other words the goal of the quest is the inner union of male and female, the great and mysterious conjunction of opposites, that Jung called the Self. This truth was presaged by Paul Heyse (1830–1914) who uses the title *Merlin* to describe the union exemplified by Merlin and Vivian.

Merlin the Prophet and Astrologer

Merlin's prophecies are intriguing. As no date is given for their supposed fulfilment, some of them may apply to our present time. Was he referring to the now fashionable births by Caesarean section, carefully arranged by busy doctors and mothers when he proclaimed: 'The bellies of mothers shall be cut open and babies will be born prematurely'? Was it the closure of the thermal spa at Bath in 1979, due to the suspicion that the waters had become poisonous, that he foresaw when he stated: 'The baths shall grow cold at Bath and its health-giving waters shall breed death'? And did he predict the proposed cutting of the M3 motorway through Old Winchester, the Iron Age Hill Fort, when he declared: 'The Earth shall swallow Winchester up'?

The most fitting of his prophecies for today is: 'The sea over which men sail to Gaul shall be contracted into a narrow channel. A man on any one of the two shores will be audible to a man on the other and the land-mass of the island will grow greater.' Is this the channel tunnel from Dover to Calais that is presently under construction together with our highly sophisticated communication system and Britain's membership of the European Community?

Some prophecies appear to allude to astrological source material, as, for instance: 'Virgo shall climb on the back of Sagittarius and so let drop its maiden blossom' (Joan of Arc?), but many more seem to be pure visionary inspirations. His most famous astrological interpretation, as recounted by Geoffrey of Monmouth, was at the time of Aurelius' death:

> **There appeared a star of great magnitude and brilliance, with a single beam shining from it. At the end of the beam was a ball of fire, spread out in the shape of a dragon. From the dragon's mouth stretched forth two rays of light one of which seemed to extend its length beyond the latitude of Gaul, while the second turned toward the Irish Sea and split up into seven smaller shapes of light.**

Merlin correctly foresaw from this the death of Aurelius and the succession of Uther Pendragon to the throne. He also predicted that Uther's future son (Arthur) would have dominion over all the lands the beam covered and that his daughters would be instrumental in establishing the royal lineage of Britain. The blood line has never flowed more strongly than it does today, in the Prince of Wales who is also Duke of Cornwall and Lord of the Isles, the first royal personage who is deeply concerned about the fate of nature and the planet.

Whom does the Grail Serve?

age of A

In *The Prophecies* Merlin tells us: 'The Gemini will cease their wonted embraces and will dispatch Aquarius to the fountains.' The forces of good and evil, light and dark, body and spirit, have their greatest conflict in the zodiacal sign of Gemini. Merlin, lover of fountains, seems to be suggesting here that when the opposing poles become differentiated, then Aquarius is called to fill its vessel and begin the work of enlightenment. It is on the Gemini–Sagittarius axis that the *Line of Advantage*, polarizing the head and tail of the dragon, is constellated. This indicates that Gemini (♊) is a gateway which leads to the exploration of inner contradictions. The resolution of the problem of duality, the tension between the mortal and immortal twin in each of us, is thus seen by Merlin to lie in the Holy Grail. It was an irreconcilable antagonism that tore asunder the previous age in which the two fishes (♓), Christ and the Antichrist, pulled against each other, tied by a cord, in perpetual conflict, like the dragons at **Dinas Emrys**. But, in our present Age of Aquarius, the fishes, who can neither be united nor separated, have become the two streams (♒ the glyph of Aquarius) that flow side by side into the cauldron of the Water Carrier. These two streams of influence – earthly and celestial – can now be reconciled in the Grail vessel to form a new attitude that radically transforms our awareness of what it means to be human. Increasingly on our journeys we found that the church doors were locked, a hint, perhaps, that the gods are preparing to vacate their man-made temples. So, finding the churches no longer open, people are turning to psychology, astrology, meditation and other paths to knowledge of the Self. On the trail of Merlin the seeker may find, as we did, that the old Celtic myth is still alive and weaves its way magically and uncompromisingly into the fabric of our own reality, which needs to encompass the human paradox that we are all children of earth and starry heaven.

England

London and the Home Counties

London

There are a number of former Merlin sites in **London**: Merlin Street near the site of his cave in Clerkenwell, Merlin's Cave in Kew Gardens and Merlin's Eyot in Chelsea.

Michel Rio has Merlin kill 500 of the Royal Guard at Walbrook to avenge the murder in **London** of his mother and Blaise. The ravens at the Tower still commemorate the burial of the head of Bran there, to defend Britain. **London** is named for King Lud (Lludd) who first found the warring dragons at **Oxford** and transferred them to **Dinas Emrys**. Merlin and Morgan le Fay can still be visited in his cave at the London Dungeons. According to some traditions, Merlin's *sword-in-the-stone* test took place outside St Paul's Cathedral and Uther Pendragon fell in love with Ygraine at his court in **London**.

Oxford
Map 35, SP 5106

Oxford is, in a sense, the birthplace of Merlin, since it was here that he first emerged into history through the pen of Geoffrey of Monmouth who taught at St George's College and whose major source for his *History* was a little book in the British language, most likely from Brittany, lent to him by the Archdeacon of Oxford.

Oxford is of particular importance to the making of Merlin, as it was here, at the geographical centre of Britain, that two dragons were caught by Lludd (see **London**) and locked in a stone chest. They were then buried at **Dinas Emrys**.

Godstow priory, opposite that most famous of **Oxford** riverside inns, The Trout, is worth a minor pilgrimage as the burial-place of Fair Rosamond, mistress of Henry II, who was caught up in a myth of Merlinesque proportions. Henry built her a magical palace at Woodstock which none could enter. His magic, however, proved less potent than Vivian's, and Eleanor of Aquitaine, the jealous queen, at whose court so much of the Merlin/Arthur material was sung and celebrated, penetrated the palace and offered her rival the sword or the chalice. Rosamond chose poison.

In the Oxford Union are a number of pre-Raphaelite murals

designed by Dante Gabriel Rossetti in 1857 which include *The Death of Merlin* by Burne-Jones.

Although **Oxford** is a Saxon foundation and seems to have had no important Celtic settlement, it is, as Britain's oldest university, the centre of that learning which was once the preserve of the druids and true home of lost causes, and has maintained its links with the Celtic origins of our culture. *The Red Book of Hergest* is preserved at Jesus College where Sir John Rhys, its nineteenth-century principal, spearheaded the revival of interest in Celtic studies.

Silchester
Map 24, SU 6261

Geoffrey of Monmouth names **Silchester** as the site of Arthur's coronation. It was once a Roman city of 100 acres and before that the sacred grove of the Celtic Atrebates. It is one of the very rare sites of a fourth-century Christian church. The present parish church of St Mary was built on a sacred precinct where at least two pagan–Celtic temples once stood. The road leading from **London** to **Silchester** is called the Devil's Highway.

Chislehurst
Map 25, TQ 4470

By road take the A222 between the A20 and A21 at **Chislehurst** railway bridge. Turn into Station Road, then turn right and right again to Caveside Close.

By rail there are regular trains from Charing Cross to **Chislehurst** main-line station (approximately 25 minutes).

By bus 227 from Bromley; also 725 Green Line.

Opening times Easter to September daily 11 am–5 pm; end of September to Easter daily during school holidays 11 am–5 pm, otherwise Saturday and Sunday only. There is a large, free car-park, a gift shop and a refreshment bar. For further information telephone 071-467 3264.

The leafy London suburb of **Chislehurst** is at first sight an unlikely place to find an ancient Celtic shrine. The approach is not promising. When we arrived a group of young people in costume were about to descend into the caves to play Dungeons and Dragons. The caves' history is now dominated by their use as an air-raid shelter for London's East-enders during the Second World War Blitz. Much attention is also paid to the *Doctor Who* TV series that was shot there. We were encouraged, however, by the presence of a sacred holly, harbinger of mysteries, above the entrance. The atmosphere inside is dry, temperate and wholesome – it has in fact been known to cure cases of asthma. As the temperature is at a constant 11°C/52°F it is advisable, on a summer visit, to take a sweater or cardigan.

Chislehurst stands on top of one of the most remarkable labyrinths of underground chalk caves and passages in the country, known as the enigma of Kent. They have been in use for 8000 years and contain no less than nine druid altars. The High Altar, where fair-haired boys were sacrificed, is surrounded, as in medieval cathedrals, by side chapels in adjacent caves, each with its own altar. Where else in Europe can you find such an elaborate druidic temple? According to *The Woman's Encyclopaedia of Myths and Secrets* by B.G. Walker (p. 651), **Chislehurst** is, along with **Brocéliande**, the most likely site of Merlin's secret cave, which may also have been the British druidic shrine of Mount Ambrosius.

The acoustics are remarkable. The resonance of an echo, produced by a blow to a tin drum, was powerfully amplified through the passages and lasted for 30 seconds. According to the official guide-book: 'If one stands on the altar and sings a note, a chord of three ensues, making a choir-like cadence.' A somewhat similar phenomenon may be observed in the cave of the Cumaean Sybil near Lake

Avernus, the entrance to Virgil's underworld.

This must be one of the most haunted sites in Britain. There are reports of children laughing, crying and playing, an old woman, a hunchback and a Roman Centurion. But most interesting to us is the story of the ghost of a woman who was said to have been murdered in the water of what is known as the Haunted Pool. She has been seen, from time to time, in her long blue gown by the water. Is she perhaps an echo of the long-suppressed Lady of the Lake? Although one might have to spend a night (no longer permitted) to experience the full mystery of the caves and their past, even a guided tour, together with a dozen or so other visitors, gives a suprisingly vivid impression of these druid catacombs.

Wessex

Uffington Castle
Map 22, SU 3087

Tolstoy makes this the setting for the great battle of Dineirth which forms the climax of *The Coming of the King*, and in which Merlin plays a notable part, confronting Wotan and compelling him to leave the field. The battle of Beranbyrg, that was the basis of Tolstoy's account and which was fought in 556, was the last action in Wessex when the Britons were not worsted. The site is usually thought to be Barbury, just south of Swindon, but never was poetic licence more justifiable than in transferring it to **Uffington**, an Iron Age hill-fort forming part of a complex that includes the famous white horse chalk figure of the goddess Epona/Rhiannon and the bald hillock where St George slew the dragon.

Wayland's Smithy
Map 22, SN 3086

This, the most famous forge of Britain, a cromlechian barrow, later identified with the Celtic myth of Gofannon and the Teutonic myth of Wieland, is the setting in Tolstoy's novel *The Coming of the King* for the reforging of Excalibur.

Liddington Castle
Map 22, SU 2179, just S. of M4 exit 15

Take the A345 south off M4 at exit 15 towards **Marlborough** then, after 1 mile take the second turning to the left towards Hinton Parva and in another mile you will see the irregular earthworks above on your right. Park here and take the path up to the very obvious 'castle'.

This, the highest hill-fort, at 910 ft., on the Ridgeway, just south-east of a village called Badbury, guarding the approaches to Wales and the West, is considered by many to be the most likely site of Arthur's great victory over the Saxons at Mount Badon. This size of the castle and its commanding position impress the visitor today – it is clearly visible from the M4.

Rosemary Sutcliffe in *Sword at Sunset* describes its 'huge hill shoulder thrust out from the main mass of the Downs, commanding the Ridgeway and the sweep of the White Horse Vale ...'. Three ancient earthwork sites in Wessex contain the syllable 'bad', possibly derived from Badi, who was a giant and the father of Wayland whose Smithy is nearby.

Southern England

Cornwall

16 Dozmary Pool
17 Castle Dore
18 Loe Pool
19 Marazion and St Michael's Mount
20 Mousehole
21 Land's End
22 Zennor
23 Killibury Castle
24 Tintagel
25 Bossiney Mount
26 St Nectan's Glen
27 Slaughter Bridge

Somerset

13 Solsbury Hill/Bath
14 Glastonbury
15 Cadbury Castle

N

Scale: 1cm = 19 miles

Home Counties and Wessex

1 Chislehurst
2 London
3 Oxford
4 Silchester
5 Uffington Castle
6 Wayland's Smithy
7 Liddington
8 Marlborough
9 Stonehenge
10 Old Sarum
11 Badbury Rings
12 Winchester

Marlborough

Map 22, SU 1969, off
M4 exit 15

This is a beautiful Georgian market town and location of a famous public school.

Thomas Heywood in his *Life of Merlin, sirnamed Ambrosius* (London 1641), states that the boy Merlin was found by Vortigern's troops not in Wales but at 'Kaier – Merlin, id est Marlbarrow' (known as Merlin's barrow in the seventeenth century). He may have been drawing on the work of the twelfth-century poet Alexander Neckham who wrote in his *Praises of Divine Wisdom*: 'Merlini tumulus tibi Merleburgia nomen praebuit, est testis Anglica lingua mihi.' The sixteenth-century historian and headmaster of Westminster, William Camden, to whom we owe so much of the early references to the Arthurian tradition, translated this as follows: 'Great Merlin's grave, the name to Marlborough in Saxon gave.'

Merlin's tomb is reputed to be the great wooded tumulus, known as the Mound, in the grounds of Marlborough College. From earliest times the arms of Marlborough, a castle argent upon a field sable, show that its ancient castle was its main claim to fame. The King of Arms of King James I added to the original crest and wrote round the shield: 'Ubi nunc sapientis ossa Merlini?' (Where now are the bones of the wise Merlin?) The Mound is 60 ft. high and covers an acre and a half. It is not unlike a smaller version of the mysterious Silbury Hill, 5 miles west on the same river, Kennet, which rises 120 ft. and covers 5½ acres. Both are artifical cones of chalk with flattened tops and have been believed to be tombs, though their real purpose remains unknown.

The Celtic Maginot Line, Wansdyke, 2000 yds. south of the mound, might well have been attributed to Merlin, but was named by the victorious Saxons for their own divine magician, Wotan. In AD556 they skirted it to gain victory at Barbury, 5 miles north and showed little interest in what was to become **Marlborough**, whose modern history does not begin until after the Norman conquest. Whether or not the Saxons feared Merlin's vengeance from the grave, the Normans had every reason to enhance their links with the Britain of old, since one third of their army came from Brittany. In 1308 those knightly guardians of the Grail, the Templars, were imprisoned in the castle, nothing of which remains.

In 1735 Frances Lady Hertford had a grotto constructed under the mound which was either the prototype or the copy of Merlin's Cave, built for Queen Caroline, at Richmond. Stukeley's perspective of Marlborough Castle in 1723 shows the mound like a grassy ziggurat with an ascending spiral path leading to a tower on the summit, with a tunnel entrance just beneath. By 1788 trees and shrubs are well advanced along the path and a walled gateway leads to Lady Hertford's grotto. The grotto was repaired in 1986 as a memorial to Harold Cresswell Brentnall and features an elaborate shell-motif, reminding us that however far from the sea we may be, Morgan is never far from Merlin and indeed, her hill is only a few miles to the west, where the Roman Way and Wansdyke meet (**Map 22, SU 0067**). In the grounds you will also find a standing stone and in the neighbourhood a dolmen called the *Devil's Den*. **Marlborough** – situated between Wansdyke and Ridgeway, **Liddington Castle** and **Stonehenge**, so near to Silbury, Avebury and the Kennet Barrows – is, whatever the realities of its Merlin connections, very close to the sacred heart of ancient magical Britain.

When we visited the college it was holiday time and there was a conference in progress, so nobody impeded our wanderings through the grounds. In term time it might be wise to clear your visit with the college. There are many places of refreshment in the town, the Castle and Ball, now a Trust House, being the traditional English inn.

Stonehenge
Map 22, SU 1343

It is a remarkable testimony to the importance of Merlin in our island story that the construction of its great prehistoric sacred centre should be attributed to him.

In Geoffrey of Monmouth's *History*, Aurelius Ambrosius, reputed to have been born at nearby Amesbury, seeks Merlin's advice for the erection of a fitting memorial to the 460 British Chieftains treacherously killed on the site of **Stonehenge** by Hengist's Saxons during a banquet. Merlin proposes a military expedition to the heart of Ireland with the aim of bringing back the stone-circle, known as the Giants' Dance, from Killaraus (cf. **Ushnagh**). Merlin accompanies the expeditionary force led by Uther and, by his craft, dismantles the circle which is then reassembled at **Stonehenge**. The known facts concerning **Stonehenge** are its original construction in about 3100–2800BC, the addition of the blue stones from the **Preseli Mountains** about a millennium later with a new alignment and a final rearrangement some time after 1800BC. Merlin's statement that the Dance of the Giants at **Ushnagh** came originally from Africa may not be so wide of the mark as it appears, considering that the first inhabitants of the British Isles, who erected the first standing stones, were a small dark people from the Mediterranean. The next wave of

Stonehenge, the sacred centre to which Merlin traditionally brought the stone circle of Ushnagh from Ireland.

invaders, the taller, fairer Beaker Folk, may have been responsible for the removal of the stones from **Preseli**. Certainly these Bronze Age sun-worshippers had an elaborate cult of the dead and seem to have made Salisbury Plain their capital. To establish the uniqueness of its status it is quite possible, as Tolstoy suggests, that they would have wished to remove the stones of a rival sacred centre and place them in the heart of their own *temenos*. One can see from the history of, for example, Egypt, how the sacred centre changes its location in accordance with new religious orientations.

The history of Christianity, too, shows that there can be but one primatial see per nation. The blue stones certainly came not from Ireland but from **Preseli**. Curiously, however, south-west Wales was occupied by Irish colonists from Leinster from the third century onwards, a fact of which Merlin-Emrys of **Carmarthen** would have been quite aware. Merlin, moreover, has left us his own signature to his handiwork in the shape of his heel-print, to be seen on stone 14, which the Devil hurled at him (see **Ushnagh** for another super-natural footprint).

It is, alas, no longer possible to examine closely either of the Hele-Stones for such evidence since the whole enclosure is strictly wired off. **Stonehenge**, now more like an internment camp than a sacred centre, has been thoroughly deconsecrated by the inroads of mass-tourism and the ill-judged efforts of bureaucracy to control it. The site is now best known for annual battles between police, druids and New Age enthusiasts at the time of the summer solstice. To gain a more profound impression of what an ancient sacred centre was like at the heart of Clas Merdin, Merlin's 'Island of the Mighty', one must go to Avebury and its surrounding barrows – but quickly, for here too the spectre of sacrilege looms.

Old Sarum
Map 14, ST 1433

Old Sarum has been claimed as the site of at least two battles involving Arthur and Merlin, including the final struggle with Mordred. Historically it was the scene of Cynric's crushing defeat of the Britons in AD552 during the second Saxon Rebellion which led to the withdrawal of the Celts to their western fastnesses. **Old Sarum** was originally an Iron Age hill-fort refortified by the Normans. It still conveys the impressive power of such defensive positions. It is on one of the oldest and best established leylines that runs from **Stonehenge** to Salisbury Cathedral, which originally stood at **Old Sarum** itself. In Roman times it was an important junction of five major trading routes.

Badbury Rings
Map 14, SY 9603 – N. of B3082 between Wimborne Minster and Blandford Forum

The spectacular approach to **Badbury Rings** along the magnificent Beech Avenue, planted by William John Bankes in 1835, leads you to the well-signposted National Trust site on the Kingston Lacey Estate. It was one of many strongpoints used by the Britons against the Saxon invaders during the sixth century and a possible site for Mount

Badon. Between AD500 and 550 the Saxon front line stretched roughly from the Hampshire Avon to the Upper Thames Valley. Most of the British fortresses hold this line from **Badbury** through **Old Sarum** to **Marlborough** and **Liddington Castle**.

Badbury Rings, which in the 1950s were wild and unorganized – a good place to take the dog for a walk – are now a well set-out Heritage site. The three rings of fortification are clearly visible and give a good impression of what it was like to defend an ancient hill-fort.

Winchester
Map 15, SU 4729

Winchester is the site of the most famous of all the Round Tables, preserved on a wall in the castle hall. It was probably built by Edward III and refurbished by Henry VIII. **Winchester**'s connection with Merlin dates back much further: it was here that Aurelius Ambrosius died by poison while Merlin was with Uther and the army. A great portent appeared in the heavens – a fiery dragon – no doubt a comet, announcing the death of the King and the succession of Uther, now to be called Pendragon. One ray from the dragon's head shone over Gaul proclaiming the coming of Uther's son, Arthur, and his victorious reign. Merlin interpreted all these signs and at his suggestion Uther had two golden dragons wrought, one for Winchester Cathedral and one to accompany the army, which should be borne by Merlin himself.

Somerset

Solsbury Hill/Bath
Map 21, ST 7464 – on the N.E. outskirts of **Bath** and N. of Batheaston

John Morris in *The Age of Arthur* provides many cogent reasons why Mount Badon should have been **Solsbury Hill**, though he fails to make the connection between the British name for **Bath**, Caer Badum and Mount Badon. **Solsbury** is a definite mons – not a spur to be taken easily from the rear, deep in British territory, with little to offer in way of support for an invading army and steep enough to be held successfully by dismounted cavalry who after three days could counter-attack on horse with the help of the terrain.

Bath, a thermal spa, was the major healing centre of Romano–Celtic Britain whose goddess, Sul or Sulis, symbolizing the subterranean eye of consciousness, had her shrine on **Solsbury Hill**. The legendary founder of **Bath**, the magician King Bladud, who was the consort of the great goddess, could fly like a bird, a peculiarity he shared with the Irish Merlin, Sweeney. He was also one of the renowned Celtic swineherds whose pigs led him to the healing waters of the goddess Sulis at **Bath**.

Glastonbury
Map 21, ST 4938

The Arthurian connection with **Glastonbury** has a long history and continues to generate much controversy. We shall confine ourselves solely to those aspects of the tradition which may relate to Merlin.

Exit 23 off M5 and take
A39 via Street.

What should not be overlooked, however, is that **Glastonbury** today is the popular Mecca of all those undertaking the Celtic mystery quest, to which Merlin is central. To begin with, its site was demarcated by a herd of pigs, his totem animals (cf. **Madley**). The other major associations to the Merlin legend are as follows:

(1) *The Holy Grail*

Merlin sends forth the knights of the Round Table on the quest of the Holy Grail. This is a cultic object which, both in its pagan and Christian form, has strong links to **Glastonbury**. In King Arthur's expedition to the underworld, described in *The Spoils of Annwfn*, a Welsh poem from about AD900, included in *The Book of Taliesin*, the main objective is to bring back a magic cauldron, which is tended by nine priestesses. In Geoffrey of Monmouth's *Vita Merlini*, Avalon, often thought to be **Glastonbury**, is said to be the abode of nine royal sorceresses. Arthur's other expedition to **Glastonbury** to retrieve something precious was his rescue of Queen Guinevere from abduction at the hands of King Melwas. It may be that both Guinevere and the magic cauldron symbolize the feminine sovereignty of the land without which there can be no true monarch, and in the absence of which the land becomes waste. Mary Stewart makes Merlin play a major role in the recovery of Guinevere just before he himself encounters Ninian who will lead him to his own otherworldly

Glastonbury Tor, where the magician-god Gwynn ap Nudd returned to the underworld with the arrival of Christianity. Here King Melwas kept Guinevere captive and Merlin devised his zodiacal Round Table.

fate. The name of this underworld dwelling is given as the fairy city or the city of glass. Both of these correspond well to **Glastonbury**:

(i) **The Tor is one of the entrances to the underworld where St Collen encountered Gwynn ap Nudd, the lord of the dead and leader of the Wild Hunt.**

(ii) **Caradoc in his** *Life of Gildas* **gives the British name of Glastonbury as** *Ynis Witrin* **or glass island.**

In the Christian myth, St Joseph of Arimathea is reputed to have founded here the first Christian church in Britain and to have buried the Holy Grail within the Tor. This may have led to the tradition of Chalice Well, described by Dion Fortune, who lived next door, as 'the wonderful Holy Well of Joseph, Merlin and the Holy Grail'.

There seems no doubt that **Glastonbury** was a sacred site long before the advent of Christianity and that St Michael's tower on the summit was earlier a druidic shrine. Recent excavations testify to the presence of cultivated inhabitants on the Tor during the Arthurian period and finds include an interesting and unique bronze head, believed to be that of a British military leader.

Bran the Blessed possessed a magic horn of plenty which was a perpetual source of nourishment. Joseph of Arimathea was supernaturally nourished by the Holy Grail for more than forty years, after which he set off with his companions to bring it to **Glastonbury**. The link between them is Brons to whom, in one version, Joseph entrusted the Grail and who then became known as the Rich Fisher King, who settled in Avalon.

Looking at **Glastonbury** today it may seem highly fanciful to regard it as any sort of island, let alone Avalon, the Isle of the Blessed and of eternal youth, so often depicted in the western seas. Up till the Middle Ages, however, the low-lying lands surrounding the Tor were indeed regularly flooded and the river Brue provided an easy access to the Bristol Channel, just south of Brent Knoll, the goddess Brigantia's sacred mountain.

(2) *Excalibur*

The southern entry to **Glastonbury**, across the Brue, is still called Pomparles, the perilous bridge, as it has been known since 1415, and probably much earlier. Here is one of the traditional sites where Excalibur was returned to the waters, whence it came, after the battle of *Camlann*. It had to follow its scabbard whither Morgan, both Arthur's sister and goddess of the Otherworld, had flung it long before, thus removing the invulnerability it had hitherto bestowed on the king.

Merlin is intimately associated with Arthur's sword, and Geoffrey of Monmouth states that Excalibur was forged in Avalon. Helmut Nickel attributes the fashioning of this sword with its runes of power to Merlin to guide Arthur to Avalon to heal him of his grievous wounds.

In connection with Morgan's otherworldly activities in Avalon, it is noteworthy that the most famous **Glastonbury** miracle is that of the hawthorn tree planted by Joseph of Arimathea on Wearyall Hill, and which continues to blossom at Christmas. Now hawthorn is the sacred symbol of the Celtic underworld goddesses, the equivalent to Persephone, who spends part of the year with Pluto and part in the world of light. The chapel of St Mary Magdalen, situated at the foot of Wearyall Hill, dates from the fifth century and lends some support to a Gnostic origin of the Grail legend. In some traditions Mary Magdalen and the sacred gnosis, imparted by Christ's kiss, is herself the Holy Grail.

(3) Merlin and Gildas

St Gildas, born in about AD500, who hailed from the banks of the Clyde like St Patrick, is one of the saints intimately connected with Merlin and the Arthurian legends. His book *On the Ruin of Britain* is the only contemporary history of the Arthurian period in Britain. He mentions Ambrosius Aurelianus and the great victory of Mount Badon, but fails to name Arthur because, according to Giraldus Cambrensis, the king had killed his brother Hueil and subdued Gildas' father-in-law, a Pict from the north. Later, Caradoc's *Life of Gildas* shows the reconciliation of king and saint when Gildas assisted in the restoration of Guinevere.

When Taliesin comes to visit Merlin (cf. **Hart Fell**) to discuss with him, among many weighty matters, the possible return of Arthur from Avalon, it is after a retreat with St Gildas the Wise at Rhuys in Brittany. According to Goodrich, Merlin himself has been identified with Gildas, one of the many saints who form the Christian face of this Celtic Janus. St Gildas is reputed to have been abbot of **Glastonbury** and to have ended his days there, though whether he was buried in the cemetery, as is claimed, or was put to sea – as would be appropriate in Avalon – is open to question.

(4) The Glastonbury Round Table

Apart from the oaken table hanging in the hall of **Winchester** Castle, most of Merlin's Round Tables have been associated with Roman remains or prehistoric earthworks. The most audacious theory was formulated by Katherine Maltwood in 1929. To her, Merlin's Round Table was a temple of the stars conceived on the principle of 'as above so below', in which the signs of the zodiac could be made out in topographical features of the landscape surrounding **Glastonbury**. **Glastonbury** itself features at the Midheaven as Aquarius, the sign of the cup bearer or the phoenix, drinking from the chalybeate water of Chalice Well (open daily to visitors).

Melkin, a prophetic bard of **Glastonbury** and proto-Merlin from the fifth century, apart from mentioning Joseph of Arimathea and the Grail, makes a reference to Avalon's island as honoured by 'chanting spheres of prophecy', which could well be interpreted astrologically.

Geoffrey Ashe in his *Avalonian Quest* finds some support for the zodiac theory in the prophecies of Nostradamus which refer to Britain as the land of the great heavenly temple.

It is easy for the rational mind to pour cold water on **Glastonbury**'s temple of the stars, but for the questor there could be few better preludes to the pilgrimage goal of the Tor than to circumambulate the putative zodiac first.

Gothic Image Bookshop in **Glastonbury** will furnish you with an itinerary and information about guided tours.

South Cadbury
Map 13, ST 6325

Park outside the church and climb the footpath signposted Cadbury Castle.

Romantic, 'many-tower'd Camelot' of Tennyson and Hollywood is a creation of the twelfth-century imagination, and none the worse for that. Chrétien de Troyes, who first writes of it in his *Lancelot*, simply tells us that King Arthur, 'one Ascension Day, had left **Caerleon** and held a most magnificent court at Camelot with all the splendour appropriate of the day'. There is a great hall where the Queen and many nobles and beautiful courtly ladies have a meal, at the end of which Sir Lancelot makes his entrance. Chrétien wastes no time on further description of the scenery, but gets straight on with the story. It is clear from this that Chrétien does not think Camelot is **Caerleon**, which seems to be Geoffrey of Monmouth's preferred site and which does apparently contain royal palaces and golden gables, as well as two churches which make it a match for Rome. Malory plumps for **Winchester**, and a recent writer has placed Camelot as far afield as **Stirling** or a holiday-campsite near Ayr, at **Greenan Castle**.

Wherever one seeks Camelot one must approach it first of all in the imagination, enriched by the white and azure images of the medieval books of hours, or seen through the inspired eyes of the poets. For Camelot is above all a city of the mind, an altered state of being. It is a city that is at one in itself, at whose Round Table all dwell together joyfully in unity. But, like the longed-for real Jerusalem, won and lost again in the century of Chrétien and Geoffrey, Camelot carried within itself the seeds of its own destruction.

Cadbury today seems far removed from the image of the ideal city. But two factors lend credence to its being the most plausible site of Camelot. Firstly, there is the historical and archaeological evidence and secondly, there is its location, just south of the main road from **Stonehenge** and east of the Fosse Way that led with Roman straightness from Ilchester to **Bath**, Cirencester, Leicester and Lincoln. Arthur's Lane northwards is now only a vestigial track, so it is best to approach **Cadbury** indirectly from the north-west as though from **Glastonbury**, to appreciate the impressive redoubtability of the citadel and to savour signposts to Queen Camel. You

may well wish to stop off for a stroll in Sutton Montis where the ghosts of Arthur and his knights still ride at Christmas or midsummer and halt to water their horses at the spring.

Once at **South Cadbury**, if it has rained at all recently, equip yourself with stout walking boots and sticks, for, as the sixteenth-century writer Camden points out, 'Camalet (is) a steep hill and hard to get up'. Outside a cottage at the foot of the rise is a large plan of the site with an up-to-date history. Flowery hedgerows give place to woodland and finally open fields, forming a domed plateau of 18

Aerial view of Cadbury Castle.

acres. Walking round it you will notice the quadruple fortifications of the earthworks rising in some places 40 ft. This was originally the most important citadel of the Durotriges, the warlike and fiercely anti-Roman tribe whose territory included Dorset, South Somerset and South Wiltshire. It was not until AD70 that it was taken by the invading Romans who founded a new settlement in what is now the village of **South Cadbury**.

Recent excavations have uncovered sensational evidence, which proves the establishment in the second half of the fifth century of re-occupation on quite a grand scale. A large timber hall had been built in the post-Roman period in Celtic style in the centre of the plateau known since at least the sixteenth century as *Arthur's Palace*. Guarding the south-western approach to the hall, at some distance away in a gap in the ramparts, the remains of a gate-house have also been found. Finally, surrounding the entire perimeter, for some three-quarters of a mile, surmounting the old earthen ramparts, a wall of the same period, sixteen feet thick, had been built in stone with wooden beams. No construction of this size or sophistication has been found anywhere else in Celtic Britain. Artefacts dug up at **Cadbury** include fragments of wine and oil jars imported from the eastern Mediterranean towards the end of the fifth century. They match those from the same period discovered at **Tintagel**. On the earthworks at the south-eastern corner of **Cadbury** the excavators found the remains of a young man thrust head downward into a pit, a fate that Merlin almost suffered to strengthen the foundations of **Dinas Emrys**.

From its height of 500 feet, **Cadbury** offers an uninterrupted view on a clear day to **Glastonbury** Tor, twelve miles north-north-west. Beacon fires could have linked it easily through **Glastonbury** and Brent Knoll to the Bristol Channel and Dinas Powys beyond. With advance intelligence, a speedily deployed cavalry force could have used the network of roads that met at Cadbury to surprise invaders. Did Arthur gallop out from here to win his famous victory of Mount Badon – whether it was at **Bath**, **Badbury Rings** or **Liddington Castle**? Certainly this connection was already old when John Leland wrote in 1542: 'At South Cadbyri standeth Camallate, sumtyme a famose town or castelle. The people can tell nothing thar but that they have hard say that Arture much resortid to Camalat.' As late as the nineteenth century an old man asked a group of visiting antiquarians if they had come to take Arthur away. For Arthur and his knights are still sleeping in a cave in the hollow limestone hill behind golden gates. And what of Merlin? It was he who built Camelot in a single night. Mary Stewart describes his connection with the city in Book II of *The Last Enchantment*. She also mentions the *Lady's Well* – 'the good spring dedicated to the Goddess.' Wells and springs are what are least likely to change and disappear at ancient sites, so, as you go back down the hill, pause for a moment half-way by the stone-covered spring under the roots of an old tree and reflect that from its waters Merlin might have drunk and the Knights of the Round Table filled their bottles for the last time as they left Camelot on the quest he had set them of the Holy Grail. There is another well in the woods if you care to explore, perhaps that of Arthur. Near its reputed site – it was too wet and steep for us to search there – we heard a rustle, and two deer, startled by a hound, bounded out of the undergrowth. Nothing that day brought us nearer to Merlin, lord of stags and wild things.

Before leaving **South Cadbury** you should pay a visit to those two indispensable centres of any true English village, the church and the pub. There was an important church at the time of the *Domesday Book* and the present Early English building is dedicated to St Thomas à Becket. The churchyard has a pair of wrens, the druids' bird, and some fine trees and the parish magazine is called **Excalibur**. The Red Lion is a tiny inn and a free house that stocks two good Somerset real ales and serves snacks. There you might be given directions to *Arthur's Well* half-way up the slope from Folly Lane, amongst the trees (cf. **Barenton**).

The pubs and churches of Queen's Camel and West Camel on the River Camel (the Celtic word for crooked) are also worth a visit. The Camelot Inn in West Camel serves a reasonably priced lunch and wines as well as excellent Wadworth's 6X Bitter. Their everyday menu includes Merlin's T-bone steak and Arthur's rump.

Cornwall

Dozmary Pool
Map 8, SX 1876

1 mile south of Bolventor and the famous Jamaica Inn of Daphne du Maurier's novel

Dozmary Pool, indicated to the left of the road at a parking space on a bend, is the second largest natural lake in Cornwall, after **Loe Pool**, but is today dwarfed by Colliford Lake reservoir on the other side of the road. Walk for five minutes down a rough path and you will come to the Pool. The farm at the end is strictly private property.

The Pool and its setting, with Brown Gelly in the background, bear a striking resemblance to **Yeun Ellez** and its **Montagne de St Michel**, much the same height as Brown Gelly though the latter has no chapel on its peak to celebrate the victory of the Archangel. Both places have a strong whiff of sulphur and an Otherworldly character. Here the wild hunt, with its hell-hounds, has become attached to Jan Tregeagle (pronounced Tregale), a local, cruel and unjust magistrate of the seventeenth century, who was pursued by the hounds all the way to Roche Rock (**Map 7, SW 9860**), the other side of Bodmin. He tried to enter the chapel there, perched dramatically on its rock, but could only get his head and shoulders through the window, leaving the rest of his anatomy exposed to the attentions of the infernal pack. Whether the cries were his or theirs, it is still proverbial in Cornwall to 'howl like a Tregeagle'. One of his post-mortem punishments, to fit his crimes, was to bail out the Pool with a leaky clam shell.

If this is indeed the pool where Sir Bedivere reluctantly flung *Excalibur* after the battle of *Camlann* – and it would have been a fair yomp if the latter were **Slaughter Bridge** – then it is also the spot where Merlin and Arthur first received it from the hand of the *Lady of the Lake* (cf. **Loe Pool**).

Castle Dore
Map 7, SX 1251 and OS 200, SX 1054

Situated to the left of the B3269 N. of Fowey near the Golant/Tywardreath crossroads. Look out for Lawhibbit Farm and you will find **Castle Dore** between it and the buildings at the crossing.

Continue on the B3269 towards Fowey. Just after the crossroads signposting Boddinick Ferry to the left, you will find the monument in about 200 yds. on the south of the road by a lay-by to your left.

Even as hill-forts go, **Castle Dore**, when viewed from ground level, without the eye of an archaeologist, is singularly uninspiring. It is, nevertheless, one of the many favoured sites of Camelot. History and legend, however, connect it more with King Mark than King Arthur and excavations in the 1930s revealed an important wooden building and sixth-century pottery fragments that link it to the post-Roman Celtic period.

Our main reason for including this area in the Merlin itinerary of Cornwall is that in the **Tristan Stone** we have the only extant sixth-century artefact pointing to the existence of any character in the entire Arthurian canon to be found anywhere in the world. The 7 ft. monolith has been moved many times and bears the inscription: DRUSTANUS HIC IACIT CUNOMORI FILIUS (Here lies Tristan son of Cunomorus). Cunomorus was a sixth-century king of Dumnonia which included Devon and Cornwall as well as parts of Brittany. His capital there seems to have been Poher or **Carhaix** which, according to the early thirteenth-century romance *Lancelot of the Lake* was also the site of King Arthur's Easter Court. It is important to stress that Cunomorus is a real historical figure recorded in a number of documents prior to the tenth century. He attempted, it seems, to unite Brittany under his rule in alliance with Childebert, son of Clovis, King of the Franks, and ruled an empire that spoke four languages. His Cornish domain was fixed on the **Tintagel–Castle Dore** axis. His names, Cunomorus (*great hound*) and Mark (*horse*), confirm his role as unifier of two clan-totems. Both these animals are guides to the underworld. He sends Tristan, his son or nephew, to bring back the Irish princess, Iseult, to be his queen. The ensuing romance between Tristan and Iseult introduces the theme of tragic, romantic and adulterous love-in-death to European literature. Mark himself, historical though he is, presents another archetypal pattern. A Celtic Bluebeard, he murders his wives at the first sign of pregnancy. He gains their lands and avoids a perilous predicted heir. One recalls Uranus forcing his children back into Earth and Saturn devouring his offspring.

Mark, who had horse's ears, not unlike horns, is one of the famous mythical cuckolds and in French idiom 'to go to Cornwall' means to be deceived by one's wife. This may symbolize the betrayal of the horned Cernunnos, god of the underworld, diabolized by the Christians. The first syllable of his name is to be found in the Cornish word for Cornwall, Kernow (see also **Mote of Mark**).

St Blazey

Between Fowey and St Austell lies the village of St Blazey, a highly Merlinesque guardian of sick and wounded animals as well as the teacher and chronicler of Merlin himself. The Celtic word *bleizh* means wolf – one of Merlin's animal companions.

Loe Pool
Map 6, SW 6225

3½ miles S.W. of Helston by B3304. As you approach Porthleven keep left and go down the road marked cul-de-sac to the furthest car-park. Take the clearly defined path above Porthleven Sands to Bar Lodge, whose gateway is the entrance to the National Trust property of which **Loe Pool** forms part. Continue until you see the Pool. Allow 1–1½ hrs. for the visit. There

Tennyson, in his *Idylls of the King*, makes **Loe Pool** the enchanted setting for the passing of Arthur. Sir Bedivere bears the mortally wounded king to a ruined chapel:

> **That stood on a dark strait of barren land:**
> **On one side lay the ocean, and on one**
> **Lay a great water.**

Three times Arthur commanded him to cast Excalibur into the Pool, and, on the last occasion, he knew from the knights' description of what had ensued that he had at last completed his mission:

> **So flash'd and fell the brand Excalibur.**
> **But ere he dipt the surface, rose an arm**
> **Clothed in white samite, mystic, wonderful,**
> **And caught him by the hilt, and brandish'd him**
> **Three times and drew him under in the mere.**

is an alternative approach from the N.T. car-park at Penrose, N. of Porthleven. The nearest point to the Pool with the best views of the Bar is from Begibna on the east side. Taking the A3083 from Helston to The Lizard, turn right at Helston Hospital, then first left and fourth right.

This was the arm of the Lady of the Lake who first brought Excalibur into Arthur's court. Later, he and Merlin had rowed on the Pool to claim:

> . . . the sword
> That rose from out the bosom of the lake
> . . . old Merlin counselled him,
> 'Take thou and strike.'

Now the King and Sword were back in the realm of her whose magic, Tennyson tells us, was subtler than Merlin's. As Arthur lay on Loe Bar three queens appeared in a dark barge to bear him away:

> To the island-valley of Avilion:
> Where falls not hail, or rain, or any snow,
> Nor ever wind blows loudly.

Loe bar still holds the Pool and ocean apart, though it was breached in the great storm of 1987, and also, according to tradition, some four centuries earlier, when a gale blew a Spanish galleon, laden with treasure, right over it, to founder in the depths of the mere. Thus we have, as so often, a story of hidden treasure associated with a sacred Celtic lake. As we scrambled down the steep banks to the edge of the still, clear water, we thought we saw shards of a broken sword. These turned out to be pieces of silvery shale glinting in the spring sunshine. **Loe Pool**, the largest natural lake in Cornwall, lends itself, as Tennyson discovered, to such flights of fancy. It lies at the bottom of a deep wooded valley, mercifully spared by the hurricane, carpeted with flowers (violets especially when we were last there), constantly changing in mood with the weather, the seasons and the time of day. To see it through Arthur's dimming eyes, it would have to be on New Year's Eve under 'the long glories of the winter moon' – a full moon at that. The river that fills the Pool comes all the way from Nine Maidens Downs, where druidesses surely presided, and, locked by the Bar, goes underground to gush forth west of it from a hole into the sea. A curious tradition links the Bar's formation to that other lake of Excalibur, **Dozmary Pool** on Bodmin Moor, far to the north-east. Jan Tregeagle, the evil genius of the place, was set the impossible task of carrying sand all the way from Berepper, half-way to Mullion, to Porthleven, across what was then the estuary at **Loe**. One day the Devil chased him and, to escape, he emptied the sack he was carrying, thus creating the Bar and the Pool. Such geographical features in the Celtic world are generally attributed to Merlin, Arthur, some local giant or the Devil (cf. **Mont St Michel** and **Baie des Trépassés**).

Marazion and St Michael's Mount
Map 6, SW 5130

As you skirt Mount's Bay by the A394 going west, turn left at Goldsithney into **Marazion** (*little market or market Jew*) for a fine view of **St Michael's Mount**. The archangel Michael appeared here to a hermit and again to some fishermen in AD495, the period of Arthur and Merlin. Here, as throughout the Celtic world, St Michael replaces the Celtic sky-god. Such shrines generally indicate a point of departure to the Otherworld. Among the Jews who came to trade for Cornish tin was Joseph of Arimathea who landed here bearing the Holy Grail, thus making it the first meeting-place between the eastern mystery tradition and the Celtic church. Merlin was later to initiate the quest for the recovery of the Grail.

Mousehole
Map 6, SW 4626 – 3 miles S. of Penzance via Newlyn and coast road

Mousehole (pronounced Mowz'l) is an attractive little port and very difficult to park in. It is the only locality in South Cornwall to celebrate Merlin's presence by name, with Merlin's Place and the famous Merlyn's Rock. This should not be confused with the prominent St Clement's Isle that guards the approaches to the harbour, gave Mousehole its original Celtic name, Porth Enys (*Island Port*), and was once the haunt of a hermit before being dedicated to the patron saint of seafarers.

To find Merlyn's Rock (marked on **OS map 203**) you must walk south by the sea for a few hundred yards (depending where you have managed to park) until you come upon a rather unexciting wave-tossed mass a short distance from the shore. A somewhat more

Merlin's Rock, Mousehole. Setting for a post-Armada Spanish raid, correctly prophesied by Merlin.

interesting but distant view may be obtained from the cliff road above, that joins up with the Cornish Coast Path. When the Rock received its name is not known, but it was the focal point of a successful prophecy supposedly made by the enchanter himself: 'There shall land on the Rock of Merlyn, those who shall burn Paul, Penzance and Newlyn'. This occurred in 1595 in the form of Spaniards seeking revenge for the Armada. They landed on the Rock, according to Camden, the Elizabethan historian. It must have been a tricky manoeuvre, but they made it, and burnt **Mousehole** for good measure to the ground, except for the Keigwin Arms (no longer a pub). After the battle of Camlann, according to one legend, the victorious Mordred chased the remnants of Arthur's army to the extreme limits of Lyonesse, when suddenly Merlin appeared in his path. The earth heaved and the waters rushed in, drowning Mordred and his host, along with the land of Lyonesse (which included Mount's Bay and 140 parishes), while Arthur's knights made good their escape to all that now survives of that lost Cornish Atlantis, the Isles of Scilly. It is hard not to think of Moses, at whose prayer Pharaoh's horses and chariots were cast into the sea, or even more vividly, Gandalf, in *The Lord of the Rings*, holding, as a servant of the secret fire, the Bridge of Khazad-Dum, while Frodo and his companions left Moria *en route* for Mordor.

The narrow strip of land between cliff and sea facing his rock is just where Merlin could have appeared. The sea made further inroads in 1099 and 1118, but the great inundation was made much earlier, perhaps contemporaneous with that which engulfed the Bay of Avranches that surrounds **Mont St Michel**, or the disaster that drowned Is in Western Brittany.

Land's End
Map 6, SW 3525 – just W. of Sennen

If you come from **Mousehole** and the magic valley of Lamorna following the side roads, you should stop, shortly after you join the B3315, and pay your respects to the *Merry Maidens*, a stone circle to the left of the road, and the *Pipers* in the fields across the road to whose tune they dance. This is an area exceptionally rich in neolithic monuments.

All the great Celtic peninsulas jutting into the Atlantic – Galicia, Brittany, Cornwall – have their **Land's Ends**, the point of departure for the souls of the dead to a better world beyond the seas. To appreciate this last bastion of Britain, which overlooks lost Lyonesse to the west, you need to walk away to the left along the coastal path, leaving the crowded car-park and tourist complex behind you. Go, if you can, out of season, as the sun sets behind the Scillies and the intervening rocks and lighthouse. If the weather is stormy, so much the better, for it is then that the voices of the drowned can be heard above the roaring waters. Do not approach too near the rollers lest you join their company, as some have done in recent times.

You can see to the south a rocky islet called the *Armed Knight* standing defiantly above the waves. Is he looking east to challenge any who would approach Lyonesse, or is he the sentinel who guards the *Island of the Mighty*? Could he even be one of Mordred's followers petrified in pursuit when Merlin let in the waters? The rock lost its crested helmet in a great storm of 1670 along with a lance placed there long before to serve some mysterious purpose.

Two things we know: one, that all who visit the Isles of Scilly, the peaks of what once formed a larger mass, are in accord with the ancients who knew them as the *Fortunate Isles*. Among them stand *Great Arthur* and *Little Arthur*. Is Merlin perhaps there, too, in the guise of St Martin (another name for Merlin) with its sacred *Old Man* stone? The other thing we know that links Merlin to this western outpost of Cornwall that has been called *his land*, is his prophecy concerning Sennen at **Land's End**: 'When the wild men from the north-east land there,' he says, 'the world will come to an end.'

Nine miles S.W. of **Land's End** is the Wolf Rock lighthouse.

Zennor
Map 6, SW 4538

As you pursue your way to the north Cornish Merlin sites, you may wish to stop at **Zennor**, 20 miles N.E. of **Land's End** by B3306. Here you will encounter Morgan, who manifests along the whole Breton coast, as the mermaid in a fifteenth-century bench-end carving. **Zennor** also has a Rocking Stone (Logan Stone) and the largest *quoit* in Cornwall, a flat cap-stone of a cromlech, covering two tombs.

Killibury Castle
OS map 200, 015739, east of Wadebridge

This is the earliest residence of Arthur recorded in the *Welsh Triads*. Only half the hill-fort now remains. The village of St Mabyn, 1½ miles to the east commemorates the sixth-century daughter of Brychan (see **St Nectan**), but is recorded in the thirteenth-century *Feet of Fines* as a male saint. This provides an interesting comment on the somewhat androgynous nature of the Celtic Apollo, Mabon, with whom Merlin is much associated (cf. **Lochmaben**).

Tintagel
Map 8, SX 0588 or OS map 200, SX 048891

At **Tintagel** we reach the heart of the Merlin mystery in Cornwall. The story is one of the best known in the world. Uther Pendragon, the High King of Britain, falls immediately in love with Ygraine, wife of Gorlois, Duke of Cornwall. Uther asks Merlin for help and Merlin, for his own purposes and the salvation of the land, spirits him into the impregnable castle – and Ygraine's bed – in the shape of Gorlois, who dies that very night in a sortie from his castle at Dimilioc. Merlin himself accompanies the King and, after Arthur is conceived, helps him make good his escape. He has forced Uther to agree that the child, who is to be born, shall be handed over at birth into his care.

This legend may be a distant echo of the magic power of the druid-astrologer to ensure the reincarnation of a hero or divine avatar at the right time. Merlin's own conception may have been the result of such calculating wizardry.

North from the tourist village of Tintagel, with its Vale of Avalon, the path leads up or down. The cove, waterfall and Merlin's Cave –

duh? the most famous in Cornwall – need no entry ticket, but are best approached when the tide is low and few other visitors are around. So go early, late, or out of season. Merlin's Cave, open at both ends, will give you shelter and food for wonder. Just after the sea has departed it leaves at its ebbing a quivering carpet of filming foam, while the western waves still beat furiously against the dark rocks and fill the cave with their Mendelssohnian music. Here Merlin received the once and future King in his infancy and bore him off to a safe haven. This glimpse of the Otherworld, beneath the great crag and its royal palace, is one of the high places of the Celtic spirit where Merlin ushered in the Age of Arthur.

The medieval castle dates from the twelfth century, the time when Arthur and Merlin re-emerged through the pages of Geoffrey of Monmouth, who visited **Tintagel** in 1134 and who first mentions the castle. But archaeology has revealed an earlier Tintagel, the site of a lordly mansion dating from between AD450–650, after the departure of the Romans and before the coming of the Saxons.

Merlin's Cave under Tintagel Castle.

Tintagel Castle is the most romantic ruin in Cornwall.

That this is hallowed ground is attested by the presence of a fifth-century Celtic Christian monastery. But the existence of a more ancient cult is clear in the dedication of the church to St Materiana, a thinly disguised successor to Modron, the great Mother Goddess of the divine son, Mabon (cf. **Lochmaben**). The patron of the ruined chapel on the island of **Tintagel** is St Juliot, who makes an interesting connection with **St Nectan's Glen** (see below). While in **Tintagel** do not neglect to visit, if you can (for it is often closed) the Hall of Chivalry. This might appear to be just the sort of kitschy tourist trap that we would normally urge you to avoid. In fact, it is a rather touching testimony to the rebirth of Arthur and Merlin at a popular, rather than literary level, on both sides of the Atlantic. Here the millionaire custard manufacturer, Frederic Glasscock, founded in 1930 his Fellowship of the Order of the Knights of the Round Table.

Bossiney Mound
Map 8, SX 0688

Bossiney Mound, between **Tintagel** and **St Nectan's Glen**, is one of the sites of Merlin's Round Table. Here it is golden and buried under a mound next to the chapel, but each year at midsummer it reveals itself with a wondrous light. One of the authors of the *Guide Book to King Arthur's Country in Cornwall* has actually seen the supernatural glow of an inexplicable light suddenly appearing inside one of the chapel windows on Midsummer Eve.

St Nectan's Glen
Map OS, 200 081886, between **Tintagel** and Boscastle off the B3263

St Juliot's feast day is 16th June and that of her brother and neighbour **St Nectan** the following day. This feast he shares with St Moling who befriended the Irish Merlin, Suibhne. So they are midsummer saints and maybe the magic waters of St Nectan's Kieve were a Jaouanc or druidical baptismal site as at the **Fontaine de Jouvence** near **Merlin's Tomb** in **Brocéliande**. The Glen is one of those ideal fairylands that one occasionally stumbles across between the bleak hills and moors of the Celtic quest. Try to be there in bluebell time and be patient enough to watch for the dippers and kingfishers that are its familiar spirits. If ever Merlin was in **Tintagel**, he would surely have come to exchange words of wisdom with the hermit, whether Christian or pagan, who dwelt here. Nowhere evokes more strongly the sense of natural religion and nature mysticism that is the hallmark of the Celtic soul, combining, as it does, forest, fountain, rock and hill. As you descend the slippery and precipitous staircase from the hermitage, suddenly at one turn of the spiral you see at last the hidden waterfall, whose roar you have heard all along, issuing forth from the rock-wall of a ravine and plunging 30 ft. into the Kieve.

Surely it is **St Nectan's Glen** that Xavier de Langlais is describing in *Le roman du Roi Arthur* when he tells how Merlin took Uther Pendragon and Ulfin into a little wood in the evening just on the outskirts of **Tintagel**. There he selected herbs whose virtues he knew well and applied them to the face and hands of himself and his companions, transforming them into the likeness of Duke Gorlois and two of his faithful servants.

Where Arthur is, Merlin is never far away, but there are so many sites with Arthurian connections where the magic has gone and which have no specific relevance to the Merlin theme, that we have had to be selective in our choice. Was Camelford Camelot; did Arthur and Guinevere live at **Killibury**; was Castle-an-Dinas, east of St Columb Major, Arthur's hunting lodge? If you have time, these, and other locations, including King Arthur's Downs and King Arthur's Hall, may merit exploration.

Slaughter Bridge

Between **Tintagel** and Camelford via the B3263 and the B3314 at the crossing of the river Camel known as **Slaughter Bridge**, is one obligatory point of call on the pilgrimage. Whether this was the scene of Camlann, as Geoffrey of Monmouth thought, or not, it may well have witnessed a last battle of sorts, as the Britons desperately fought to keep the Saxons out of their last furthermost redoubts in AD823.

For *Arthur's Grave*, turn into the gates by the bridge and a little way up on your right you will see a notice on a tree saying 'The Stone'. Park your car here, walk to the stream and climb down the steep bank, and there, as if forgotten for a few hundred years, lies the stone, on the edge of the fast-running stream. The inscription reads: CATIN HIC JACIT – FILIUS MAGARI (Here lies Catin, the son of Magarus). It may be significant that the 1989 Gaia conference, held to discuss the future – if any – of the planet, was held at **Slaughter Bridge**.

One mile east of **Slaughter Bridge** is Collen's Cross, commemorating the saint who gave his name to **Llangollen**. (See also **Glastonbury**.)

Northern England

The main link between Merlin and Northumberland lies in the visits he paid to his companion and chronicler Blaise, the hermit and grey wolf, who lived there. The site of his hermitage is unknown (Goodrich's guess is **Fast Castle**), but there are other associations to Merlin in the province.

Bamburgh Castle
Map 85, NU 1834

Sea-girt **Bamburgh Castle** was the British stronghold of Din Guayrdi and is for this reason the most likely site of Sir Lancelot's castle of *Joyous Garde*. In one tale, *Childe Rowland*, Merlin masterminded the rescue of Burd Helen from the Dark Tower of the King of Elfland. Burd Helen had disappeared on Midsummer's Eve whilst trying to retrieve her brother's ball from the trees. Merlin, who was living at the castle of the *Joyous Garde* at the time, explained to Burd Helen's oldest brother how to release her. But he did not pay attention and failed. The second brother failed likewise. Only Childe Rowland heeded Merlin's instructions, overcame all the obstacles and finally confronted the King of Elfland himself, wielding the sword that once belonged to his father, King Arthur, on which Merlin had engraved magic symbols. He slew the King, thus setting free his sister and two brothers.

The castle, magnificently perched on its rock, was originally known as Dolorous Garde and was under an evil spell from which Lancelot freed it. No doubt, this is the spell related in the *Laidley Worm of Spindlestone Heugh*, a story not dissimilar to *Childe Rowland* but without the direct Arthurian connections: a beautiful maiden is turned into a loathly serpent by her wicked stepmother and is later

Bamburgh Castle, Lancelot's castle of Joyous Garde where Merlin helped Childe Rowland to free his sister from a spell.

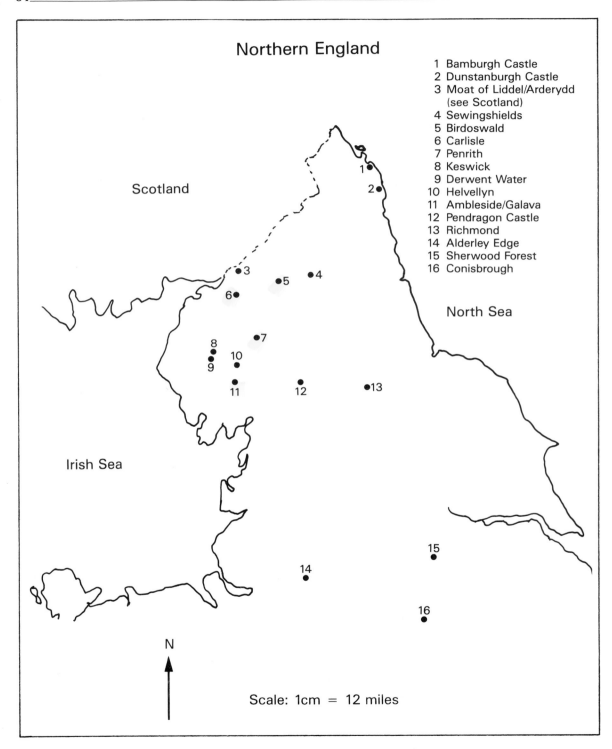

Northern England

1 Bamburgh Castle
2 Dunstanburgh Castle
3 Moat of Liddel/Arderydd
  (see Scotland)
4 Sewingshields
5 Birdoswald
6 Carlisle
7 Penrith
8 Keswick
9 Derwent Water
10 Helvellyn
11 Ambleside/Galava
12 Pendragon Castle
13 Richmond
14 Alderley Edge
15 Sherwood Forest
16 Conisbrough

Scotland

North Sea

Irish Sea

N

Scale: 1cm = 12 miles

rescued by her brother, Sir Owain, who transforms the stepmother into a toad.

Spindlestone lies almost 3 miles south-west of **Bamburgh**. The trough where the maiden–serpent used to drink the milk of seven cows every evening and the cave where she dwelt have been destroyed by quarrying, but the Spindle Stone is still standing.

Dunstanburgh Castle
Map 85, NU 2623 – 8 miles N.E. of Alnwick

The stark ruins of the castle, which changed hands five times during the *Wars of the Roses*, are visible from the B1339. To get there drive to Dunstan (map 79, NU 2419) and follow the signed footpath to the castle which is an ancient monument, controlled by English Heritage.

Sir Guy the Seeker came on his quest to **Dunstanburgh Castle** and at midnight the doors were opened to him by an old man – surely none other than Merlin – surrounded by flames, his hair hanging long and white and around his waist a flaming chain. He held a wand of red-hot iron and invited the knight to enter. After passing through a labyrinth of horrors he entered a black marble hall in which one hundred knights with their steeds lay sleeping. At the far end he found a sleeping beauty in a glass coffin guarded by two giant skeletons. Merlin had decreed that she could only be awakened by a knight brave enough to face the sinister mysteries of the castle and wise enough to decide whether first to draw the sword or blow the horn. As in all similar stories, his choice proved to be the wrong one. The next morning, like Parzival at the Grail Castle, he awoke outside the castle empty-handed. It is said that his ghost still continues the search for the maiden and the treasure which would have been his. Thus Merlin's spell remains unbroken.

Alnwick
Map 79, NU 1813

Similar stories are told of **Alnwick Castle**.

Richmond
Map 72, SD 1701

Between **Richmond Castle** and the river Swale is reputed to be a cave where Arthur and his knights are seated asleep at a Round Table. As usual, the intruder, Potter Thompson in this case, has to choose between drawing a sword or blowing a horn and inevitably he makes the wrong decision (cf. **Chepstow** *et al.*)

Sewingshields
Map 78, NY 8170

As you follow the B6318 from Corbridge along Hadrian's Wall towards **Carlisle**, you will see the car park for Carrawburgh and Temple of Mithras. The next location on the Wall, comprising turrets and a milecastle, is **Sewing-shields.** After a minor road on your left to Haydon Bridge, you will come to an isolated house on your right by a gated

The crags are impressively precipitous and down below one can see a lake, said to be full of hidden treasure which can only be recovered by dragging it with twin horses and twin oxen, using a chain forged by a seventh son of a seventh son. Beyond are two sandstone ridges to the north-west, named locally *King's* and *Queen's Crag* for King Arthur and Queen Guinevere. They and the knights lie sleeping in a cave within the crag, according to a story that is much the same as that told at **Dunstanburgh**.

One agreeable variation to be found in this version is that the failed hero, a shepherd, is watching his flock and knitting – as they all did until quite recently – when called to undertake his subterranean adventure. This must be the wildest, most dramatic and least frequented barbican of Rome and a marked contrast to the rolling uplands the other side of the border.

Birdoswald, the most likely scene of Camlann.

road. Proceed along this road until you reach a T-junction with a group of farm buildings in front of you. Park there, walk into the farmyard and turn sharp right along a wall (signposted by yellow arrows) and over the steps of another wall ahead of you. Then turn left and follow the path up to the Roman wall and fort with the crags below right.

Birdoswald/ Cambloglanna (Cumbria)
Map 78, NY 6266

2½ miles W. of Greenhead on minor road off B6318, well signposted by English Heritage

Scholarly opinion increasingly favours **Cambloglanna** as the site of *Camlann* (crooked river), Arthur's last battle. The excavations of the Roman settlement, reoccupied after the withdrawal of the legions – since when it has been continuously inhabited – are extensive and impressive, as are the magnificent views over the southern crags to the bends of the river Irthing. If *Camlann* is here it reinforces the claims of the border region to be the epicentre of Merlin's and Arthur's exploits. Local folk tradition recounts that after *Camlann* Merlin cast in his lot with paganism under King Gwenddolau, a course which led directly to *Arderydd* (see **Moat of Liddel**).

Cumbria

Carlisle
Map 71, NY 4055

Carlisle (Luguvalium, the fortress of the god Lugh, ancient capital of the Kings of the North), like **Caerleon**, retained its impressive Roman architecture intact for many centuries after the Roman withdrawal. In an early text **Carlisle** appears under the name of Cardeol and was the capital of Urien, King of Rheged and patron of Merlin/Taliesin. If it is indeed Carduel then it was also the city where Arthur was crowned and besieged by six kings. Merlin assisted him on this occasion and later set up the Round Table here.

Penrith
Map 71, NY 5130

(1)   See Owain's grave in St Andrew's churchyard. **Map 71, NY 5228**.
(2)   See the Round Table situated 1½ miles south at Eamont Bridge. Park your car at either the Beehive or the Crown Inn.
   In the field across the minor road from the Crown and opposite the Beehive is a prehistoric earthwork known as the Round Table which was already well known as such by 1538. There was an old tradition that jousting had once taken place there and as late as the eighteenth century it was used for military training and games (cf. **Pendragon Castle**).

Pendragon Castle
Map 71, NY 7802

We stayed at the Fat Lamb Inn on the Sedbergh–Kirkby Stephen Road and took the adventurous narrow moorland track that leads from Ravenstonedale to Mallerstang Common. (Turn right after second cattle-grid going east, from the Fat Lamb, towards Kirkby Stephen.)

As you come down from the high moors to the river Eden you will notice some ruins on your right, between the river and the B6259. This is all that remains of the only place in Britain to bear the name *Pendragon*. It was built by Robert de Clifford who took part in the siege of **Caelaverock Castle** in 1300 and was rewarded with lands and castles by King Edward I, the *Hammer of the Scots*. Robert himself had married into the old Welsh royal line descended from Arthur and Uther Pendragon. This was a period when interest in the prophecies of Merlin and all things Arthurian were enjoying great popularity.

We arrived as dusk was approaching, when the moors appeared particularly haunted and the dark silhouette of the castle ruins stood out boldly against the fading light.

Lake District

The **Lake District**, where the Cymry found a refuge from the Anglo-Saxon invaders, preserves a powerfully Celtic atmosphere despite the inroads of mass-tourism attracted to this area of outstanding natural beauty. Both Mary Stewart and Tolstoy make it an important Merlin centre.

Keswick
Map 70, NY 2623

Keswick Carls. Stone circle which Merlin would have visited during his stay in the Lake District.

As you approach **Keswick** from **Penrith** you pass the village of Threlkeld. Somewhere amongst the fells and crags to the south, Arthur was borne from *Camlann* (his last battle) and still lies sleeping. The Wolf Crags to the east and the Castlerigg Stone Circle to the west form a suggestive Merlin landscape. Merlin, the great authority on planetary movements, would surely have come to this neolithic observatory.

Derwent Water
Map 70, NX 2722

According to Geoffrey Ashe's educated guess, **Derwent Water** was the home of the Ladies of the Lake. Derwent is etymologically connected to the Celtic word for oak and more distantly to that for druid.

Mary Stewart in *The Hollow Hills* describes the lake-island under a crag where the youth Arthur, guided by Merlin, follows his hound, Cabal, in pursuit of a white stag to discover *Excalibur*. Derwent Isle under Friar's Crag and Lord's Isle to the south are both possible settings for this initiatory adventure.

Helvellyn
Map 70, NY 3315

Between **Keswick** and **Ambleside** stands **Helvellyn**, the central mountain of the Lake District. If it is indeed Mount Mellun of Tolstoy's *The Coming of the King* then it is here that Merlin and Taliesin play on a magical chess-board before Merlin descends to the underworld to sacrifice his eye and discover his true identity.

Grasmere
Map 70, NY 3307

In *The Hollow Hills* Mary Stewart places the island cave in a small stretch of water to the north of **Ambleside** about 1 mile long and ⅓ mile wide with an island in the middle. This description fits **Grasmere** quite well, though much of the forest she describes has now gone. Some confirmation for her siting may be found in the hill called Stone Arthur, 1½ miles north-east of **Grasmere**. We are reminded of Merlin's presence in the neighbourhood by near and far Swine Crag and Hart Crag.

Rydal Water
A more likely alternative from Mary Stewart's description is Rydal Water, whence the Rothay flows out towards **Galava** and the great lake Windermere.

Ambleside/ Galava
Map 71, NY 3704

About **Galava**, in Mary Stewart's terms, there is no doubt; she places there the seat of Arthur's foster-father, Sir Ector, and speculates that it may also be Merlin's fountain of *Galabes*. The remains of this old Roman fortress are impressive. There are ancient oak-trees growing out of its walls and the adjacent rocks near where the spring (**Galava** meaning strong spring) flows fast and clear into Lake Windermere. This is another meeting place of two rivers, the Rothay and the Brathay and another Merlin site where an oak grove grows out of a mass of tumbled rocks.

Merlin's successor and Teutonic alter ego Wotan looks down on **Galava** from the great height of Wansfell Pike to the east. It may be that Merlin outflanks him in *Applethwaite Common*, 'the clearing where apples grow', a couple of miles further east beyond Troutbeck.

Many parts of the Lake District have, at least in the green language of the birds, beloved of punning troubadours and bards, an echo of Arthur and Merlin. Arthur's Pike looks down on Ullswater and its splendid Sharrow Bay Hotel, while 1½ miles south-west are

Galava. Likely setting for Merlin's Fountain of Galabes.

Ambleside

Martindale and its common. Martin is one form of Merlin and provides a cover for him in the Christian era. At the southern extremity of Ullswater, St Patrick's Well and its protective crag, the Knight, introduce the Irish/Celtic mysteries into the Cumbria of the North.

Cheshire

Alderley Edge
Map 57, SJ 8478

Take the B5087 to Macclesfield. The first path on your left, after you leave the built-up area, leads you in 300 yds. to the *Wizard's Well*.

When you reach *Castle Rock* on your right, turn left down the path until you come to an overhanging rock where water drips into a trough at the base. On the rock can be seen the carved face of Merlin as an old man and the following inscription: 'DRINK OF THIS AND TAKE THY FILL FOR THE WATER FALLS BY THE WIZARD'S WILL.'

Alderley Edge must be the most surprising Merlin site in England, situated as it is in the opulent suburbs of Greater Manchester. It bears a worthy name, the alder being the sacred tree of the god Bran whose legend is at the root of much of the Arthur/Merlin tradition. The story of Merlin the Wizard at **Alderley Edge** is similar to those at other sleeping hero sites, but has some interesting variations:

One misty autumn morning a farmer from Mobberley was riding his white horse to Macclesfield market in order to sell it. All of a sudden a tall old man in a black cloak loomed out of the murk and offered to buy the horse. The farmer refused, hoping for a better price at Macclesfield. The old man predicted that he would find no buyer and should meet him in the same place that evening. All turned out as the wizard had foretold and at sunset the two men met again. The wizard led the farmer by way of the *Seven Firs*, the *Golden Stones* and *Stormy Point* to a wall of rock. He touched it with his wand to reveal a great pair of iron gates which opened with a mighty clanging. Having reassured the terrified farmer and his horse, he led them through many caverns to where a host of men and white chargers lay fast asleep. In the innermost cave lay a great treasure hoard from which the wizard bade the farmer to take whatever he wished as the price of his horse. He then explained that one more white horse was needed to complete the number so that at the right time the army could sally forth to save the country. Merlin (for it was surely he) finished by saying: 'Go home in safety – leave your horse with me. No harm will befall you; but henceforth no mortal eye will ever look upon the Iron Gates. Be gone!'

The prophecy became attached to an era when George, son of George, should be on the throne of Britain. In 1745, during the reign of George II, the Scottish army of Prince Charles Edward Stuart did, in fact, cross **Alderley Edge** during their advance on Derby. No Hanoverian cavalry charged out to confront them, but the invaders did seize all the horses that were to be had in Manchester and the surrounding countryside. Merlin, Arthur and the knights evidently refused to do battle against their kinsmen, the men of the North.

We had heard in our researches at the Trafford Arms Hotel and the excellent Wizard Bookshop of another magus who maintained a Merlin tradition on the Edge in the 1930s. This was John Evans who lived in a cave surrounded by wild animals whom he had made his friends. He dedicated his life to introducing children from the slums of Manchester to the world of nature with which he was at one. We spent a hot, though not entirely fruitless, couple of hours vainly searching for any trace of him. At last, on our third attempt, we found the warden of the National Trust at home. He at once led us to the cave behind and to the left of the Wizard Restaurant, through a gate into a fairy-like enclosure of rocks, trees, freshly planted grass and flowers, up a long well-tended path to a comfortable dry cave in the rock-face where this neo-Merlin had lived. The warden, who is a true guardian of the forest and its secrets, had spent two years lovingly restoring this now semi-mythical abode to its pristine state. He told us of two other faces of Merlin as well as the one we had seen above his spring. These, which are difficult to find and also apparently old, show the wizard in his Mabon form as a young boy and as a man in the prime of his life. He confirmed our first impression on entering the forest that it is a place of healing. The area is honeycombed with mine-workings including a tunnel which they say led all the way to the Trafford Arms. There are many caves, springs and great trees, but the essence of the place is stone. The great craggy Edge, with its

Wizard's Well, Holy Well, Devil's Grave and *Druid's Circle*, forms a natural barbican against the creeping tentacles of the great city of the North.

The mysteries of the area have been celebrated in the epic fictions of Alan Garner.

Sherwood Forest

Fountain Dale
Map 49 SK 5956, near Blidworth but not marked. OS map 120, 576568

Go north from Ravenhead on the A60 and take the first turning on your right, Rickets Lane. Fountain Dale is the third drive on your left. Take the public footpath through the field on the left before the drive, signposted to Harlow Wood, and then turn right to Friar Tuck's Well.

Ancient **Sherwood** was once Britain's greatest *nemeton*, stretching from Lear's city of Leicester up to Lincoln and **Conisbrough** where Ambrosius and Merlin won a famous victory against Hengist. It would be surprising if the wizard were not to put in an appearance in this sacred forest and, sure enough, he does, one snowy Candlemas, garbed in a russet gown and black sheepskin, carrying a bow and arrow and some wild geese he had just shot. The forest was the haunt of Merlin's stag-god Cernunnos before Robin Hood, whose story bears some similarity to Merlin's, took over its glades with Marian and his Merry Men.

We had to decide where in **Sherwood** to seek Merlin. The characteristic habitat would be likely to include a holy well with pagan-Christian connections. The obvious site was Friar Tuck's Cell near his spring in Fountain Dale. From the description of Merlin in **Sherwood** (see above), he could well have been the model for Friar Tuck himself. It was here that Friar Tuck carried Robin across a stretch of water and dumped him in the middle of it. If Robin Hood is, as some suspect, a folk memory of the god Wotan, then an older deity, Merlin of the woods and the stags, does metaphorically carry him on his shoulders until, in the course of time, much of their myths become entangled. Merlin's Saxon name is Rof Breoht Woden, Bright Strength of Wotan.

The supernatural is far from having vanished from Fountain Dale. The lake, where Merlin might have bagged his geese, was cursed by the monks evicted from the nearby abbey at the Reformation. To this day, we were told by the lady in whose property it stands, the lake alternates between seven years of total dryness and seven years of fullness. This spell has worked without fail for the twenty-eight years her family has lived there. When we were there it was dry which made it an easier walk to the spring than through the obstinate rhododendrons on its banks. The spring, flowing from its housing into the wooded glade where footpaths form a T-junction, was also dry on our visit. All that remains now of Friar Tuck's Cell are the foundations and a few stones at the beginning of the rhododendron plantation near the present house. It should be stressed that this is private property, but the spring can be reached by public footpath.

This is the heart of Robin Hood country: he and Maid Marian were married in Blidworth church where the grave of Will Scarlett, the most elegant of his Merry Men, can still be seen. Near Kirkby in Ashfield, to the west, there is a Robin Hood's cave, now a disused coal-mine, and Southwell Minster, to the east, possesses, in addition to the finest collection of carved green men in Europe, an elusive trysting stone in a pillar with the names of Robin and Marian.

Just north of the A617–A614 crossroads, the first turn on your right after Bilsthorpe, is the bridge, by a lay-by, where Little John (who plays Thor to Robin's Woden) blocked his future master's path and knocked him into the stream.

Major Oak
Map 59, SK 6266

Take the path from Sherwood Forest Centre, well signposted, at Edwinstowe.

The Sherwood Forest Centre at Edwinstowe preserves the mighty remains of **Sherwood**'s ancient oaks. For a Cernunnos experience one cannot do better than gaze at the tortured outlines of the antler trees as dusk approaches on a fine, late autumn evening. The Major Oak, too easy of access and buttressed against the ravages of time to be as numinous as Ponthus' beech in **Brocéliande**, remains, nevertheless, the undisputed monarch among the trees of England.

In his *White Goddess*, Robert Graves makes an interesting connection between Robin Hood and Merlin. Merlin was originally the lover of Marian, the May bride, but Robin Hood took his place and Merlin became an old bearded prophet.

Conisbrough
Map 59, SK 5098

It is here, at the Fort of Conan the Celt, on the banks of the Don, sacred to the goddess Danu, that Mary Stewart, after careful research, places the great battle in which Ambrosius and Uther, with the assistance of Merlin, won a decisive victory over Hengist and the Saxons.

The Don valley is now thoroughly industrialized, but **Conisbrough**'s great treasure, its Norman castle, which features in Sir Walter Scott's *Ivanhoe*, still stands intact on its ancient mound overlooking the town and river.

Wales and the Marches

Welsh Marches

Alleluia Stone/Mold

Map 56, SJ 2464 – 1 mile W. of **Mold** on the Pant-y-mwyn road

Having left **Alderley Edge** later than planned, we had no time to get any further than the small town of **Mold**, just over the border into Wales. The first thing we discovered was that *The Birth of Merlin*, a play attributed to Shakespeare, had had its first showing in 300 years at the Theatr Clwyd and we had missed it by a few days. The next thing we discovered was an obelisk, known as the **Alleluia Stone**. This monument, which commemorates a victory by the Britons over the Picts and Saxons in AD430 or, as has been suggested, AD447, was a real find for us. Here was lapidary evidence of an event which took place in Vortigern's time in the presence of two highly important historical characters, St Germanus of Auxerre and St Lupus of Troyes. It brought to mind the statement of the Norman historian, Orderic Vital, that Merlin had once prophesied before St Germanus, no doubt during his apostolic mission to Britain to combat the Pelagian heresy, for which a British monk, Morgan, was responsible.

Dinas Bran/Llangollen

Map 46, SJ 2142, marked as Castell

There are a number of ways up **Dinas Bran**. We left **Llangollen** by the Din Brin road and turned right up the cul-de-sac, just before a 'Major Road Ahead' sign and parked by the footpath sign to **Dinas Bran**.

In her book *Albion*, Jennifer Westwood makes out a strong case for **Dinas Bran** being the Grail castle, if ever there was one. Its other names, Corbenic, could also suggest *corps bénit*, the Blessed Body, i.e. of Christ, in the church's Grail Sacrament of Communion. Another meaning might be Cor-abenig, the chair of sovereignty, but the simplest origin is probably the twelfth-century French word *corbin*, meaning crow or raven. In the medieval romance Fulk Fitzwarren comes like Perceval/Peredur, to the Chastel Merveil – also known as Chastiel Bran – in the Welsh Marches. Whoever the hero and wherever the battle, it is Merlin who initiates the quest for the Holy Grail. A clue to his involvement with the site is that here, as at **Dinas Emrys**, there is a buried treasure which only a fair-haired boy can discover. The situation of the castle is outstanding, not unlike Montsegur, the Grail Castle of the South. The ascent is no less steep and the views from the ruins on the summit equally spectacular. We observed that Bran's totem ravens still haunt the weathered ram-

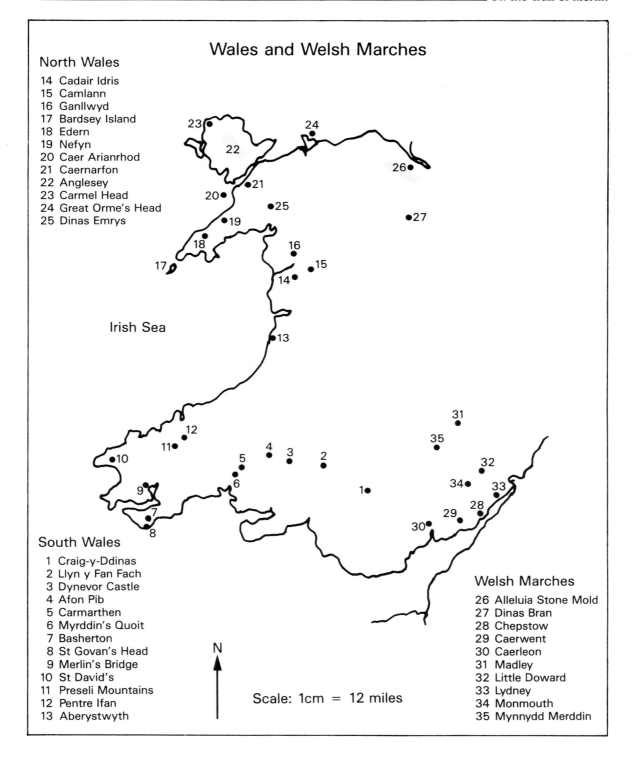

Wales and Welsh Marches

North Wales

14 Cadair Idris
15 Camlann
16 Ganllwyd
17 Bardsey Island
18 Edern
19 Nefyn
20 Caer Arianrhod
21 Caernarfon
22 Anglesey
23 Carmel Head
24 Great Orme's Head
25 Dinas Emrys

Irish Sea

South Wales

1 Craig-y-Ddinas
2 Llyn y Fan Fach
3 Dynevor Castle
4 Afon Pib
5 Carmarthen
6 Myrddin's Quoit
7 Basherton
8 St Govan's Head
9 Merlin's Bridge
10 St David's
11 Preseli Mountains
12 Pentre Ifan
13 Aberystwyth

N

Scale: 1cm = 12 miles

Welsh Marches

26 Alleluia Stone Mold
27 Dinas Bran
28 Chepstow
29 Caerwent
30 Caerleon
31 Madley
32 Little Doward
33 Lydney
34 Monmouth
35 Mynnydd Merddin

parts. To the north the amazing range of crags, that constitute the Eglwyseg Mountains, are clearly visible, though to admire Craigh Arthur (**map ref. 2348**), one must drive along the narrow scenic road off the old Horseshoe Pass that leads to World's End. Craigh Arthur lours imposingly, immediately above the Tan-y-graig Dog Kennels on your right as you go north, and confirms an Arthurian presence in the area. The patron and founder of **Llangollen** is St Collen who freed the people of the Vale from a giantess. He also visited **Glastonbury** where in the heart of the Tor he encountered Gwynn up Nudd, lord of the underworld, Leader of the Wild Hunt and brother of one of Merlin's saintly analogues, St Edern, the Lord of the Stags (see **Glastonbury** and **Lannédern**).

Chepstow Castle
Map 33, ST 5393

It is worth stopping at this attractive gateway to Wales to visit its romantic cliff-top castle above the Wye.

From the Watergate, if you lean over the parapet, you will make out a cave amid the rocks below. Once there was a stairway that led from it into the castle, but to explore it now would be difficult without a boat. In this cave, it is said, as of many others, Arthur and his knights lie sleeping. Barber relates the same story of this cave concerning Potter Thompson's discovery of King Arthur and his sleeping knights as Ashe tells of **Richmond Castle** in Yorkshire. According to the tale, Thompson 'took a bugle from the wall and picked up a sword,' but fled from the cave when the men at arms awoke, with the words ringing in his ears – 'Potter Thompson, hadst thou drawn the sword or blown the horn You would have been the luckiest man ever to be born.' The castle's custodians knew nothing of any such legends.

Caerwent
Map 21, ST 4790

Take exit 22 on the A48.

If Merlin lived in South Wales in the late fifth century he would almost certainly have known **Caerwent** well. The Romans made it the administrative centre for the important tribe of the Silures in AD73–78 and much of their town-planning is visible to this day. Along with **Silchester** it is the only site of a Romano/Christian church in Britain. It may have been the see of St Dubricius, Merlin's Christian *alter ego*, as well as the seminary attended by St Cadoc, also much associated with Merlin. Michel Rio's map in his novel *Merlin* shows **Caerwent** as Carduel, to which Uther Pendragon transferred his capital in honour of Merlin. Today little of Merlin's magic remains amid the neat Roman ruins.

Caerleon
Map 20, ST 3391

According to Geoffrey of Monmouth, **Caerleon** played a prominent role in the story of Arthur, who chose it as the setting for the plenary court he held there, attended by kings and great men from all parts of Britain and Europe. He had a tower so high that from its top one could see, beyond Christchurch Hill and the Bristol Channel, the beacon peaks of Somerset. The nearby Iron Age fort, Lodge Hill, is said to have been reoccupied in the sixth century by King Arthur. Guinevere fled to **Caerleon** and took the veil in one of its two great churches when Arthur returned to Britain from his campaigns on the Continent. Merlin's connection with **Caerleon** would, surely, apart from whatever functions he may have performed at court, have concerned the college of two hundred astrologers who practised there. One of Merlin's clearest prophecies concerns the passing of the archiepiscopal primacy from **Caerleon** to **St David's**. His Round Table has been shown, thanks to the excavations of Sir Mortimer Wheeler, to be one of the best preserved Roman amphitheatres in Britain, though this need not preclude its use for other purposes in Arthurian times.

The twelfth-century chronicler Giraldus Cambrensis has left us an admiring description of the impressive vestiges of **Caerleon**'s former splendour, the Roman central heating system particularly catching his fancy. Giraldus also tells of a contemporary of his named Melerius, magician and prophet, who evidently maintained a Merlin-esque tradition of soothsaying in the area.

There is much of interest to be seen in the museum and excavations at **Caerleon**, but it is chiefly of the Roman period as befits the *City of the Legions*. The British associations, though important, are invisible with the exception of the Round Table. Macsen Gwledig, the imperial Roman ancestor of Uther and Arthur, allegedly founded **Caerleon** as one of the three great cities he promised to his beloved Welsh dream-maiden Helen, though in reality it was already an important camp three centuries before his time. It later became the see of St Dubricius (cf. **Madley**).

As you come into the town from the south you pass the Priory, now an hotel, where Tennyson once stayed while writing his Arthurian poems. To visit the Round Table, look for the signs to Amphitheatre on your left.

Hours of admission to the amphitheatre are:
15 March–5 October: 9.30–18.30 every day. 16 October–4 March: 9.30–16.00 weekdays; 14.00–16.00 Sundays. Closed Christmas Day, Boxing Day and New Year's Day

Madley
Map 33, SO 4238

This is the birthplace of St Dyfrig, who is, however, better known internationally by his Latin name Dubricius. He is the closest to Merlin of all the saints whose stories have become intertwined with his. So close an *alter ego* is he that Goodrich considers them to be one and the same person. The parallels are remarkable: Dubricius was of the royal line of the Demetae, which claimed descent from the emperor Maximus; he was born of a pious mother who, like Merlin's, was sentenced to death during her pregnancy; he was of unknown paternity, named for his royal grandfather, with a miraculous or possibly scandalous element underlying his nativity – was the grandfather, King Brychan (see **Tintagel**), also the father? Reputedly born in the same year as Merlin, AD450, he crowned Arthur king and inspired his armies on the battlefield. He founded the college for 200 astrologers, philosophers and scientists at **Caerleon** and was guided by helpful pigs to Archenfield where he founded his monastery. He was also tutor to Merlin's protégé, Gawain. Finally he retired to **Bardsey** where he ended his days. Tennyson refers to him as 'Dubric, the high saint, Chief of the church of Britain'.

His church at **Madley** has a number of interesting features. It was an important centre of pilgrimage until the Reformation, most probably to venerate the relics, not of Dubricius himself, but of his mother, Efrddyl. This theory is underlined by the rare alternative dedication of the church to the Nativity of the Virgin. The Chilstone Chapel in the southernmost aisle, was added in 1330 and contained a famous statue of the Virgin which was destroyed during the Reformation. The Chilstone or Childstone, which marked Dubricius' birthplace, one mile north of **Madley**, is now incorporated in the village cross.

Other churches dedicated to him in the area are: Moccas (pig moor), Ballingham, Wormbridge, Llanwarthyn, Henllan and Archenfield near Weston-under-Penyard, where there was a miraculous tomb of a son killed by his warrior father, Arthur.

Little Doward
Map 53, SO 5316, marked as 'Fort', off the A40 at Ganarew

This remarkable fort is difficult to reach since it is on private property. The area is confusing and there are no signposts. We were lucky enough to be shown the way by a local house-owner who lives just below the fort.

When the child Merlin prophesied the forthcoming downfall of Vortigern, the tyrant took refuge in this unassailable natural stronghold, rendered well-nigh impregnable by the hand of man.

Geoffrey of Monmouth, who no doubt knew the area well, since it is less than three miles from his home-town, recounts the vain efforts of Aurelius Ambrosius and Uther to lay siege to this stronghold of Genoreu (Ganarew, i.e. pass of the hill) on Mount Cloartius (**Little Doward**). Eventually it was only through fire that Vortigern and his tower were destroyed. This fulfilled the prophecy of Merlin: 'Run from the fiery vengeance of the sons of Constantine . . .. The first thing they will do will be to burn you alive, shut up inside your tower.'

A visit to the site is truly memorable. The triple ramparts are clearly visible, vast, steep and overpowering, but the most impressive feature was designed by no human hand. As you walk down a track to the south-east, you suddenly emerge through a narrow, natural postern-gate in the sheer rock face, with a cave like a guard-room at the base of the cliff. Below, the path widens into an avenue of magnificent beeches leading down to the wall of the estate, whilst above loom the tremendous crags.

King Arthur's Cave
OS 162, SO 545155

From Whitchurch, drive between **Little Doward** and Great Doward following signs to *The Biblins*. Leave your car in the public park at the entrance to the private driveway which leads to the youth camp and take the path downhill to the right (west).

King Arthur, in flight from his foes, hid his treasures here and Merlin enchanted the cave so that nobody should ever find them. The cliff has an unmistakeable double cave which you will find after ten minutes' walk on the footpath through the woods.

Little Doward, Vortigern's last stronghold, destroyed by Ambrosius and Uther as predicted by Merlin.

Lydney
Map 33, SO 6303

Open Easter Sunday and Monday, Sundays, Bank Holidays and Wednesdays from 23 April to 11 June. 28 May–4 June open every day, 11.00–18.00. (Enquiries from the Estate Office, Tel: Dean (0594) 42844.)

   Entrance off A48 (Gloucester to Chepstow) between **Lydney** and Aylburton.

Lydney is a rare example of a Romano-British temple to a purely Celtic god whose cult continued in the post-Roman period. Not surprisingly, Mary Stewart, in *The Last Enchantment*, makes it the scene of an important visit by Merlin to pay a debt to the King of the Otherworld who had guarded the sword which the enchanter had brought from **Segontium** (see **Caernarfon**) before the time came to place it in the Green Chapel.

   The God whose healing shrine can still be seen at **Lydney** was Nodens. He is much better known as a pan-Celtic divinity: Nuada of the Silver Hand in Ireland, Nudd of the Silver Hand in Welsh, who is also the Lludd who gives his name to Ludgate in **London**.

   It seems that **Lydney**, which was erected late in the fourth century, represented a reaction against Christianity, which had been the official religion of the Roman empire since AD324. The excavations revealed that it was a healing sanctuary which incorporated hydrotherapy and diagnostic dreams, as in the temples of Asclepius and at **Lochmaben**. One aspect of the Lydney god is the divine youth of healing, prophecy and fertility, Mabon, whose major shrine was a few miles up the Severn, at Gloucester, where he was delivered from captivity by Arthur's knights. Lud/Nodens appears to have succeeded the goddess Tamesis (Thames) as the major water deity of Britain and it may well be that, as Anne Ross suggests, his Silver Arm is the river Severn herself.

The museum at **Lydney** Park contains much precious evidence of the nature of Noden's cult – the Lydney dog, the guide of souls to the Otherworld and back, being the most famous. There are many ex-votos representing the nature of the affliction for which the votary sought healing. But, as usual, it is the site itself which best conveys the nature of the divinity. As we walked down from the mansion we were first aware of the magnificent trees – oak, copper-beech and sweet chestnut – which animate the parkland. Then, from beneath them, there was a movement, and a great herd of deer stirred and moved off at a dignified pace to a more distant patch of deep shade. We then climbed the steep path up to the top of the hill where the excavations of the temple are to be found. There is a sheer drop on the far side with an iron-red stream flowing at the foot. Beyond, the rolling hills of the magical Forest of Dean stretch away for a dozen miles to the north.

Monmouth
Map 33, SO 5113

The present capital of the old kingdom of Gwent is an attractive town of interest to our story as the home of Geoffrey of Monmouth who became its Archdeacon in 1151 and introduced Merlin to the pages of history. What is called Geoffrey's Window can still be seen in the old priory, now a youth hostel, between the church and the river. The window dates from two centuries later than Geoffrey, but there is no reason to doubt that he would have had his quarters in the priory.

The King's Head, a delightful old coaching inn, might be a good headquarters for touring the Marches, though we ourselves stayed at, and strongly recommend, the Crown at Whitebrook, four miles south of the town, a wonderfully secluded inn, in a wooded valley, with delicious food and excellent Welsh wine from Tintern Parva, which Geoffrey, no doubt, appreciated.

Mynnydd Merddin
Map 33, SO 3427

Mynnydd Merddin (1060 ft.) is one of the reputed sites of Merlin's tomb. It is a twin peak, unimpressive compared with the neighbouring Black Mountains, modest as Merlin hills often are. Its magic lies mainly in its confusing topography and difficulty of access. It is like the centre of a maze or spider's web. We drove round and round the circle, passing through places with names like Great Bilbo, New Bilbo, Cwmbologue, Wigga and Arcadia, before we finally reached the peak, or rather a plateau of farmland with fine views to the west over Offa's Dyke and the Black Mountains.

South Wales

Craig-y-Ddinas
Map 29, SN 9007

Craig-y-Ddinas, the Rock of the Fortress, jutting out prominently where two rivers meet, last refuge of the fairy folk in Wales, where they were reported as late as the nineteenth century, is also a sleeping hero site with a Merlin connection. A man from those parts, while crossing London Bridge, encountered the wizard who asked him where he had cut his hazel stick and promised that there he would find great riches. They travelled together to **Craig-y-Ddinas** and went down an underground passage to a cavern where Arthur and his knights lay asleep. The wizard told the Welshman to help himself to as much treasure as he wished, but to be careful not to touch the bell near the exit, which he did, and the story, as usual, ended badly.

Local tradition suggests that **Craig-y-Ddinas** was the rock from

Llyn y Fan Fach. Welsh home of the Lady of the Lake.

which Merlin persuaded Arthur to draw *Excalibur*. The magnificent falls of the Neath have also been associated with Merlin (cf. **Alderley Edge** *et al.*)

Llyn y Fan Fach (pronounced chlinnuh van vach)
Map 32, SN 8122

Turn off the M40 towards Myddfai. This is a spectacular drive on narrow and steep paths to Llandeusant. When you come to a T-junction by a church, turn left and look for signs to **Llyn y Fan Fach**. You eventually come to a cattle-grid which you can cross by car. Follow the path on the other side as far as permitted. From then on you should allow approximately 1½ hours for the excursion.

This remote lake in the Black Mountains is the centre of Welsh traditions concerning the Lady of the Lake, as well as the home of seven centuries of renowned physicians descended from her. Her story, which dates from the twelfth century, is a familiar one with typical interdicts in the Mélusine tradition: a water-fairy marries a mortal on condition that if he strikes her thrice or touches her with iron she will disappear. He eventually breaks the interdict and she disappears into the lake with all her possessions. This, incidentally, may also demonstrate the liberalism of traditional Celtic divorce laws.

The familiar legend suggests that druidical healing practices dating back to Merlin and Vivian continued up to the twelfth century and even the nineteenth century in this remote mountain region. The cultivation of herbs is a living art to this day at Myddfai, long famed for the skill of its doctors and the beauty of its women. Some of the ancient remedies have survived in the *Red Book of Hergest*, preserved in the library of Jesus College, Oxford.

The climb south-east out of Myddfai to **Llyn y Fan Fach** is a typically confusing and at the same time magical experience. Although the bottomless lake has now been transformed by the water authorities into a reservoir, the menacing wildness of its mountain framework still preserves much of its original mystery. It is more awesome in its dark splendour than the other waters associated with the Lady of the Lake and her cult, and well worth the long walk. On the way up we were accompanied by dippers, wheatears and stonechats as well as the inevitable mountain sheep.

Dynevor (Llandeilo)
Map 31, SN 6222

Edmund Spenser, in *The Faerie Queene*, following an unknown, probably local tradition, places the cave, where Merlin is interred and still clanks his iron chains, at **Dynevor**:

> **That dreadful place.**
> **It is an hideous hollow cave (they say)**
> **Under a rock that lyes a little space**
> **From the swift Burry tumbling apace,**
> **Amongst the woody hills of Dynevawr.**

As with many sites associated with Merlin, privacy is strictly enforced. The new castle is now corporate territory but the evocative ruins of the old castle on a summit where Merlin may have prophesied from a natural rock-throne, are best viewed from the south bank of the Tywi (not the Barry, as Spenser thought). They are also impressive when viewed from the drive leading to the modern castle. The location of Merlin's cave here is uncertain.

Afon Pib
(Merlin's Cave)
(Map 31, SN 4832. You will need OS map 146 – 485320.

The easiest way to visit the **Afon Pib** valley with its waterfall and cave is to obtain a key to the gate of the nearest forest approach road from the Forestry Commission in Brechfa. Turn west off the B4310 by the side of the Forestry Arms and keep following this road until you come to a white bungalow on your right. The forest gate is immediately to the right. Drive up this path until you see the river-bed on your left and start looking out for the waterfall. If you come to a sharp left turn you have gone too far. Park your car before this bend and make your way down the bank.

Carmarthen
Map 31, SN 4120

Dynevor does not just consist of the two castles and their grounds at Llandeilo, but comprises the whole area from **Llyn y Fan Fach** to Brechfa and the **Afon Pib** between **Carmarthen** and **Llandeilo**. Although no cave has been found under the ruins of **Dynevor** Castle, above a well-protected and strikingly beautiful double waterfall on the **Afon Pib** there are what seem to be the remains of a collapsed cave which Barber says is sometimes referred to as *Ogof Myrddin* – Merlin's Cave.

This is one of the most remote and most difficult Merlin sites to find and to approach. Assuming you get the key from the Forestry Commission and are able to follow our directions, you will need good equipment in the way of sticks, boots and leg covering in order to negotiate the dangerously steep slopes and rocks that lead to what was once the cave. The difficulties of climbing up and down precipitous rocks to the place where the river forms a natural pool by the cave before plunging down, are considerable and bear out Spenser's description of the perils, but it is only from here that you will gain what is plausibly a Merlin's-eye view southwards through **Dynevor** to the Vale of Tywi.

Carmarthen – Caer Myrddin – bears the name of Merlin and was his birthplace. It is suggested that he is not named for the town, but vice versa, the ancient name *Moridunum* (sea-fort) being the origin of Merlin's. In fact, when one considers that the oldest appellation for Britain is, according to the *White Book of Rhydderch*, *Clas Merdin*, Merlin's enclosure, the title sea-fort seems quite in keeping with one who was both god of the island and, as his incarnate prophet, its staunch defender.

According to Geoffrey of Monmouth, Merlin's mother lived among the nuns at St Peter's, still the mother-church of **Carmarthen**, though rebuilt in the fourteenth century. Merlin would have lived with her until, when he was seven, they were both taken away to **Dinas Emrys** by the messengers of the tyrant Vortigern.

Merlin's links with **Carmarthen** remain strong. The remains of his oak were tenderly preserved in the middle of the town until quite recently in order to avert his dire prophecy:

> When Myrddin's Tree shall tumble down
> Then shall fall Carmarthen town.

A relic of it is still preserved in the town museum and **Carmarthen** remains standing, though the disaster of a train plunging into the Tywi evoked some unease locally since Merlin had predicted a water catastrophe:

> Llanllwch has been
> Carmarthen shall sink
> Abergwili shall stand.

and:

> Carmarthen then shalt have a cold morning,
> Earth shall swallow thee, water into thy place.

One prophecy of Merlin's concerning **Carmarthen** which has come true was that a bull would go to the very top of St Peter's Church. One day a calf actually accomplished this feat, perhaps presaging the return of the old horned god of the Age of Taurus from his exile and repression. On the cathedral of Laon, one of many famous European cities named in honour of the Celtic god Lugh, who has so many affinities with Merlin, one is struck by the number of carved stone oxen, apparently intent on climbing the exterior of the great towers.

In 1819 the first eisteddfod of the modern era was held at the Ivy Bush (now the Ivy Bush and Royal) Hotel in **Carmarthen** and a Gorsedd (conference of bards and druids) was held in a stone circle especially erected in the garden. Presiding over these proceedings was the old man responsible for the restoration of druidism and traditional Welsh culture, Iolo Morgannwg, truly a figure in the Merlin tradition. The druidism refounded is far from being a joke – the Queen was installed in the order of bards at an eisteddfod before her coronation, and the regimental druid still celebrates the leek-eating rites of St David's Day for the Royal Regiment of Wales.

Merlin's Hill
Map 31, SN 4120 –
3 miles E. of
Carmarthen on A40

Readers of Mary Stewart's inspiring trilogy will feel they know this hill, the site of the *Crystal Cave*. According to local gossip she gained her familiarity with the area from a friend, an Austrian countess, who married a local landowner called Morris, in the 1920s. The couple lived at Bryn Myrddin, the big house, clearly visible on the **Carmarthen** side of the hill from the Tywi Valley below the A40. The humpback hill, the throne where Merlin prophesied, will have already attracted your attention as you drove along the road from Llandeilo, but your exploration might well begin by taking the first turning to the left after *Whitemill*. There is a lone standing stone in the field opposite the hill on the other side of the road belonging to Tyllwyd Farm (the next farm is called Glynnmyrddin). This is Merlin's Stone about which he prophesied that one day a raven would drink a man's blood from it. In fact a young treasure-hunter was crushed to death when the stone fell on him while he was burrowing underneath it. The owner of the land in proper Celtic tradition promptly re-erected

Merlin's Stone under Merlin's Hill, Carmarthen.

it. This blue stone was not quarried locally, but probably in **Preseli**.

If you look up at **Merlin's Hill** from his stone, you will see three small houses facing you across the A40. To the right of the third, left-hand one, look for some tall ash-trees half-way up the slope, which will give you your line for seeking Merlin's spring and cave. It is a very steep and difficult scramble, to the right of the garden belonging to the last house, through almost impassable forest, but if you persist you may find, depending on recent rainfall, a green patch of water-cress and the hint of a spring. Most of the water has now been syphoned off for farm use, but remnants of a cave-like formation can still be seen. If you follow the line up, it is said, you will come across, with luck, a more likely candidate for the title of *Crystal Cave*, but at midsummer the undergrowth made further exploration impossible.

The mill described by Mary Stewart, where *Stilicho*, Merlin's Sicilian amanuensis, married the miller's daughter, is still producing whole-meal flour, though, alas, the mill-wheel is no longer functioning since the water authorities imposed a charge for use of the stream. Above the village of Whitemill with its agreeable inn, drive up the Pantiwog road until you come to a farm belonging to Mr Ben Jones. He may allow you to look at the disused and water-logged lead-mines in the field just above the farm buildings. Somewhere on the hill above is a vertical shaft guarded by a grille leading down to the old mine-workings, up which Merlin made his dramatic escape from death in *The Last Enchantment*, but we were unable to find it. Mr Davies of the

B. and B. near Merlin's Stone told us that as a child he used to drop pebbles down the shaft to see how long they took to land.

It is worth the climb to the top of **Merlin's Hill** to appreciate the special quality of the surrounding countryside, not unlike that of New Grange in Ireland, as you look south to the serpentine coils of the river Tywi, and immediately below you can pick out Merlin's Stone in the lap of the river goddess.

Very recently there was a demonstration by local residents against the cutting down of trees, to widen the A40, on the slopes of the hill, lest this should disturb the prophet's shade and arouse his vengeance.

Myrddin's Quoit
OS 159 – 378161

Yet another memory of Merlin, **Myrddin's Quoit**, is to be found outside **Carmarthen** on the B4312 to Llangain where you pass the chapel at the crossroads and just past the next lane to Dolaumeinion, in a field on the right through the first gate. This cromlech has now lost its capstone or quoit, but three of the supports are clearly visible with two more hidden in the hedge.

Bosherton
Map 30, SR 9694

This lily-lake – in shape not unlike **Loe Pool** – linked to the sea by a short stretch of creek, is the site in South Wales of the source and destination of *Excalibur*, or *Caledfwlch*, and Arthur's point of departure for Avalon.

St Govan's Head
Map 30, SR 9703

It is said that Sir Gawain, one of Arthur's knights and the friend of Merlin, later achieved the odour of sanctity. If so, this sharp corner of Wales would have been a worthy setting for the apotheosis of this fearless warrior. The sea pounds into the narrow cove with its pillars

St Govan's Head. Here Merlin's friend Gawain retired to live as a hermit.

of rock and reaches up to the tiny chapel, squeezed between two sides of a ravine. Celtic supernatural beings were traditionally hostile to the bells of saints and churches, but here the sea-nymphs rescued one which had been looted by pirates and hid it in a rock which itself rings when struck. A few yards below the chapel is a healing well, particularly efficacious for afflictions of the eyes. The Casterton artillery ranges, which ensure that nature here is undisturbed and unexploited, except during firing-practice, would have been a source of interest to the old soldier, Gawain.

Merlin's Cross (Pembroke)
Map 30, SM 9801

On the parallel route to the south of the Tenby Rd (A4139), three roads meet by a small triangular green called Merlin's Cross.

Merlin's Bridge (Haverfordwest)
Map 30, SM 9515

Just upstream from where Merlin's Brook flows into the Cleddau, at the top of its navigable stretch, and at the site of its first ford, is a suburb of Haverfordwest, called **Merlin's Bridge**, at the foot of Merlin's Hill. Much scholarly opinion holds that this was originally Magdalen Bridge, the site of a medieval hostel for lepers. Nevertheless, it is surely a point in favour of the present name that the brook was known as the Merthyn before the arrival of Viking, Norman and Fleming. Here, Gruffydd ap Rhys, the last independent chieftain of the district, had his castle of *Abermeirthin*. The old village of **Merlin's Bridge**, that still existed at the beginning of the century, has now been obliterated by the progress of dual carriageways,

Haverfordwest, Merlin's Bridge.

housing-estates and industry – except, that is, for the area around Haroldston, with its delightful example of an old Pembrokeshire Bridge. We knocked at the door of the most attractive house there, which turned out to belong to the Whalleys, whose newly published *Guide to Haverfordwest* we had just purchased at the County Library. Mrs Whalley told us that at high tide the meadows around Merlin's Brook are flooded, lending the two hills on either side the semblance of islands.

The site of St Caradoc's Well now seems to have been lost, but, as late as the beginning of the twentieth century it was still known as a wishing-well, whose story is similar to that of **Barenton** where Merlin encountered Vivian. St Caradoc, a harper like Merlin, and one of the last great Welsh saints, who died here AD1124, decreed that any true lover casting a pin into the fountain on Easter Monday and gazing into it would see his or her future partner.

St David's
Map 30, SM 7525

On a bridge over the River Alyn there used to be a marble slab called the *Stone of Loquacity*. Merlin prophesied that a king of England, returning from the conquest of Ireland, wounded by a man with a red hand (presumably an Ulsterman), would die on it.

Preseli (Prescelly) Mountains
Map 30, SM 1035; OS 145 – 130325

The nearest turning off to the mountains is ½ mile S. of Crymych. After you have gone 2 miles you will see, just past the wood, a drive leading to a white farmhouse on your right called Glanrhyd. Take the path to the left of the farm and you will see ahead of you the impressive crags of Carnmenyn.

No area in Britain is richer in Arthurian references than the **Preseli Mountains**. Its special significance for the Merlin trail lies in its being the most likely source of the blue stones of **Stonehenge**. Obviously, these pre-date the historical Welsh Merlin and his technology by some 2000 years, but the association between Merlin and the memorial for the slain Celtic chieftains is central to the tradition (cf. **Stonehenge**, **Caerleon** and **Ushnagh**).

Tolstoy has argued convincingly the need for a High King to transfer to the sacred centre of his own realm holy symbolic objects of defeated foes, in order to integrate their powers (cf. the stone of Scone at Westminster).

According to Geoffrey of Monmouth it was from **Ushnagh**, the heart of Erin, that Merlin and Uther brought the *Giants' Dance* to Salisbury Plain, but south-western Wales was also at various times subject to the rule of Irish invaders. Thus it may well have been a victory of Aurelius or Uther over a Hibernian king in Wales with which Merlin is implicated. Certainly, the three hill-tops castellated by extraordinary rock formations at Carn Meinyn form a landscape straight out of Tolkien – some Weathertop where the Company of the Ring encounters dread enemies from another world. Many of the stones look half-quarried or dressed and just to the west of Carn Meinyn, near Arthur's Tomb (Carn or Bedd Arthur), there is still evidence to be seen of ancient quarrying. Along the line of the summits lies the *Golden Way*, the medieval pilgrimage route to **St David's**. Far in the distance to the north-west we were able to make out in the clear evening light the unmistakable cone of **Bardsey** where Merlin lies. Monks in the middle ages were ferried there for burial across Cardigan Bay with its lost cities. From Preseli Head you can also see to the south-west the Otherworld haven of Grasholm where Bran – or his head – spent many years on the return journey from Ireland to the **Tower of London**. But it is above all with the stones of **Preseli** you need to commune in their Rorschach variations.

Pentre Ifan
Map 30l, SN 0937 (indicated by red M) – between Bryn Berian on B4229 and Felindre Farchog on the A483

This, the largest in Dyfed, along with many other Welsh cromlechs, has also been known as Arthur's Quoit and is a dancing ground for fairies. Originally it was enclosed to form a darkened initiation chamber known as the *Womb of Ceridwen*. **Preseli** has more to offer than stones, peaks and Otherworlds. Next to this famous burial chamber you will find an enchanted forest – miniature in comparison to **Brocéliande** or **Huelgoat** – where rock and tree interplay in magical and contorted shapes that speak to the imagination directly of Merlin and Cernunnos. These oak groves were once the site of a flourishing druidic school.

In 1988 a mother took her two year-old son, Robin, to the forest. Suddenly he called out: 'Mummy, the man with the horns is looking at us!'

Aberystwyth
Map 44, SN 5881

Nanteos is an eighteenth-century mansion, 4 miles S.E. of **Aberystwyth**.

As unsensational a source as the *AA Illustrated Roadbook of England and Wales*, 1966 edition, states: '… [*Nanteos*] preserves the historic healing cup, the legendary Holy Grail, taken from Strata Florida Abbey'. In 1966 it was still shown to the public but now, like many Grails, it has been withdrawn from view. The cup was made from wood, much eroded by the bites and nibbles of the faithful, and had a long and well-established reputation for healing. Wagner stayed at *Nanteos* in 1855 and began there the long gestation of *Parsifal*.

North Wales

Cadair Idris
Map 45, SH 7113

This is one of the magical mountains of Wales. Anyone spending the night on its summit comes down the next day, if still alive, either a bard or a madman. Idris was a giant, a bard, an astrologer and philosopher, obviously a proto-Merlin. In the Welsh *Triads* the riddling poet says of himself: 'I have sat in an uneasy chair; I know the names of the stars from north to south.' Robert Graves, in *The White Goddess*, has no difficulty in naming this character as Idris, who in the same poem reveals himself as Taliesin and Merlin the diviner. **Cadair Idris**, the chair of Idris, also boasts a bottomless lake, Llyn Cau, with a man-eating dragon, and a Rock of the Evil One on the south side of the mountain, where the devil used to play cards and dice with sabbath-breakers on the Lord's Day.

Camlann
OS map 124,
SH 815163

On the OS map this site is marked along the A470(T) and in the OS Motoring Atlas along the A45B(T)

Many sites are claimed as that of Arthur's last, fatal battle: **Birdoswald**, the Pass of Arrows in Snowdonia, Camelford in Cornwall, **South Cadbury**, Salisbury Plain and **Slaughter Bridge**. There is, however, a place near Dolgellau which actually bears the name of **Camlann**. This feels a convincing place for a battle, a swampy valley, where a number of streams flow into the Afon Cerist. It lies beside the only way over the narrow, forbidding pass guarding the approaches to the harbours along Cardigan Bay.

Some traditions date Merlin's disappearance before the battle of **Camlann**, about AD539. Others make him a participant in the battle or one of those who accompany the fallen king to Avalon. If they were able to transport Arthur over the pass to the Afon Clywedog, then they could have ferried him past Dolgellau into the Mawddach, past Barmouth and across to **Bardsey** or wherever Avalon was to be found.

Ganllwyd
Map 45, SH 7224

Mention should be made of a second potential Camlann in the area, some four miles north of Dolgellau on the A470(T). Here the river Gamlan, a possible distortion of Camlann, flows into the confluence of the Eden and the Mawddach. This would have been a more convenient site for the ferrying away of Arthur on his last journey. The wooded area to the east of the river is to this day known locally as the King's Forest. Whilst in this area, do not miss the Rhaiadr Du (black waterfall), which is up the gated path, opposite the car-park by the King's Forest (**OS 718247**).

Bardsey Island
Map 44 SH 1221

Bardsey is now owned by the Bardsey Trust and is run as a farm and nature reserve. The best official way to see the island is a one-week, self-catering, visit. You will need to bring your own food for one week, and longer, in case your return is delayed by bad weather. Boats depart from Pwllheli on Saturday or first suitable day following and you need to book in advance. For further details, contact Mrs Helen Bond, 21a Gestridge Road, Kingsteignton, Newton Abbot, Devon.

Bardsey Island, island of bards or birds, or to give it its British name, *Ynys Enlli*, the *Isle of the Current*, is where Merlin lies, guarding the thirteen treasures of Britain. These are:

1 The Sword of Rhydderch Hael
2 The Hamper of Gwyddno Garanhir
3 The Drinking Horn of Bran
4 The Chariot of Morgan
5. The Halter of Clyno Eiddyn
6 The Knife of Llawfrodedd
7 The Cauldron of Dyrnwch
8 The Whetstone of Tudwal Tydglyd
9 The Coat of Padarn Red-Coat
10 and 11 The Crock and Dish of Rhygenydd
12 The Chess board of Gwenddolau
13 Arthur's Cloak of Invisibility

Bardsey was from early times a burial isle. Monks in the Middle

Tel: 68580; or contact the secretary of Bardsey Island Trust, Stabal Hen, Tyddyn Du, Criccieth, Gwynedd, LL52 0LY. Tel: Criccieth 2239.

The hotel on the seafront of Aberdaron is a good place to stay and if you are lucky you might find someone to take you across to **Bardsey** on a short day-trip.

To reach Ffynnon Fair, go west through Aberdaron, take the first road to your left and continue, over a cattle-grid, to the end of that road until you reach a large car-park. Follow the path to the left which leads down alongside the stream, a steep, grassy and rocky slope, to the spring gushing into the sea.

Ages were still ferried there for interment all the way from Cardigan. Once the waters between were a fertile land 40 miles in length with sixteen fine cities, but in the reign of Gwyddno Garanhir, Seithenin, 'one of the three great arrant drunkards of the isle of Britain', left open the sluice gates, like Dahud at Ker Is (see **Baie des Trépassés**), and flooded the fertile land. St Dubricius, who is Merlin's closest parallel saint in Wales, a contemporary Bishop of **Caerleon**, who crowned Arthur king, was also buried on **Bardsey**. The journey across **Bardsey** Sound is not easy. To begin with, the Welsh title *The Island of the Current* is no idle one and the coasts of the Lleyn Peninsula bear witness to its treachery in the great number of vessels wrecked there over the centuries. We thought we had established how to get there from Pwllheli and even had the telephone number of the ferryman. By the time we reached the Lleyn Peninsula, however, this service was no longer working. So, somewhat despondently, we journeyed to Aberdaron, the nearest port to **Bardsey**. There, after some enquiries, we found a golden-haired Merlinian youth prepared to take us across the six-mile strait in his tiny boat. Already we had glimpsed the magic isle, smothered in a dollop of Manannan's white mist from the west when, the evening before our voyage, we travelled to Ffynnon Fair, the spring of Mary, a freshwater source bubbling up from the sea between perilous rocks, dangerous and difficult of access.

If you drink from the spring and run three times round the remains of the ruined chapel, whose foundations are still visible upstream, your wishes will come true. Pilgrims would stop here before the last lap of their journey in small open boats across the treacherous waters to reach sanctuary in the monastery of **Bardsey**.

We set sail for **Bardsey** on an idyllic morning with great excitement in our hearts. The experience the island offered us was unexpected, but much in accord with the Celtic religion of nature. As we walked up the west coast towards the ruins of St Mary's Abbey, one of us said: 'I wonder if there is a seal out there.' Immediately, what had seemed to be a rock, moved and dipped and re-emerged to reveal the unmistakable geometry of a seal's head. It accompanied us, a watchful sentinel, all the way along our path. Later, when we returned for a picnic on the beach at Porth Solfach, opposite the tiny islet of Carreg yr Honwy, we became aware of a remarkable sound across the water. A full Welsh choir, from treble to bass, of about twenty-five seals, were singing a magical mermaid's chorus while sunning themselves on their rocky fastness. We swam out towards them under the watchful eye of a pair of sentries who allowed us to approach repeatedly within seventeen feet before they ducked down and bobbed up again, in precision formation. We also saw many of those Celtic birds, the choughs, symbols of Arthur, and saluted the nesting-holes of the Manx shearwaters who had escorted us on our passage from Larne to Stranraer.

Edern
Map 54, SH 2739

Some 10 miles north-east of Aberdaron on the B4417 the village of **Edern** announces the presence in these parts of the saint and Lord of the Stags, closely linked with Merlin (see **Lannédern**).

Nefyn
Map 54, SH 3040 –
2 miles N.E. of **Edern**

Giraldus Cambrensis (1146–1220) in the *Itinerary through Wales* writes tantalizingly, but unequivocally: 'We slept that night at Nevyn, on the eve of Palm Sunday, where the Archdeacon, after long inquiry and research, is said to have found Merlin *Sylvestris*.' It would appear that Giraldus is referring here to the writings of Merlin rather than a body or grave, although he also refers in the next paragraph to **Bardsey**, Merlin's reputed final resting-place. Vortigern's Valley lies approximately 4½ miles north as the crow flies, just west of Llanaelhaearn, under two rocks called The Rivals.

Caer Arianrhod
Map OS 123 – 423546
– ¾ mile S. of Dinas
Dinlle, off A499

Park your car at the beach car-park from where the submerged castle-rock is visible at very low tide, or, better, take the first turning left, after you cross the Afon Llifon going N. on A499 and make your way to the shore beyond the farm buildings (private property).

This is the magical, revolving, glass castle of the goddess Arianrhod, where souls make their purgatorial sojourns between incarnations. In the same poem where he states: 'I was called Merlin the diviner,' Taliesin also claims: 'I was three periods in the castle of Arianrhod.'

Caer Arianrhod, though seldom visible above the surface, looks, Janus-like, to both worlds. Could Merlin have been thinking of **Caer Arianrhod** and the conflict of two eras, two races and two religions, ending in the disappearance of the old order, when he made his prophecy that links Ariadne (Arianrhod) and Janus (the god of the old and the new year)? 'After this Janus shall never have priests again. His door will be shut up and remain concealed in Ariadne's crannies.'

When we visited the beach of Dinas Dinlle, there were no postcards of it and those who had heard of it said it was seldom to be seen. For a rare glimpse it is worth consulting the tide table and asking permission of the farmers to cross their fields.

On the A499 south of Caernarfon, near **Caer Arianrhod**, you will notice the Merlin Nature park.

Caernarfon/ Segontium
Map 54, SH 4862

Caernarfon figures in the Merlin legend as the site of the forge where the lame master-smith, Wayland, fashioned and engraved the cups which King Rhydderch offered Merlin as an inducement not to return to the wild (cf. **Dumbarton**).

Mary Stewart, who has devoted much scholarly research to the crafting of her Merlin tale, makes **Segontium** the hiding place of all the treasures of Britain, buried, according to the *Anglo-Saxon Chronicle* for the year AD418, when the Roman legions departed. Amongst these she includes a sword made by Wayland the Smith which was presented to Merlin by a Welsh king. The smith would really have been the Celtic Hephaestus, Gofannon, who, like Merlin-Lailoken, was responsible for the death of his own nephew. Mary Stewart makes Caer Seint or **Segontium** an important centre for her narratives, understandably, since it was the birthplace of Elen of the Hosts, the dream Empress of Maximus (Macsen Wledig), who came to seek her there. He built a city, worthy of her, on the site, along with others at **Carmarthen** and **Caerleon**.

It is difficult to recapture the **Caernarfon** of the fifth century, so imposing is the splendour of the thirteenth-century castle, where the first English Prince of Wales was presented, as an infant to the cowed populace, by his father, Edward I, who swore to them that the new Prince of Wales spoke no word of English.

The Roman fort of **Segontium** (on the A4085 to Beddgelert) is a neatly laid-out excavation site which tells us something of Rome, but little of post-Roman Gwynedd.

The seat of the Celtic chieftains was on the hill of Llanbeblig, near the road to **Segontium**, where the mother-church of **Caernarfon** now stands.

Mona/Anglesey
Map 54

Mona, or as the Saxons called it, Anglesey, after their victory in AD818 over the Welsh, led by a chieftain called Merddyn, was the centre of the British religion, where the druids and druidesses made their tragic and heroic last stand against the Roman legions in AD61. Perhaps their spirits live on in the chambered cairn of Bryn-Celli-Ddu (**Map 54 SH 5171**).

Carmel Head
Map 54, SH 2894;
OS 114 – 309924

Approximately 1½ miles walk from Mynachdy

This is a desolate, isolated spot, especially difficult to get to. The best views can be gained from Cemlyn Bay, with a nuclear power station on one side and a nature reserve for 850 pairs of terns on the other.

Carmel Head, the north-western promontory of Anglesey was, according to Goodrich, the location of Carmelide, seat of King Leodagan, the father of Queen Guinevere. One tradition tells of Arthur's need for King Leodagan's support in a war against King Rion and, to ensure Leodagan's alliance, Merlin advises Arthur to marry Guinevere. The Round Table, which had been made by Merlin for Uther, who had passed it on to Leodagan, was part of her dowry.

The ensuing great battle was fought on the site of Carmelide, with Merlin himself bearing the banner of the flaming dragon, and summoning a magical wind and floods to ensure Arthur's victory.

According to E. Schuré, Carmelide was also the name of Merlin's mother, and is sometimes considered to be **Carhaix** in Brittany.

Great Orme's Head
Map 55, SH 7684

You can either take the dramatic scenic route by car, or the more exciting and enjoyable tramway or cabin lift to the summit.

This is one of a number of places, including **Edinburgh** and **Dinas Emrys**, where the child Merlin is believed to have declared his prophecies to King Vortigern. Like many another Merlin site, it is now a nature reserve and geographically resembles the head of the great worm or dragon for which it is named. The cliff scenery is spectacular, with fine views of the **Isle of Man**. There are prehistoric stone remains on the peninsula and the chapel and well of St Tudno (Llandudno). He built his cell here in the sixth century after living at first in the cave of Ogof Llech, with its spring of crystalline water. He used to preach from a rocking stone and is said to have had in his possession the magic whetstone which could tell a brave man from a coward and was one of the thirteen treasures of Britain. These traditions clearly link Tudno, like many another saint, to the Merlin legend (cf. **Bardsey**).

Dinas Emrys
OS map 115 – 605492 – 2 miles N.E. of Beddgelert, Gwynedd, off A498

This isolated ancient hill fort stands in the valley of Nant Gwynant, in the wild mountains of Snowdonia opposite the old Sygun Copper Mine, which is signposted.

It was at **Dinas Emrys** (the fort of Emrys/Ambrosius) that Merlin saved his own life as a boy by establishing himself as a powerful prophet. According to one tradition, the tyrant, King Vortigern, sought refuge from the Saxons in Snowdonia with his druids. He intended to build an impregnable fortress on **Dinas Emrys**, but mysteriously the building materials crumbled during three successive nights. Vortigern summoned his magicians to establish the cause of this and was told that the building of the fortress could only proceed successfully if the blood of a fatherless boy was sprinkled on its foundations. Such a lad, the seven-year-old Merlin, was eventually found at **Carmarthen** and brought before the king. Merlin, who had learnt that the druids had advised Vortigern to sacrifice him, asked them whether they knew the cause of the mysterious interference with the building of the fortress. When they could not answer this question Merlin told them that there was a pool beneath the foundations in which two dragons were fighting, one, white, representing the Saxons and the other, red, representing the Britons. The red one would eventually regain the sovereignty of the land. He told King

Dinas Emrys, where Merlin embarked on his career as prophet and magician.

Vortigern to seek a safe stronghold (**Little Doward**) and took over **Dinas Emrys** himself.

It is said that Merlin buried his treasure here in a cave, covering its entrance with a large stone, earth and green turf. He further prophesied that one day a blond, blue-eyed youth would find it. He will know that the treasure rightfully belongs to him when the cave opens to the sound of bells at his approach. The treasure may well be the head of Emrys, whether of Merlin himself or another, which is said to be buried here.

The first time we visited **Dinas Emrys** it was on a cold, damp and windy morning in March. As far as we could make out there was no marked path leading to the top. We simply did our best to climb up its steep side. Eventually we reached the summit where we found the remains of the ancient fortress and the famous hidden pool. There is a natural hollow here, an ideal shelter from the harsh weather conditions, where a coven of old, gnarled, stunted oak-trees still marks the site of long-forgotten ceremonies.

The descent was even more perilous than the ascent. Although this hill is not very high, it is steep, and as we could not see any definite paths leading down we followed a very narrow sheep-trail which led us around the hill to a point where we had just enough room to put one foot in front of the other, holding on to the side to stop ourselves plunging down a 30 ft. sheer drop. We should have turned back at this point, but it seemed more dangerous to do that than to continue in the same direction. In the end we managed to slide on all fours to safer ground and found our way to the road.

On another visit to **Dinas Emrys**, this time in high summer, we found the easy way up and down: Go along inside the wall to the south-west of the hill until you reach a path leading up to your right to the summit. On this occasion the pool had dried up and was full of bracken and reeds, but the ramparts of the hill-fort, re-inhabited in the fifth century, stood out clearly from below through the summer foliage. As we approached the summit we were vouchsafed a rare vision – a tawny-haired goddess, Rhiannon, Morgan or Vivian, stepped forth, quite naked and unashamed, into the high meadow, squatted down and did a pee.

Isle of Man

The **Isle of Man**, the navel of the British Isles, is named after *Manannan*, son of Lir, the Celtic sea god. He was a notable wizard and shape-changer who ruled an island paradise, Emain of the Apple-trees, identified with Arran and **Man** among other sites. He is also famous for his herd of pigs which nourish the gods. Like Merlin, he is the guardian of the treasures of Britain, though in an earlier form, including the Cup of Truth and a magical spear. One of his powers is the ability to summon up mist, rendering islands and armies invisible. An arch-magician, he once appeared to the queen of *Dal Araidhe* while her husband was away at the wars and threatened that unless she slept with him the King would die. He offered the King victory in the battle on condition that he might spend the night with the Queen, which he did, disguised as the King. The outcome of these arrangements was the birth of Mongan who ruled Ulster until his death in AD625. Mongan was also the name of the swineherd who killed Sweeney.

Such stories – concerning apples, pigs and arranged conceptions – are enough to demonstrate the considerable parallels that exist between Merlin's deeds and those of *Manannan*. In the **Isle of Man** these become even more explicit.

South Barrule
Map 64, SC 1576;
OS 95 – 259759

Park your car on A27 just S. of the crossroads with the A36 and climb the steep direct path to the summit (1585 ft.).

This is the most important site on the island directly connected with Merlin, so we lost no time in getting there. It had been a fine day when we started out. No sooner had we set foot on his mountain than *Manannan* summoned up a thick mist, driven by a biting wind from the north. We nevertheless discovered the Manx Round Table, a Celtic hill-fort surrounding the summit and forming the main stronghold of southern **Man**, and which is reputed to be the dwelling place of *Manannan*. But Merlin too is here and keeps a number of giants imprisoned in their graves at the foot of the mountain. In a cave near by called the *Devil's Den* there also lies a great prince still alive but bound for centuries by magic spells. Furthermore, a huge dragon has been sighted there and no animal, it is said, will willingly go near this entry to the underworld.

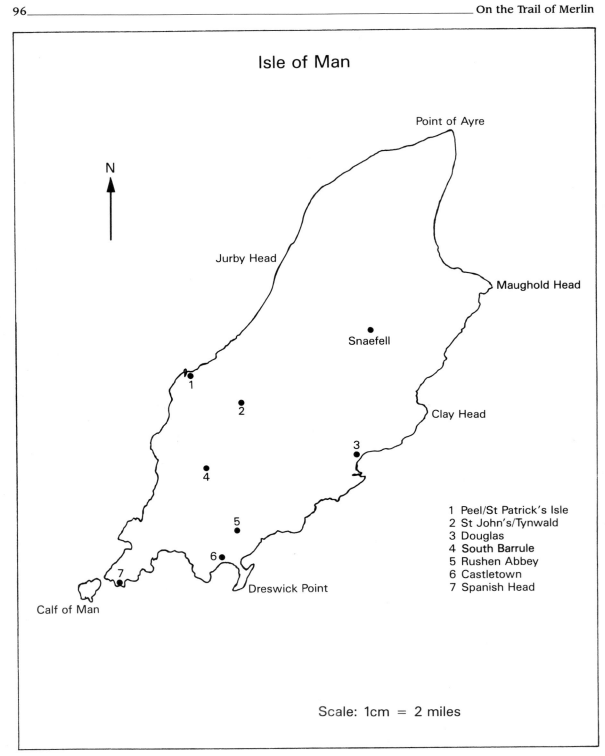

Isle of Man

Point of Ayre

N

Jurby Head

Maughold Head

Snaefell

Clay Head

1 Peel/St Patrick's Isle
2 St John's/Tynwald
3 Douglas
4 South Barrule
5 Rushen Abbey
6 Castletown
7 Spanish Head

Dreswick Point

Calf of Man

Scale: 1cm = 2 miles

England

Merlin's Cave at Tintagel, where Merlin received the infant Arthur, conceived in the castle above. Merlin took him away to be educated in a safe place, as Uther had agreed, in exchange for his night with Ygraine.

Left *Loe Pool. Here Merlin counselled Arthur to claim his sword Excalibur which the King, before his departure for Avalon, commanded Bedivere to return to the Lady of the Lake.*

Left *Alderley Edge. Three faces of Merlin carved into the cliffs bear testimony to the lingering presence of the Wizard and Arthur's hosts behind the Iron Gates.*

Right *St Nectan's Glen, the hidden waterfall in a magical valley near Tintagel, a favourite retreat of saints and hermits.*

Wales

Left *Dinas Bran, Llangollen, the most likely site of the Grail Castle in Britain.*

Below left *View from Dinas Bran.*

Right *Afon Pib, the little known alternative setting for Merlin's cave in the region of Dynevor, the remains of which are above the fall to the right.*

Overleaf *View from Dinas Emrys, Snowdonia, over Llin Dinas. This view must have changed little since the child Merlin was brought to the summit to confront the tyrant Vortigern and his own likely sacrifice. Merlin's treasure is still said to be hidden nearby where only a golden-haired boy can find it.*

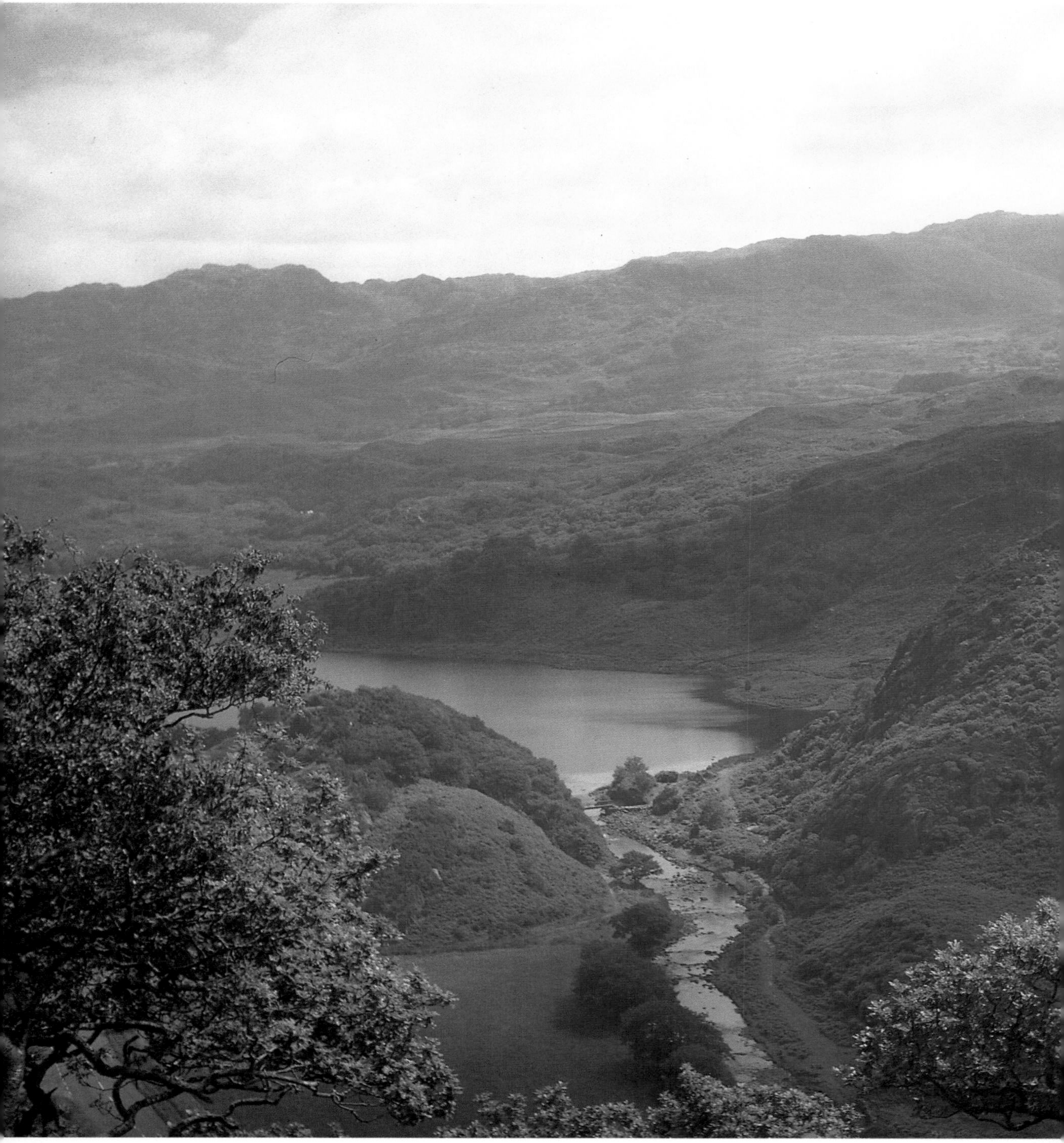

Isle of Man

Above *Rushen Castle, Isle of Man. Merlin enchanted and entombed some giants in the castle dungeons. Galahad is believed to have been trained here.*

Right *St John, Tynwald. The Giant's Grave is located beside the Manx Parliament and may commemorate the Green Knight at whose hands Gawain underwent a Merlinesque initiation.*

Ireland

River Aughavaud at St Moling's, separating the Madman's Well, where Sweeney lived, from the Celtic Christian community.

Above *Slieve League, the highest sea-cliffs in Europe, provided a rough resting-place for Sweeney.*

Right *Dunseverick. Sweeney was at last freed from the unwelcome attentions of the Hag of the Mill when he induced her to jump from the cliff onto the rocks below.*

Killaney. Sweeney's wild career began here when he threw St Ronan's psalter into the lough and was cursed by him.

Scotland

Right *Clochmabenstane, Gretna Green. This famous Mecca for eloping couples is associated with the cult of the divine youth Mabon, whose fertility stone is all that remains of a pagan temenos.*

Below *Drumelzier. Here, where two rivers meet, Merlin suffered his threefold death and lies buried at the root of a thorn tree. It was correctly prophesied that when his grave was flooded the thrones of Scotland and England would unite.*

Dumbarton, the court on Clyde Rock of King Rhydderch and Merlin's sister, Queen Gwenddydd, where the prophet spent three enforced stays during his madness.

Brittany

Above *The Mirror of the Fairies in the Val Sans Retour where Morgan imprisoned faithless lovers until the true and fearless Lancelot broke the spell.*

Right *Mont St Michel and Tombelaine. Merlin was indirectly responsible for the creation of these two isles when he told Gargantua's parents to carry the rocks, from which they were formed, to impress King Arthur with their strength.*

Left *The Beech of Ponthus, monarch of Brocéliande, marking the site of the castle of the Galician knight who challenged all comers in the nearby Camp du Tournoi as guardian of the fairy ladies of Barenton.*

Right *Fountain of Barenton, the wish-fulfilling fountain of the fairies and trysting-place of Merlin and Vivian. Water poured there on his stone may still bring a sudden downpour.*

St Edern at Lannédern who, like Merlin, rides a stag, carries a book and whose sister is also his soul partner.

The eerie chasms near Spanish Head, Isle of Man.

Spanish Head
**Map 64, SC 1765;
OS 182658 –S.W. from
Barrule**

Here Sir Gawain, often to be found close to a Merlin site, still walks, bearing the marks of the Green Knight's axe on his neck. On the way, passing the carefully preserved village of Cregneish, we stopped at the *Chasms*, a remarkable series of fissures in the rock which lead a couple of hundred feet down to the foaming sea. As soon as we neared the cliffs, we became aware of an eerie and unearthly keening as of lost souls awaiting their passage to the *Isle of the Blessed*. This sound came from thousands of seagulls, whose tenement-nests clung to the precipitous crags of *Sugar Loaf*. We recalled other Land's Ends, in Galicia, Brittany, the Lleyn Peninsula, Cornwall, Donegal and above all **St Govans**, but nowhere were the sound effects so impressive. Here, as so often, we saw and heard Morgan's tutelary raven.

Castle Rushen/ Castletown
Map 64, SC 2667

The citadel of **Castletown**, **Castle Rushen**, dating back to 1153, is in a magnificent state of preservation. It has only been captured twice: first by Robert the Bruce in 1313, the year before Bannockburn, and secondly by Cromwell's forces in 1651. Goodrich states that Galahad was raised there by his father Lancelot and the Grail King's daughter Elaine.

We discovered in the castle David Freke who has supervised the excavation of many sites on the **Isle of Man**. He had found no trace of habitation there during the Dark Ages but considered the area to the east, where the playing-fields of King William's College meet the boundary of Ronaldsway Airport, to have been one of the three major settlements on the island, there being no real capital prior to the Viking invasions.

According to a local legend Merlin, having been summoned to the island to deal with troublesome giants, enchanted them and laid them out here in the dungeons of the castle, rather than at the foot of **South Barrule**.

Rushen Abbey/ Ballasalla
Map 64, SU 2769

Another ancient centre of learning is to be found in **Rushen Abbey**, once a girls' school, beautifully situated on the banks of the Silver-burn, where the earliest history of **Man** was written. The twelfth-century ruins stand peacefully in a public garden and contain a most interesting monument listing the names of the Kings and Lords of **Man** who are buried there. These include a number of important figures from the fifth and sixth centuries such as Rhun, the heir of King Maelgwn, Cadwallan, Cadwallader and above all Maelgwn himself, nephew of King Arthur, who died in AD520. He was king of Gwynnedd in North Wales and was much traduced by St Gildas for his pagan backslidings and bigamous marriages. The great Welsh poet Taliesin, whose story is so intimately intertwined with that of Merlin, was raised at Maelgwn's court and gave, as a child, like Merlin, sage answers to the King's questionings. In Tolstoy's *The Coming of The King* this story is attributed to Merlin himself.

St John/Tynwald
Map 64, SC 2781

This is the sacred centre of the **Isle of Man** and seat of its open-air parliament. Goodrich sees St John's Church and Tynwald Hill as the likely site of the Green Chapel where Gawain underwent his test of ritual beheading. She also points out that the ceremonial Celtic axe was known as a *merlin*. Other scholars have considered that the gigantic Green Knight, who administered the initiation, was Merlin himself in his wild man form. Perhaps some of the Green Knight tradition lives on a few yards down to the left of the Tynwald Parliament where there is a flat stone with a plaque in the wall, dating from 1000BC, which has been called the *Giant's Grave*.

Peel/St Patrick's Isle
Map 64, SC 2484

St Patrick's Isle, with its castle and the ruins of St German's Cathedral (cf. **Mold**), was the birthplace of Christianity on the **Isle of Man** in AD450. Goodrich has aroused widespread enthusiasm on the island by her claim that this was the seat of the Rich Fisher King and the Arthurian castle of the Holy Grail which, she further asserts, was re-established by Merlin and Arthur as a Christian centre.

The island has been thoroughly excavated under the direction of David Freke and interesting remains of Celtic occupation during the Dark Ages have been revealed. He considers, in support of Goodrich's thesis, that there is some evidence for the existence during the fifth and sixth centuries on the **Isle of Man** of a British fleet, for which **Peel** Harbour would have been the obvious base.

Whatever the facts may be concerning the presence of the historical Merlin and Arthur on the island, there can be no doubt that magical beliefs and the cult of nature continue to thrive here more strongly than anywhere else in Britain.

A highly cultivated professional woman of our acquaintance cut down an elder-tree that was overshadowing her garden, despite the strenuous protests and warnings of her gardener. Within a week she had the experience of being picked up by an invisible force and hurled to the ground, breaking her leg severely in two places.

The best and least expensive way to pay a short visit to the **Isle of Man** is to take a ferry as a foot-passenger and hire a car. For further information about new developments and literature, consult John Shakespeare at Legends Bookshop, 6/8 Michael Street, Peel.

Ireland

Introduction

Apart from a cave and a tower named after him, Merlin's main association with Ireland is his legendary feat of dismantling the Giants' Dance at **Ushnagh** and shipping it back to **Stonehenge**. There is, however, another figure, so similar to Merlin in so many respects that we decided to devote a special itinerary to cover his journeyings. Consider the parallels between Suibhne, whom we shall Anglicize as Sweeney, and Merlin-Lailoken.

The story of each begins with a strongly anti-Christian, or at least anti-clerical, attitude; both are kings; both go mad as a result of a disastrous battle and receive their nicknames, *Geilt* and *Wyllt* in consequence. Both live a life of hardship in the wilderness, nourishing themselves on whatever berries and other natural produce they can find. Both are afraid of being captured and taken back to civilization and when that occurs each escapes back to the wild. Each has a wife who remarries, with whom each maintains an ambiguous relationship. Both have a bird-like preference for tree-top refuges and Merlin retreats to his mysterious *esplumoir* which sounds like an aviary for moulting. Both are poets who apostrophize apple-trees. Both have an affinity with stags, wolves and other wild creatures, manifesting a love of nature that was to become a rarity as the Christian era developed. Both prophesied their own deaths. Both were reconciled to Christianity by sympathetic saints. Both died at the hands of herdsmen.

For the history of the texts and their sources we must refer the reader to J.G. O'Keeffe's 1913 bi-lingual edition of *Buile Suibhne*, without whose notes and glossary of place-names our quest would have been impossible, as well as Seamus Heaney's summary in his introduction to his 1983 translation *Sweeney Astray*. The historical Sweeney was king or, more probably, regent of Dal Araidhe, a small state comprising Antrim, west of the mountains and east of the river Bann, including an area south of Lough Neagh. His principal residence seems to have been **Rasharkin**, a hill-town overlooking the

Ireland

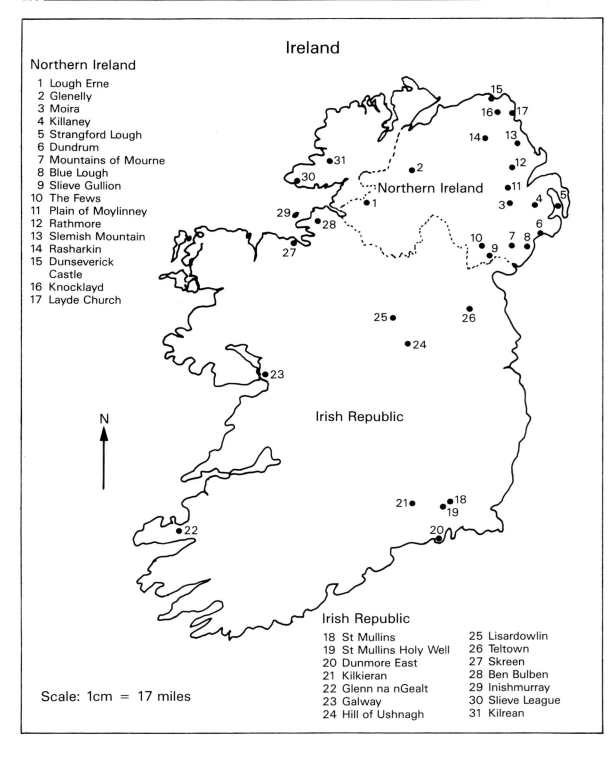

Northern Ireland

1 Lough Erne
2 Glenelly
3 Moira
4 Killaney
5 Strangford Lough
6 Dundrum
7 Mountains of Mourne
8 Blue Lough
9 Slieve Gullion
10 The Fews
11 Plain of Moylinney
12 Rathmore
13 Slemish Mountain
14 Rasharkin
15 Dunseverick
    Castle
16 Knocklayd
17 Layde Church

Northern Ireland

Irish Republic

N

Scale: 1cm = 17 miles

Irish Republic

18 St Mullins
19 St Mullins Holy Well
20 Dunmore East
21 Kilkieran
22 Glenn na nGealt
23 Galway
24 Hill of Ushnagh
25 Lisardowlin
26 Teltown
27 Skreen
28 Ben Bulben
29 Inishmurray
30 Slieve League
31 Kilrean

Bann valley, but his sphere of influence evidently extended as far south as **Killaney**, since it was there that he tried to prevent St Ronan from establishing a church. He arrived in great haste, stark naked, his wife having pulled his cloak off in an attempt to detain him, and threw the saint's precious psalter into the nearby lake. During the altercation a messenger appeared, summoning Sweeney to battle at **Magh Rath** (**Moira**) some twelve miles to the west. St Ronan's psalter was returned intact by an otter and he cursed Sweeney to roam Ireland naked and mad. At **Magh Rath**, St Ronan had a further confrontation with Sweeney who hurled a spear at his bell and slew one of his favourite psalmists. Ronan repeated the curse and prophesied that Sweeney, too, should die by a spear.

The rest of the long poem recounts the working-out of the curse. Sweeney, overtaken by madness during the battle, began his amazing aerial life, visiting all parts of Ireland, especially the mountains and streams, crossing over to Ailsa Craig, Islay and Eigg in Scotland, and spending a year in Britain with a sympathetic fellow lunatic called Alan. Twice his madness seemed to be healed: on the first occasion he was egged on by the Hag of the Mill into demonstrating his aerial skills, with the result that they flew round the country, the hag ever in pursuit, until he manoeuvred her into jumping to her death off **Dunseverick Head**.

His final relapse was due to the vindictiveness of St Ronan who summoned up five disembodied heads in the **Fews** to hound the fugitive like Furies to the last phase of the journey. This led him to St Moling's Abbey near New Ross where the saint befriended him, and enjoined him to return each night so that he could write down his story, as St Blaise did for Merlin. He also told the wife of his swineherd (or cowman) to put out milk for him every evening, which she did by pouring it into a hollow she made in a cow-pat with her heel. One day, the swineherd, roused to jealousy by gossip, speared Sweeney as he was drinking his milk. As Tolstoy points out, there are similarities here to Merlin's triple death – spearing, drowning with his face in the milk (and dung) and impaling himself on a hidden deer's antler. St Moling blessed him and promised that they would meet again in heaven.

The most remarkable thing about our Sweeney journey was to discover how many of the sites must still be as he would have known them. His *Madman's Well* at **St Moling's** is still there, the other side of the river. By the watercress beds of **St Kieran's** we found an ancient yew which the caretaker of the graveyard, who was born there, had never noticed before. From one of its ancestors Sweeney would have had his dialogue with the priest, so brilliantly translated by Seamus Heaney.

In **Gleann na nGealt**, Tom O'Connor told us, madmen still came from all over Ireland in his grandmother's time, and he showed us the hollowed stone where the farmers' wives – or fairy-women – would pour milk for them, together with two distinct hand marks on either side, where for centuries lunatics had steadied themselves to drink. There are still otters in the three loughs at **Killaney**, though this being the Protestant North, the man who owned the field where Sweeney had his ill-fated confrontation with St Ronan, had never heard of either.

Tracing Sweeney's flight of madness across Ireland is perhaps one of the most exciting and interesting ways to see the island, for this trail leads to many relatively unknown sites that the traveller would not normally seek out or hear about.

Republic of Ireland

**St Mullins/
St Molings,**
Co. Wexford
Map L10 – N. of New Ross, left off R729 at Drummin to Borris

Of all the sites associated with Sweeney, none is more certain and few more beautiful than this. It was here by the *Madman's Well* – so named in his honour – by the banks of the fast-running Aughavaud, richly green with Sweeney's favourite watercress, that the wanderer spent his last days under the benign care of St Moling. Except for a small, ivy-smothered oratory next to the well, the ecclesiastical buildings are on a hill, across the river. Brooding over all the north-west stands the imposing mass of Brandon Hill. This name recalls the great navigator and contemporary of Merlin's whose mightier mountain marks the end of the world on the **Dingle Peninsula**, beyond that other *Madman's Well* (see **Gleann na nGealt**). St Moling confined his nautical exploits to establishing the ferry on the nearby river Barrow, which still runs to this day.

For us the focal point was obviously the well, and very remarkable it is, quite unlike those we have seen in other Celtic countries and indeed in Ireland itself. It is a square stone construction, open to the sky, entered through a narrow doorway, designed to keep out animals – most essential, to judge by the two inquisitive ponies who followed our every move. Water pours into the well-house through two sluices from a beautiful clear pool above and behind the well. The arrangements of the edifice, which include a flat stone, convey the impression that it was used for liturgical purposes, no doubt baptism and services of healing. St Moling himself, who loved and admired Sweeney and may have been the author of some verses about him, describes the scene:

> Dear in sooth is he whose tomb this is,
> often were we two – happy time! – conversing
> one with the other along this pathway.
> Delightful to me was it to behold Suibhne –
> he whose tomb this is – at yonder well.

> The *Madman's Well* is its name, for often would he eat of its
> watercress and drink its water, and so the well is named after

him. Dear, too, every other place that Suibhne used to frequent. (O'Keeffe)

There is still a farm adjacent to the well, the same, no doubt, where Mongan, Moling's swineherd, lived with his wife Muirghil. She it was who, on the saint's instructions, put out milk every day for Sweeney in an unusual receptacle, formed by digging her heel into a cow-pat. (Tolstoy makes the interesting suggestion that this practice may be due to some lost memory of Merlin, whose original name, *Merdinus*, links him with dung.)

One night during a milking-yard quarrel, a woman accused Muirghil of preferring Sweeney to her husband. The herd's sister overheard and taunted Mongan. He seized his spear and transfixed Sweeney as he knelt to drink his milk. St Moling gave Sweeney absolution, Holy Communion and the Viaticum and buried him, raising a cairn in his honour. Moling promised him, before his death, that they would meet again in heaven and spend an equal period together there. The jealous herdsman, on the other hand, he consigned to hell.

Sweeney's tomb and the place of his death are unknown but one might guess from St Moling's description that the little oratory by the well is probably the right place. The relics of St Moling himself, who

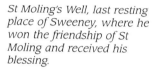

St Moling's Well, last resting place of Sweeney, where he won the friendship of St Moling and received his blessing.

died in AD697 still lie in the ruined, but locked, chapel near the present church in its vast graveyard. His Gospel book, admired by Giraldus Cambrensis in the twelfh century, still survives in the library of Trinity College Dublin and gives the plan of his original monastery. Like many Celtic saints he was in tune, as were Merlin and Sweeney, with the natural world and had a pet fox.

Allow time to wander round the remarkable ancient monuments in the churchyard. Just below it, on a steep path which leads down to the river, are the remains of St Moling's Mill. The great motte above the churchyard is said to contain the ships in which the Norsemen sailed up the Barrow. The pub/post office is a good place to get information, a drink and a fishing permit, should you need one. The landlady directed us to the guest house, *Teac Moling* (a beautiful place to stay), on the banks where Sweeney's river flows into the Barrow and which is signposted from the common.

St Mullin's Holy Well, Co. Kilkenny

Map K 10 (not marked) and OS 19 – 6233 (essential)

To visit this alternative St Mullin's Well, take the road to Graiguenamanagh where you turn left and S.W. to Inistioge. From here take the road to Mullennakill. If you see signposts to Holy Well follow them although they stop before you get there and you will need to look out for a large statue behind a hedge by the side of the road. However, if you do not spot the signs ask in Mullennakill for directions.

A rocky hillside overlooking Glen Arrigle; a sacred spring; a fairy thorn-tree now the home of a Marian cult – there could be no better illustration of Celtic-pagan Christianity than the other **St Mullin's Well**, across the Barrow and the Nore, where Sweeney's friend would retire to be alone with nature and God. Surely Sweeney, fired by the same yearnings, would also have used his power of flight to perch on this tree and drink from this well.

St Mullin's alternative Holy Well. Fine example of a pagan–Christian tree-cult.

Dunmore East,
Co. Waterford
Map L 11

This was the scene of one of the more elaborate tricks that Merlin has played on us. At **St Mullin's Holy Well** the car was causing us grave anxieties, indicating an immediate stop at the nearest Volvo garage. This turned out to be at Waterford. It was lunch-hour and amazingly hot and we sat in the forecourt for 1½ hours until the mechanics returned to their labours. There was nothing wrong, merely a loose connection. So we set off again, cursing the delay, towards the west. A couple of hours further on, idly flicking through the pages of the 1963 *AA Illustrated Road Book of Ireland*, we noticed that **Dunmore East** boasted a Merlin's Cave overlooking the sea on the cliff path that leads to Swine's Head. We were much disappointed at not having asked ourselves why Merlin had wanted us to stop in Waterford and on our return to England we wrote to Southeast Tourism in Waterford requesting further information. The Senior Tourism Officer, after investigating the matter with a number of people in **Dunmore East** who had lived there for a considerable time, could find no one with any knowledge of the cave. On this occasion we had reluctantly to confess ourselves defeated by Merlin's famous elusiveness and no doubt his laugh echoed over Waterford Harbour all the way from Arthurstown to Hook Head.

Kilkieran,
Co Kilkenny
Map J 10

3½ miles N. of Carrick on Suir on L26. Turn right at the foot of the steep wooded hill and the graveyard is signed on your right.

The parishes of Ahenny and Kilkieran are noted for their ancient High Crosses, but we went there in search of the yew tree and the watercress beds where Sweeney had one of his most touching encounters with a representative of the new religion. Let Seamus Heaney take up the story:

One day Sweeney went to Drum Iarann in Connacht where he stole some watercress and drank from a green-flecked well. A cleric came out of the church, full of indignation and resentment, calling Sweeney a well-fed contented madman, and reproaching him where he cowered in the yew tree:

CLERIC: Aren't you the contented one?
You eat my watercress,
then you perch in the yew tree
beside my little house.

SWEENEY: Contented's not the word!
I am so terrified,
so panicky, so haunted
I dare not bat an eyelid.

The flight of a small wren
scares me as much, bell-man,
as a great expedition
out to hunt me down.

Were you in my place, monk,
and I in yours, think:
would you enjoy being mad?
Would you be contented?

Kilkieran. On a yew tree at this spot Sweeney had an altercation with the priest who lived there.

We were examining the well-tended ancient graveyard when we noticed a man scything thistles in the field beyond. As he shouldered his implement like old Father Time and began to head for home we dashed after him. It was well met indeed. He was born in the farm below the cemetery and after forty years as a civil engineer had returned to become the unofficial and unpaid guardian and sexton of this sacred place. It was he who kept the graveyard and its approaches so beautifully and who, to the annoyance of the Department of Antiquities, had carried out some notable excavations, including that of a Celtic *lingam* and *yoni* which we had already admired. He was a fund of information about the legends of the district and confirmed that there had indeed been a small hermitage there at the time of Sweeney's visit. The hermit's sister had been killed by wolves, in the great forest that surrounded them, while gathering firewood to cook the hermit's porridge one winter morning.

Our guide showed us the watercress beds, much more extensive when he was a boy and the cows were kept out of it, and the stones of old monastic buildings. But he had no memory of any yew tree in the grounds. As we were about to take our leave of him we noticed in a corner of tumbled walls, quite overgrown with briars, brambles and thorn-trees, a skeletal remnant, like the mast of a shipwrecked vessel, poking up above the undergrowth. We went to investigate and, sure enough, there it was, Sweeney's yew or its son or grandson, still putting forth its green needles – hidden for sixty years from the eyes of one who knew the land perfectly and was proven to be no mean observer. Thus the ancient text of *Buile Suibhne* was once more confirmed.

Gleann na nGealt, the Glen of the Madmen and the Dingle Peninsula, Co. Kerry
Map C 11

Take the R559 from Tralee. The Glen lies between Camp and Lougher on your right and left as you reach the top of the hill where the railway crosses under the road.

It was rather too late on a golden evening in late June when we arrived in what we believed to be the area of Gleann na nGealt, with the welcome of Benners Hotel in Dingle still some twenty miles off. The trouble was that we did not really know what we were looking for, except for the usual watercress beds. After our finds at **St Mullin's** and **Kilkieran** we had little hope of striking it lucky for the third time in a day and experiencing how accurate a guidebook a ninth-century poem can still be. The indications were tenuous – one sentence in O'Keeffe's notes stating: 'Perhaps we have here some confusion between Gleann na nGealt in Kerry and Glenn Bolcain.' Glen Bolcain figures prominently in the text and usually refers to Sweeney's home stronghold just outside **Rasharkin**, Co. Antrim. By a fine piece of literary detective work, O'Keefe tracked down in another Irish poem, The Battle of Ventry, a reference to a Glenn Bolcain, whither the King of France, defeated in the battle, literally flew 'with the wind, and with madness before the eyes of the hosts of the world, and did not stop till he came to Glenn Bolcain in the east of that territory'. Ventry is at the south-west tip of the **Dingle Peninsula** and **Gleann na nGealt** in the north-east.

When Sweeney flew from the Battle of **Magh Rath** he visited all parts of Ireland till he reached '... ever delightful Glen Bolcain. It is there the madmen of Ireland used to go when their year in madness was complete, that glen being ever a place of great delight for madmen'. The text goes on to describe the springs of clear water with watercress, sorrels, wild garlic and sloes. The madmen were, it seems, an unruly lot, who used to 'smite each other for the pick of the watercress and for the use of the couches that the Glen afforded'.

Our map of Gleann na nGealt, which should make it easier for you to find Sweeney's landmarks.

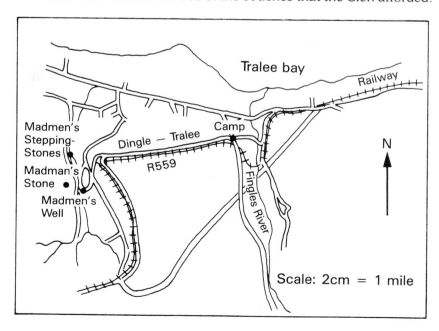

We had thrashed about aimlessly for some time, far too high up the mountain, when we decided to call it a day. As we crossed the pass between Corrin and Knockbeg for the third time, having elicited more suspicion than information from the local inhabitants, we saw a woman getting out of her car and asked once more about **Gleann na nGealt**. She said, 'It's Tom O'Connor you'll be wanting', and told us how to find him. Not without further difficulty we came at last to a low-built, white Kerry farmhouse at the end of a lane and knocked at the door. A tall, upright, fair-complexioned man, glowing with health, emerged. This was Tom O'Connor, and he agreed to be our guide to the sites of the Glen of which he is both the greatest authority and tutelary spirit. He is in his mid-eighties, but still herds his flocks high on the mountainside, and has a memory that is long and clear, as well as being a great raconteur. He told us the story of the Battle of Ventry as though it had been the Somme and made it even more topical by making the royal refugee the King of the Belgians (in other versions he comes from Greece). As recently as his grandmother's time madmen still came once a year from all over Ireland, and he had some grand tales to tell of them and their obstreperous behaviour as he led us in search of the treasures of the Glen.

The most striking of these to us was the *Madman's Stone*, hollowed out to form a basin where the farmers' wives or fairy-women had poured milk for at least 1500 years of madmen, and there, as silent witnesses to them on either side, were two perfect hand-prints. *Bullauns*, standing stones with hemispherical depressions, probably used as mortars, are not uncommon in Ireland, but the hand-prints are! We were now accompanied by Mr O'Connor's 15-year-old grandson, a golden lad, who, if ever he went to **Dinas Emrys**, would

Glenn na nGealt, the Madman's Stone, which shows the hollow and the handmarks where for 2000 years madmen from all over Ireland drank the milk provided for them by the fairies.

be just the one to find the treasure. May his grandfather pass on to him the lore of the Glen. This also includes the *Madmen's Stepping-Stones*, the *Madmen's Well* and remarkable, ancient, subterranean homes, which are more likely to have been *pecht*-houses than barrows for the dead. These would have been the couches which the madmen disputed among themselves in winter. As for the watercress that used to grow in Mr O'Connor's field as big as cabbages, ten years ago a local farmer dug it all up.

As we drove, much too fast, to Dingle, to beat the dinner deadline of 9.30 pm, we came as near as nothing to hitting a wall over a steep drop, when suddenly, round a bend, silhouetted in the setting sun, we saw for the first time the unmistakable outline of *Skellig Michael*, Ireland's *Merveille* and entry to the underworld, more than 30 miles to the south-west. Some people say that the madmen of **Gleann na nGealt** were really the spirits of the dead waiting for their final departure to the *Isles of the Blest* (cf. **Skreen** and **Pointe du Raz**), but we prefer to accept Tom O'Connor's story, that this was indeed the Valley of the Madmen. Certainly the Glen is a poor point of departure for the Skelligs or any other likely insular abode of souls. Skellig is even harder to reach than **Bardsey** and has no clear Sweeney or Merlin connection, so we had to give it a miss. The Celtic monks maintained the practices of the Egyptian desert there long after the remainder of the West had yielded to the standardization imposed at Whitby.

We finally arrived at Dingle to find traffic at a standstill for the annual plastic duck race and just made it to Benner's Hotel in time for an excellent dinner (lobster on the table d'hote and a fine old Midleton whiskey).

Next day, heavy rain and dense low cloud prevented us from visiting important sites in the far west of the peninsula, such as Ventry, Sybil Head, Gallarus Oratory and Brandon Mountain, but not from taking the splendid and hair-raising Brandon Pass, with its magnificent waterfalls, back to Tralee. Brandon, in this western point, may commemorate the great Celtic navigator and guide of souls, St Brendan. It was either he or his near namesake, Barinthus, who ferried Merlin to Avalon.

Galway
Co. Galway

Merlin's Tower and Merlin's Gate
Map E 8

4 miles W. of Oranmore on the R338 in the grounds of the Merlin Park Hospital, opposite the Merlin Pub. A

The Merlin Tower is a mystery: no one has been able to explain its name to us. During Cromwell's wars it was known as the water-tower because the English soldiers, parched with thirst, killed the local inhabitants who, speaking only Irish, failed to understand their request for water. For further literature consult Kenny's Bookshop in **Galway**.

In fact, there seems to be a mystery surrounding any Merlin site in Ireland. When we wrote to Southeast Tourism in Waterford concerning Merlin's Cave south of **Dunmore East**, they told us that this cave was not known in the area. We were advised, however, to footpath to the left of the drive to the Reception building, between the morgue and the Alcoholics Treatment centre, leads through thick woods, over boulders and a stream to a crossing where four paths meet. Go straight ahead and you will see this impressive square tower on your left.

The Hill of Ushnagh/ Uisneach, Mount Killaraus, Co. Westmeath
Map J 7

write to Ireland West Tourism for information regarding a certain Merlin's Gate, a cave somewhere along the Galway Coast and which is listed in *The Caves of Ireland* by Jack Coleman. But they, too, had never heard of any Merlin's Gate or Cave.

We anticipated few problems in finding **Ushnagh**. It was, after all, the sacred centre of Ireland where the High King, Tuahal Teachtmhar, built his palace in the first century. It was also here that the god Lugh met his triple death and where the first druidic Beltaine Fire was lit from which all others throughout Ireland were kindled. But we had not counted on the trickster element that so often plays its part in the Merlin quest. When we were almost at the site we spotted an official signpost to it, unexpectedly directing us to turn left. A long, confusing Irish lane it turned out to be. We at last found a farmer and asked him where we had gone wrong. He smiled and said that there were people about with 'twisty fingers'. In Ireland they turn the signposts. In **Brocéliande** they uproot them.

It was showery and extremely muddy when, an hour later than expected, we reached what seemed to be the right place, where another Tourist Board signpost pointed ¼ mile up a hilly field to something called the *Cat Stone*. There was a rather disappointing looking cleft boulder at the top of the meadow which we solemnly photographed, and then we nosed around for what we could find. In the next field to the left was a circular clump of trees, brambles and nettles, that, on closer inspection, was clearly man-made, though too big, too old and too low to be an enclosure for cattle or sheep. In the middle was a large stone and round the perimeter were suggestions that there might still lie buried, or once have stood, an impressive henge. Now, however, there was nothing to see but its toothless gums. Surely, to the eye of faith at least, this was the site of the *Dance of the Giants* on *Mount Killaraus* which Merlin despoiled and removed to **Stonehenge**.

There is one account of Merlin's exploits at **Ushnagh** that is more pleasing to pan-Celtic ears than the usual tale of his imperialistic plundering of the sacred stones. At night, when all the labourers were exhausted by their vain attempts to budge even one of the great monoliths, Merlin entered the circle by moonlight, his harp in his hand and began to sing an incantation which the bards called. 'The Enchantment of the Precious Stones'. The petrified giants stirred, swayed to the music and moved into a dance that led them to the sea and across it to the isle of Britain where they resumed their former positions in their new home at **Stonehenge**. There the returning warriors of Uther's army found them ready for the funerary ritual. 'Behold', they exclaimed, 'Ireland is visiting Britain!'

At the top of the road, between two small houses, we got out of the car and followed in the well-manured and squelchy wake of a herd of bullocks up the path that led through two corrals to the ruins of the palace of the High Kings, overlooking much of central Ireland as well as a peaceful pond fringed with reeds and white flowers. On the very summit above stand the remains (marked on the Irish OS map) of a cromlech where St Patrick made his bed. Was it from here that he cursed the stones of **Ushnagh** so that they could no longer heat or hiss in the fire of Beltaine? His more interesting and personal memento we only discovered later. We wandered back to the car, inspecting a well with an iron railing, but failed to find the cave, also marked on the map, which, as at Delphi and other sacred centres with reputations for being the navel or cervix of the earth, would have provided a hot line to the source of chthonic inspiration and rebirth.

All the best research is carried out in pubs and we would have saved ourselves much time and trouble if we had gone straight to the excellent Ushnagh Inn, but even with our delayed arrival it had seemed rather early for the first Guinness of the day. There we met the man, who an hour earlier we had forborne to hail and stop as he bicycled through the rain. He and the landlord gave us much precious information and the landlord threw in for good measure an invaluable local guide. To begin with, the *Cat Stone*, where President de Valera had stood like an ancient High King to address the representatives of an Ireland once more free, was there, looking at us proudly through the window of the saloon. This is *Ail na Mireann*,

Ushnagh, Sacred Centre of Ireland, whose missing circle of stones was spirited away to Stonehenge by Merlin.

the 30 ft. *Stone of the Division*, which marked the meeting place of the five ancient provinces of Ireland: Ulster, Munster, Leinster, Connaught and Meath, the midpoint. Beneath this stone, Eire, the queen who gave her name to the land, lies buried, after her death at the battle of **Teltown**. As for the abandoned stone circle, it was indeed a place of importance, and it was not so long ago that the priests had celebrated Mass there once a year.

Less known, is a stone on the left-hand side of the bridge at the foot of the hill below the pub as you travel west towards Mullingar, on which is imprinted St Patrick's footprint. We found it as described. What is one to make of these foot and hand marks (cf. **Gleann na nGealt**), forever captured in an empty space of stone? One thing is sure – they smack of a magic older than that of saints and priests of Rome. Did some Merlin or Sweeney leave a visiting card or was it the launching pad of *Connla of the Golden Hair*, the Celtic hero who left **Ushnagh** for Tir na nOg, land of everlasting youth, beguiled by a beautiful woman in a glass boat? Encouraged and refreshed by our visit to the inn we set out conscientiously once more to find the real *Cat Stone*. But the trickster had one more card up his sleeve. We were put ignominiously to flight by a herd of about thirty bullocks who, halted for a while in their curiosity by halloos and stick waving, broke into an ambling but intimidating charge that soon had one of us face down in the mud, and both of us content to call it a day and scramble over the wall to safety. If you go east towards Mullingar pay your respects at Loch Ennell to the shade of Malachy (d.1022), last truly Irish High King who wore 'the collar of gold which he won from the proud invader'.

Teltown, Co. Meath
Map L 6 – 4 miles S.E. of Ceanannus Mor

Sweeney, who normally avoided crowds, journeyed at Lammastide to **Teltown**, along with much of the population of Ireland and Scotland, drawn there by the Celtic equivalent of the Olympic Games, and in search of a marriage partner. The games and the town were instituted by the legendary Queen Tailtiu, daughter of the King of Spain. The games were held in honour of her foster-son, the great god Lugh (Lughnasadh = Lammas), around the graves on the hill of Tailltinn. Tailtiu died, it is said, as a result of clearing the great forest of Meath and the town was named in her memory. The games were held there until 1st August 1169 and the tradition of **Teltown** marriages lingered on into the nineteenth century.

Lisardowlin (Ard Abhla), Co. Longford
Map I 6 – 2 miles S.E. of Longford; OS 12 – 107705

Lisardowlin is a green, rather dull plateau, either side of the N4, the **Longford** side of the Fountain Blue Hotel, by a river crossing and a pond to the north, one mile beyond the golf course. Sweeney complains to this wife about the coldness of the beds here. The name in Celtic suggests the presence of a high ring-fort which may perhaps be further up towards Ardagh.

Skreen/ Alternan, Co. Sligo
Map F 5

We knew from O'Keeffe that the place we were looking for was near **Skreen**, but not being sure where, we followed signposts to the right off the Ballysadare–Ballina road to *Beach Bar*. This pub turned out to be a good deal further than we had anticipated, but a much more attractive old harbour inn than its name suggested and as usual a valuable source of information. O'Keeffe in his notes had simply stated of this highly important Sweeney site: 'The place referred to is Alternan, which was the only place between **Kilkieran**, where he had his altercation with the cleric and **St Mullins**, his final resting place, that Sweeney had found peace.' He described a delightful valley where he was at one with nature and on friendly terms with the community of saints who lived there. The indications were somewhat contradictory, suggesting that he may have been referring to an extended area rather than pinpointing one spot. For example, he mentions a 'beautiful, green-streamed river, dropping swiftly down from the cliff'. A delightful stream does indeed flow into the little inlet next to the pub, but the land between the Ox Mountains and the sea is all low-lying, and includes nothing that could be dignified with the name of cliff. On the other hand, six miles west of **Skreen**, at the entrance to Dromore West, the Dunneill River forms a dramatic and beautiful, though much littered, stepped waterfall, banked by great trees and much ivy, just as Sweeney described the scene. And yet he also commented on the 'many fat seals that used to sleep on that cliff after coming from the main beyond'. The coast is still famous for its seals today, especially at the entrance to Ballysadare Bay where there is an islet named 'Great Seal Bank'. So it must remain an open question whether Sweeney's stopping-place was at Dromore, next to *Beach Bar* or somewhere else: 'I sleep 'neath a tree at yonder waterfall'. He was entranced with the place and wrote a poem

Skreen, one of Sweeney's favourite watering-holes.

praising its hazels and nuts, 'and fair, heavy-topped apple-trees'. Merlin also wrote a poem to apple-trees. Apples or an apple-bough were the passport to the Celtic Otherworld, itself known as the Apple Isle – *Emain Abhlach* or Avalon.

One important tradition we learned at the pub was that the dead of the area used to be buried in the beach outside during the winter, awaiting fair weather before they could be ferried the twelve miles across Sligo Bay to the funerary island of **Inishmurray**, which Sweeney had also visited. This story, which strongly recalled that of the **Baie des Trépassés** in Brittany and **Bardsey Island**, suggested to us that accounts of ancient traditions concerning disembodied spirits may have been interwoven into the legend of Sweeney.

On a lighter note, we learned something else of value in the *Beach Bar* – how to persuade an Irishman to have a drink, a feat which until that time had eluded us. A young man with a nice twinkle said that you must repeat the invitation at least five times and then round it off with the line: 'You might as well, we may never meet again', and order the pint firmly. Somebody suggested that if we were looking for the community of saints who befriended Sweeney, it would surely make sense to start with **Skreen** itself, which we thought we had already passed through. How could we have missed it, on its little road parallel to the N59? As soon as we saw **Skreen** we knew we were on firm ground. This was clearly the place of the saints – two of them very famous. The first, Colum Cille (Columba) counselled Sweeney in the poem:

> **Colum Cille offered thee**
> **Heaven and kingship, O splendid youth,**
> **eagerly thou hast come into the plain**
> **from the chief prophet of Heaven and earth.**

The full name of **Skreen** is *Scrin Adhamnain* and it is there that the well of St Adamnan is to be found on the right as you enter the village from the east. Like Colum Cille, whose biography he wrote, he was Abbot of Iona. He mentions, in his book, the **Battle of Magh Rath** and confirmed its date, AD637, by reference to his own thirteenth birthday. He also introduces the Loch Ness Monster to the pages of history. His other notable publication, *De Locis Sanctis*, should make him the patron saint of guidebook writers, being an itinerary to the Holy Land, written by someone who probably never travelled south of **Skreen** or east of Wearmouth.

The water of the well is still good, the doctor in the old rectory assured us, since he drinks it himself, although the watercress, as at **Gleann na nGealt**, was recently grubbed up. In the corner of the churchyard opposite the well is a ruined oratory that probably marks the site of one of the monasteries that Sweeney knew. It is no doubt just a coincidence that the area later became a stronghold of the MacSweeneys.

Ben Bulben,
Co. Sligo
Map G 4

Under bare Ben Bulben's head
In Drumcliff churchyard Yeats is laid.

Thanks to Yeats's poem which contains the epitaph now gracing his tomb, this must be the best-known mountain in Ireland. The poem starts with the Gnostic and Essene sages of Alexandria and a company of phantom horsemen who:

... ride the wintry dawn
Where Ben Bulben sets the scene.

Perhaps his poetic and prophetic predecessor, Sweeney, formed part of this wild hunt of familiar spirits. As Yeats tells us: 'ancient Ireland knew it all', the mysteries of life and death, which the druids shared with eastern sages. Like many another sacred mountain, **Glastonbury** Tor, Montségur and Canigou, **Ben Bulben** dominates a vast area with its fascinating and tremendous presence. From the evidence of Evans Wentz it is undoubtedly the major fairy-mountain of western Ireland. It continued to command our attention from the moment it hove into view on the road west from Ballysadare all through Co. Sligo till we crossed into Leitrim. We stopped in Drumcliff churchyard to gaze up at its scarred crags and pay our respects at the graves of Yeats and his wife. The magnificent High Cross, which Yeats refers to in his last verse marks the site of the monastery established by St Colum Cille, *c.* AD575. He, too, like Sweeney had a dispute over a psalter with a fellow saint, Finian. In the ensuing *Battle of the Books*, fought near by, 3000 men were killed, which makes Sweeney's row over St Ronan's psalter seem tame in comparison. At the period when Sweeney arrived 'before eventide in bitter Benn Gulbain', he was still not fraternizing with the clergy, so would have foregone whatever comforts were offered by the monks who might already have settled in the valley.

Inishmurray,
Co. Sligo
Map G 4

From Sweeney's vantage point on **Ben Bulben** he would have had a grand view of the funerary isle of Inishmurrary, another haunt of his, an easy hang-glide away to the north-west. Between **Inishmurray** and the mainland is a mysterious island that becomes visible once every seven years. Sweeney, surely, frequented it too, but we mortals would have to take a boat with Rodney Lomax from Mullaghmore (8 miles north-east of Grange, turn left at Creevykee Cross Roads), or from Streedagh Strand (1½ miles west of Grange).

Slieve League
and Kilrean,
Co. Donegal
Map F 4

Sweeney's only reference to this site comes in the long lay he utters during a remission of his madness in the care of his nephew just before his fateful encounter with the Hag of the Mill:

For certain am I Suibhne Geilt,
one who sleeps under the shelter of a rag,
about Sliabh Liag ...

These are the highest sea cliffs in Europe, looking south from the wild mountains of West Donegal. Our way there led through Killybegs where O'Keeffe placed Sweeney's first stop, when he flew from the yew-tree at Ros Bearaigh (see **Rasharkin**), immediately after the *Battle of Magh Rath*:

> Then as they were closing round the tree, Suibhne rose out of it very lightly and nimbly (and went) to *Cell Riaigain* (Kilrean) in *Tir Cannail* where he perched on the old tree of the church.

To get to St Catherine's Well turn left immediately at the western end of the village at Roshene Rd and go on until you come to dead end. Park here and walk through the gate up the path.

Here, at **Kilrean**, he finds himself once more surrounded, this time by Domnhall, the High King and victor of **Magh Rath** and his men, and flies off on the hejira that was to continue the rest of his life. In the busy harbour town of Killybegs we found the Garda station, but they had never heard of a Kilreagan or **Kilrean** within the parish. Nevertheless, one officer kindly led us in his car to a malodorous sewage farm. There we went on foot to an ancient and neglected ruined church in the midst of a graveyard, with what must have been monastic buildings and many a tree that Sweeney would have been proud to perch in. Thence to the sixth-century St Catherine's Well with a fine path leading up to it, still very obviously the object of a living cult, adorned, if that is the right word, with a modern statue. Above it on a summit overlooking the bay were the stone remains of what might have been a hermitage. All this was evocative and interesting, but, as we discovered later, not the **Kilrean** we were seeking.

Meantime we drove along the beautiful coast road to Carrick and then up a seemingly endless gated track to the best views of **Slieve League**. They are literally breath-taking, as a party of elderly German tourists who had had to abandon their coach a mile down the hill, discovered. Apart from their height the cliffs are remarkable for the variety of colours they display. We saw many caves where Sweeney might have lain under his rag. A day spent exploring **Slieve League** is rewarding and the energetic quester will need to take the sensational One Man's Path from Bunglass to reach the oratory and the Holy Well at the summit. We finally returned to Carrick and sat in the sun outside one of its pubs with a Guinness. There, gazing at the map to see our next port of call, we suddenly noticed across the peninsula to the north-east a place named **Kilrean**. So we leapt into the car and drove off across the Glengesh Pass.

Kilrean,
Co. Donegal
Map H 3

22 miles N.E. of Carrick.

Kilrean is an area rather than a village and we had some difficulty in finding the old churchyard until some builders put us on the right track. The churchyard, itself now a pasture for cattle, contained the ruins of an old church and, as we so often found, had been, until recently, the place where people chose to be buried alongside their ancestors. Immediately opposite the graveyard was a house with

Take the Carrick–Ardara road and then the T72 to **Kilrean** where you follow the main road to Donegal. Turn left in ½ mile until you see the only two-storey house, set back a little distance from the road. Take this path which leads to the churchyard.

three fine yew-trees in its garden. The owner, who was hard at work in her rockery, told us of a holy well, not far up the path. We drove on a bit and persuaded ourselves that a green patch at the far end of a boggy field was all that was left of it in a hot summer. Luckily the lady had followed us on foot and noticed our mistake. She led us further up the track and showed us where out of a rock on a bank a spring was still bubbling into an overgrown natural basin. This was surely, to judge by other sites, the place where one would have been most likely to encounter Sweeney when he abandoned his yew-tree perch in search of sustenance.

Northern Ireland

Lough Erne, Co. Fermanagh
Map I 4/5

Lough Erne's hills provided Sweeney with a wet bed and a sleepless night. It is a big lough – or indeed two, upper and lower – and one can only hazard a guess as to where Sweeney would have landed. Our guess is Devenish Island, a sacred centre of the old and new religion with its Round Tower and High Cross. Not so long ago it was reported to have been a hiding-place of the Grail. Wellesley Tudor Pole, the founder of the Chalice Well Trust at **Glastonbury**, considered it to be, along with Iona and **Glastonbury** one of the three holy islands of the United Kingdom. Devenish Island was another of the places we never got to, though we peered wistfully at it across a narrow stretch of intervening water that almost tempted us to swim it. Monday is the one day the ferry does not operate.

Enniskillen is a good centre for touring both sides of the border and, if you really wish to get a feel of Ulster's heartbeat, as opposed to being cocooned in tranquil isolation, you could not do better than stay at the modestly priced Railway Hotel where Catholic and Protestant meet to dine, drink, dance and make merry in an atmosphere of great conviviality.

Glenelly, Co. Tyrone
Map K 2

On your way between west and east you should take the B48 north out of Omagh and turn right at Plumbridge along the beautiful Glenelly Valley (the scenic route is to the south of the river), with its wooded slopes and water-meadows and its bare rounded mountains above. Sweeney writes of the cry of the herons there and the coming and going of migratory birds. He was obviously there in winter since he comments on the cold of the high glen.

Moira/Battle of Magh Rath, Co. Down
Map N 4 – near Belfast just off the M1, motorway exit 9

The **Moira** of today is a neat seventeenth-century plantation town with fast-growing suburbs and housing estates. In the midst of one of these, in Killnore Road, stands the seventh-century hill-fort that would have been the focal point of the great **Battle of Magh Rath** in AD637 – lasting at least two days – and which determined the separate destinies of Ireland and her Scottish offshoot, as well as providing the launching-pad for Sweeney's flight of frenzy. It provides the fixed historical point in time of our story, 64 years after Merlin's turning point at the battle of **Arderydd**. Here, as there, much of the preliminary bloodshed would have taken place at the river crossing; there of the Esk and Liddel, here of the Lagan.

To get a good view of these killing-fields, take the lane by the side of the Police Station until you come to the farm. If the farmer allows it you can drive through a gate towards the river. The fort lies almost due north and one can well imagine how the battle raged to and fro between it and the valley.

Moira today vaguely remembers the great battle, but not Sweeney. In the text his behaviour leaves much to be desired. Despite his unquestioned martial courage he emerges as a truce-breaker, constantly upsetting St Ronan's attempts to humanize and resolve the conflict. It was here that he hurled a spear at Ronan and when the saint's bell deflected its thrust, slew his follower and foster-son with a second cast. Sweeney, at this stage, is arrogant, rash and violent; the remainder of his history, under Ronan's curse, is a rectification of these vices and an archaic process of refinement of the soul through suffering.

Killaney, Co. Down

Map O 4 and OS of Northern Ireland Map 6 358580

The most direct route from **Moira** would be to take the minor road to Dromore, then the B2 to Ballynahinch, then the A49 north towards Baileysmill/Lisburn. Take the Lough road at **Killaney** until you come to the second house on the right. You will see a gate to a field and a path leading up to a clump of trees.

The story begins at **Killaney**. Sweeney, who must have been quite near, heard the bell of St Ronan, who was marking out the site for a new church on his territory. Sweeney was enraged and dashed off to stop him, leaving his cloak in the hands of Eorann, his wife, who had tried to prevent him. Finding St Ronan singing psalms he seized the psalter and threw it into the Bow Lough. As the naked and furious king was dragging Ronan away a messenger came summoning him to the **Battle of Magh Rath**. Ronan, deeply upset, remained *in situ*, bewailing the loss of his precious psalter and his dignity. When, after a day and a night, an otter restored the book to him unharmed, he cursed Sweeney: 'He shall roam Ireland, mad and bare . . .'

There are three churches in **Killaney** and a fourth, now in ruins, marks the place of confrontation between saint and king. It is an old densely overgrown graveyard with a remarkable plantation of yew-trees. It was interesting to note that the modern protestant community had also chosen to bury its dead in this ancient Catholic *temenos*. The lake was still there at the foot of the hill, a good psalter's throw away, and the owner of the land confirmed that there were still otters in the vicinity, but he knew nothing of the story of Sweeney and Ronan.

Strangford Lough, Co. Down

Map P 4

On our way from **Killaney** to the **Mountains of Mourne**, we stopped first at Downpatrick, the holiest Christian site in Ireland, whose two greatest saints, Patrick and Brigid, lie buried here. Just to the north is Sweeney's shimmering **Strangford Lough** with its

Take the B2 S.E. of
Ballynahinch to
Downpatrick.

Dundrum,
Co. Down
Map O 5

Mountains
of Mourne,
Co. Down
Map N 5

*Blue Lough, Mountains of
Mourne, magical natural
lough in the wild mountains
haunted by Sweeney.*

multitude of islets and its *Temple of the Winds*. Thirteen swans glided hieratically over the silver surface between us and the silhouette of a distant castle.

From **Strangford Lough** we took the pleasant A2 coast road to **Dundrum** with the outline of the **Mourne Mountains** looming ever larger through the heat-haze. **Dundrum** possesses a fine castle overlooking a sea-lough and a bay where Sweeney listened to the sound of the billows.

The **Mountains of Mourne** that 'sweep down to the sea' are famous throughout the world for their quintessentially Irish beauty, but to Sweeney they were a place of storm and endless snow, no place for food or milk, a bitterly cold abode for a blighted man. It was, nevertheless, in Heaney's translation, a good place for a madman, and it is mentioned five times in the poem, so was clearly a favourite refuge, despite its discomfort. In Sweeney's dying speech it is the last place he mentions except his beloved Glen Bolcain.

When we were there it was a midsummer day in the midst of a heat-wave so obviously we could not recapture Sweeney's experience, but we still wanted to try and find the kind of site he might have frequented. He might well have chosen the highest peak in the range, Slieve Donard, renamed from a princess of Ulster who became St Patrick's disciple, but earlier commemorating Slaine, the Celtic Asclepius, buried on its summit. The text, however, refers to a mountain-couch above the lake. Most of the lakes in Mourne are now reservoirs, but in the lee of Slieve Donard there remain three untouched by bulldozers and concrete. Of these the most impressive for its shape and position is Blue Lough.

The authors in the Blue Lough.

Blue Lough
OS of Northern Ireland Map 9, 327253

North-west from Mullartown, follow the road round to the left along some wooded slopes and stop in the first car-park on your right. From here a path leads up past Annalong Wood on your right to Blue Lough along a stream. Keep going north-west. Without the OS map you should ask for directions in Annalong.

Slieve Gullion, Co. Armagh
Map M 5

S. from Newry on Forkill road. Look out for signs to the right to *Killevy Old Church A.M.* (Ancient Monument)

This Lough forms an almost perfectly round basin or mirror in which the faerie loveliness of the surrounding mountains is reflected back to them with photographic exactitude. Contemplating its depths, a madman would find a soothing balm for his soul.

By the time we arrived there the hikers had all come down and we had the Lough entirely to ourselves, though the sun had not yet dipped behind the rim of the silent, encircling hills. We took off our clothes and immersed ourselves in the tranquil water. A pair of ravens confirmed that the old gods had not yet abandoned this sacred enclosure. Avalon echoes, too, in the name of the bay nearest to our hotel at the foot of Mourne north of Annalong – *Arthur's Port*. If you want to stay in Mourne and enjoy luxury and amazing service (where else has the car been washed without our asking?), do not hesitate to spend the night at Glassdrumman House, Annalong BT34 4QN. Tel: 039 67 68585.

Slieve Gullion, 1893 ft. high, is the magic mountain of embattled South Armagh, visited on a number of occasions by Sweeney. On the summit there is a lake between two cairns, one of which marks a passage-grave, where the fairy-woman guardian of the mountain dwells invisibly. Sweeney often preferred hillside sacred wells to mountain summits and if you have only limited time you could probably rendezvous with his shade at Killevy Old Church which was founded by St Monenna during his lifetime. Her sacred well is up a path to the right-hand side of the two impressive monastic buildings, one of which is of the ninth century. We were encouraged in our belief that this might be the right place by the discovery that we had arrived here on 5th July, the eve of the saint's feast. St Monenna herself, who died in AD518, founded the original community for nine nuns, clearly a Christianization of the numerous earlier pagan colleges of nine druidesses.

The Fews (Slieve Fuaidh), Co. Armagh
Map M 5, the hilly area N. of Newtownhamilton on B78

We had great difficulty in finding the **Fews**; many people had heard of them but nobody seemed to know exactly where they were, except finally a council employee whom we met at Killevy Old Church. This wooded, hilly area to the north of Newtownhamilton is the setting for one of the most dramatic incidents in Sweeney's story. After the death of the *Hag* at **Dunseverick**, Sweeney came again to his senses, but the vengeful malice of St Ronan continued to enforce the curse to the bitter end. The saint conjured up severed heads and

The Fews. Here St Ronan conjured up the furies to destroy Sweeney's returning reason.

headless bodies to haunt Sweeney as he crossed the **Fews** on a dark starless night. Driven by these furies Sweeney fell once more into madness and escaped to Feegile (Portarlington, near Kildare) on the last leg of his flight of frenzy.

We visited the **Fews** on a day of brilliant sunshine, but it was not difficult to imagine how sinister Dead Man's Hill by Dog Street might appear as twilight settled on the dark forest. Is there a memory perhaps of Sweeney, in the very name Slieve Fuaidh, the **Fews**, so close to the Irish root meaning a wanderer? Officially woods, but also the mountain is traditionally named for Fudd, a Milesian hero, slain on its slopes.

The **Fews** were also the birthplace of the sea-god Lir, perpetuated in Shakespeare's *King Lear*. To counterbalance this pagan influence St Patrick set foot on Carrigatuke, the highest mountain of the range.

Moylinney, Co. Antrim
Map N 03

Travelling north from Belfast you cross the plain of **Moylinney**, between Loch Neagh and Carrickfergus, much frequented by Sweeney.

Rathmore, Co. Antrim
OS of Northern Ireland Map 6, 185 873

The remains of the old palace of the kings of Dal Araidhe (Sweeney's kingdom), just north of **Rathmore**, are worth a visit, although the area is much affected by the motorway and suburban sprawl. Various remains are marked on the OS of Northern Ireland (**Map 6: 871d8**). But Sweeney's own favoured citadel seems to have been **Rasharkin**.

Slemish, Co. Antrim
Map N 3

On the road north from Antrim to Rasharkin, as you look right from the Ballymena bypass, you should see, some 7 miles to the east, **Slemish** (1437 ft.), the highest mountain of South Antrim. This was the mountain in all Ireland that was most frequented by Sweeney. It was also where St. Patrick spent his youth as a swineherd.

Rasharkin, Co. Antrim
Map M 3

'Suibhne of Ros Earcain is my name': thus Sweeney introduced himself early in the poem. Later it is named as one of his three main residences in his own country, whither he was wont to return after his madness. Glen Bolcain, when it does not refer to the **Glen of the Madmen (Gleann na nGealt**) in Dingle, denotes, according to O'Keeffe: 'Dunbolcain (or Drumbolcain) about a furlong north of **Rasharkin**'. Ros Bearaigh, where a yew-tree in the churchyard was one of his refuges of predilection from the day of the **Battle of Magh Rath**, is near by.

Sad to relate, **Rasharkin** is today a dreary little town where few would choose to linger. Nevertheless, to our surprise, the young barmaid in the pub knew the part called Dunbolcain – up the hill at the new housing estate, past the cricket-ground to the left, through the rubbish-dump. We followed an overgrown path through a dense thicket and climbed up eventually on to open moorland looking down on the town and the church, away from the disagreeable smell that had pervaded the woods. There, more or less where O'Keeffe had indicated, were the remains of a steep-sided hill-fort, though it is not shown on the Republic of Ireland's OS map. It stands in a commanding position overlooking the valley of Sweeney's beloved Bann in the heartland of Dal Araidhe. The road to the west led to the neighbouring kingdom of Dal Riada, which was to give birth to Scotland, some eight miles away.

On the intervening high moors are a number of ancient standing stones and an altar. But here, as so often in the Plantation lands of the Protestant North, it feels as though some vital link has been severed.

Dunseverick Castle, Co. Antrim

Map M 2, OS 2 – 9845 on B146 from Bushmills

Park your car in the lay-by on the left-hand side of the road and take the steep staircase down to the cliffs.

The Giant's Causeway, the Antrim coast road and the Glens of Antrim are justifiably world renowned and form the major tourist area of Northern Ireland. Time should therefore be allowed for visiting some of the major scenic attractions as well as the oldest working whiskey distillery in the world, Bushmills. At the eastern end of the path which leads past the wonders of the Giant's Causeway, stand the ruins of **Dunseverick Castle**. It was from this cliff that the hag-ridden Sweeney finally rid himself of the unwanted companion who had trailed him the length and breadth of Ireland. It was the Hag of the Mill who had tempted him to demonstrate his powers of flying during his first recovery from madness and brought on a new bout of frenzy. In *Sweeney Astray*, Seamus Heaney describes the final episode of their *folie à deux*:

> We coursed all over Ireland then ...
> But always look before you leap!
>
> Though she was fit for bog and hill,
> Dunserverick gave her the spill.
> She followed me down off the top
> of the fort and spread-eagled
> her bitch's body in the air.
> I trod the water, watching her
> hit the rocks, and I was glad
> to see her float in smithereens.

Knocklayd, Co. Antrim

Map N 2, OS 2 – 1236, S. of Ballycastle

One of Sweeney's favourite watering-holes was the spring-well of Lethed Lain which Heaney translates as **Knocklayd** (1695 ft.), the northernmost mountain of the Antrim chain. Some two dozen streams course down its slopes. One, from very near the summit, flows into the Glenshesk River to the east. A good impression of the glen and mountain may be obtained by driving south along one bank of the river and back by the other, which will necessitate the crossing of this and other streams. If you are feeling energetic, you could follow one of them up the mountain whence on a clear day there are fine views towards Mull of Kintyre, where Sweeney also landed.

Scotland, as we know it today, owes its very existence and its name to invaders from these glens who set up the kingdom of Dal Riada in Argyllshire, in AD501.

Layde Church, Co. Antrim
Map N 2

Follow signposts at north end of Cushendun for ½ mile to **Layde Church**.

O'Keeffe differs from Heaney and suggests that Lethed Lain is **Layde Church**, with its stream flowing into the sea, rather than **Knocklayd** mountain. When, with the usual difficulty, we at last discovered the site, we were inclined to agree with him. Going down a path from the car-park you suddenly glimpse from behind a mass of fuchsias the romantic ruins of a church set amidst a multitude of MacDonnell tombs, underlining Scotland's Antrim origin. Behind the church a row of trees marks the course of a rushing burn which enters the sea not far below. Of all the Sweeney sites we visited in Ulster, none conveyed a more sacred atmosphere than this.

Travelling south down the spectacular Antrim coast road, one passes through Glenarm where the Madman's Window may commemorate an unchronicled visit by Sweeney who knew this country so well.

At the end of the road lies the port of Larne, also a Sweeney site, which he, like us, would have found a convenient point of departure for Scotland.

Other sites visited by Sweeney

Airgeadros (on the Nore, parish of Rath Beagh), Co. Kerry
Assaroe, Co. Donegal
Benevenagh, mountain, Co. Derry
Benn Boghaine (Bannagh), Co. Donegal
Borona (on the Shannon near Killaloe), Co. Clare
Cloonburren, opposite Clonmacnoise, Co. Roscommon
Cooley, Co. Donegal
Croagh Patrick (Holy Mountain of St Patrick), Co. Mayo
Derry Colmcille (Londonderry), Co. Derry
Drum Lurgan, Co. Armagh
Dun Cernan (Old Head of Kinsale), Co. Cork
Edenterriff, in parish of Annagh, Co. Cavan
Emly, Co. Tipperary
Feegile, in parish of Clonsast, near Portarlington, Co. Laois
Galtee Mountains, Co. Limerick and Co. Tipperary
Inishboffin, off the coast of Co. Mayo
Inishowen Peninsula, Co. Donegal
Knockmealdown Mountains, Co. Waterford
Lough Diolair, Belleek, Co. Fermanagh
Lough Rea, Co. Galway
Lough Ree, Co. Longford, Co. Westmeath and Co. Roscommon
Maghera, Co. Derry
Moy Fevin, south of Cashel, Co. Tipperary

Moylurg, near Boyle, Co. Roscommon
Muirthemne, plain of, Co. Louth
Portarlington, Co. Laois
River Lagan, Co. Monaghan
River Liffey, Co. Wicklow and Co. Dublin
River Suck, Co. Roscommon and Co. Galway
St Dervil's Chapel, near Erris, Co. Mayo
Slieve Aughty, Co. Galway
Slieve Bloom, Co. Laois and Co. Offaly
Slieve Lougher (near Castle Island), Co. Kerry

Other relevant sites of interest in Ireland

**Lough Derg,
Co. Donegal**
Map I 4

St Patrick's purgatory is one of the most ancient and famous sites of Christian pilgrimage that almost certainly incorporates pagan initiatory rites. Merlin called King Arthur back from undergoing the full experience of descent to the nether regions here.

**Hill of Tara,
Co. Meath**
Map M 7

Seat of the High Kings of Ireland where St Patrick defeated the druids in a battle of magic, assuming the form of a deer.

**New Grange,
Co. Meath**
Map M 6

Burial place of the High Kings, entry to the underworld, residence of the goddess Boyne, the Dagda and his son, Aengus Og, the divinely youthful god.

**Glendalough,
Co. Wicklow**
Map M 8

Beautiful pilgrimage site, associated with the Christian druid St Kevin, who had a tame deer and a tame otter as well as a blackbird that laid an egg in his hand. He gave a psalter to St Moling, Sweeney's patron.

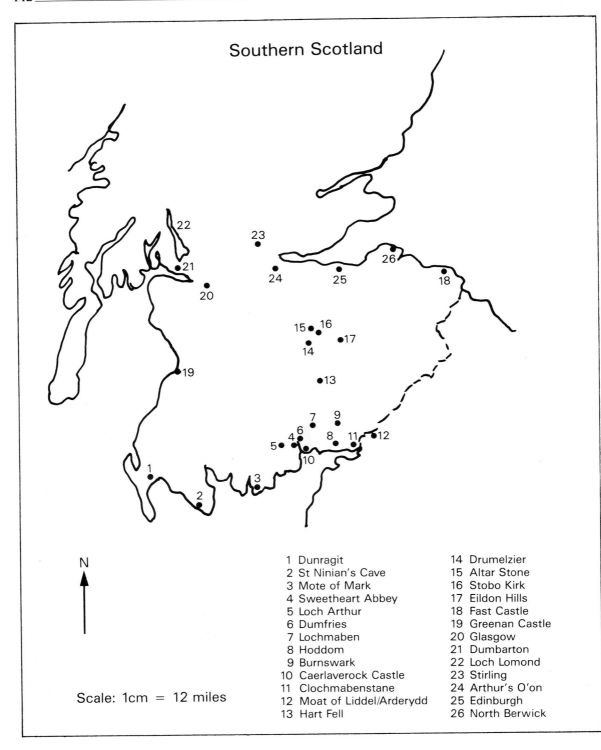

Southern Scotland

Scale: 1cm = 12 miles

N

1 Dunragit
2 St Ninian's Cave
3 Mote of Mark
4 Sweetheart Abbey
5 Loch Arthur
6 Dumfries
7 Lochmaben
8 Hoddom
9 Burnswark
10 Caerlaverock Castle
11 Clochmabenstane
12 Moat of Liddel/Arderydd
13 Hart Fell

14 Drumelzier
15 Altar Stone
16 Stobo Kirk
17 Eildon Hills
18 Fast Castle
19 Greenan Castle
20 Glasgow
21 Dumbarton
22 Loch Lomond
23 Stirling
24 Arthur's O'on
25 Edinburgh
26 North Berwick

Scotland

Dumfries, Galloway and the Borders

In Galloway, home of the northern Welsh or Strathclyde Britons, we are approaching the homeland of the historical Merlin-Lailoken. As the ferry moved away from Larne, our last port of call in Ireland, we were soon aware of a great conical shape to the north-east that formed the major landmark on our voyage. This was Ailsa Craig, quarry of a million curling-stones, on whose inhospitable crags Sweeney perched for six weeks.

At this meeting point of two great Celtic nations the histories and myths of Merlin and Sweeney come close to overlapping. But already in the time of Arthur, Loch Ryan was, according to Goodrich, the chief naval base of the great ruler. There is some archaeological evidence

Dunragit, last vestige of the great kingdom which stretched form Dumbarton to Rochdale.

Dunragit
Michelin Map F 19,
OS 82 – 149 579

Coming from Stranraer, turn left in the village to 'Home Farm' and left again at the farmhouse. Park your car at the end of the lane and go through the gate. After about 100 yds. you will come to a hawthorn clump in the middle of a hill-fort.

St Ninian's Cave
Map 75 NX 4535;
OS map 83–422361

Coming from Stranraer, turn right at Glenluce on A747 and after passing the village of Glasserton take the fifth turning on the right, including farm tracks, down a magnificent beech avenue to the car-park and follow signs to **St Ninian's Cave**.

pointing to its importance as a harbour at the relevant period. If you arrive as late as we did at Stranraer, the North West Castle Hotel is very comfortable and convenient for an overnight stay.

This is all that survives of the *Dun of Rheged*. The name bears testimony to the once mighty kingdom of *Rheged* which stretched from the Mersey to the Clyde. King Urien, husband of Morgan and its most famous monarch, was the patron of the bard Taliesin, the friend of Merlin, who shares much of his legend. Despite the scantiness of the remains of the ancient fort, one is somehow closer here to the forgotten war-lord halls of the sixth century than in Urien's great capital of **Carlisle**, now a modern city. This unassuming, unimpressive and unfrequented pastureland leads one unexpectedly to the heart of the Dark Ages. This is a good place to begin the Merlin trail in Scotland.

Goodrich asserts, without much supporting evidence, that **St Ninian's Cave** is really Merlin's cave. Other scholars have been puzzled by the coincidence of Merlin's lover sharing the name of Scotland's first evangelist. Certainly, Merlin's story becomes much entangled with that of numerous saints from Brittany to Strathclyde, but St Ninian's foundation of the *Candida Casa*, the first Christian church in Scotland, pre-dates by some two centuries Merlin-Lailoken's exploits (see Introduction). It is known, however, that the cave was both occupied and visited as a place of pilgrimage until the eighth century. So it is perfectly possible that Merlin himself, as a semi-Christian druidic sage, came here, and unquestionably the site has much to commend it to one of Merlin's tastes. The moment one walks down the long path, the entrance to which is guarded by holly, through the woods towards the sea, one is on familiar Celtic sacred ground. As we entered the *nemeton*, our nostrils were titillated by the pungent aroma of wild garlic, a sovereign remedy in any healer's or magician's chest. Alas, we came a few hours too late and loose earth on either side of the path revealed the depredations of some local garlic hunter. The path was dappled with sunlight, and a stream, rich in watercress, accompanied us until it lost itself in the sands of Port Castle Bay.

After such a promising approach, the cave in itself, sad to relate, was something of an anticlimax. It looks impressive at the far end of a beach of magnificent stones, but when we got close we discovered that much of it had collapsed.

Some ancient engraved crosses can still be seen on the walls of the cave that has shrunk to a mere twelve yards in depth, but the best have been removed for safety to Whithorn Museum.

While in the area it is worth visiting St Ninian's Chapel *Candida Casa*, on the Isle of Whithorn, as well as the Abbey, Museum and excavations in the town of Whithorn.

Mote of Mark, Rockcliffe

Map 75, NX 8454,
OS 84–845540

Is this the real **Tintagel**, fortress of King Mark, uncle of Tristan? Increasingly, in the minds of scholars, the action of the Arthurian legends is moving north. The **Mote of Mark** – like **Tintagel** and **South Cadbury** – is a Celtic stronghold, inhabited during the fifth–seventh centuries, to which quantities of luxury foreign goods were imported, including fragments of pottery from Bordeaux, glass from Germany, iron objects from the Lake District, bangles made from Yorkshire jet and pieces of gold (all now in the National Museum of Antiquities of Scotland in **Edinburgh**).

The citadel, atop its impregnable crag, was burnt out and vitrified in the seventh century by invading Angles, who sailed up the Solway Firth and Rough Firth, which the Mote commands. Nothing is known of the identity of the British defenders, but the names **Mote of Mark** and *Mark Hill*, in conjunction with **Loch Arthur** and *Troston (Tristan?) Hill*, a few miles to the north, lend credence to the notion that this may indeed be *Tintagel North*. Celtic tribes often extended their rule over considerable distances. (e.g. Dumnonia which included Devon, Cornwall, most of Brittany and part of Scotland). The **Mote of Mark** is an exceptional hill, well worth the steep – and sometimes wet – climb through thick undergrowth, affording magnificent views over Rough Firth to the distant Galloway Highlands. Below the summit, a mass of tumbled masonry bears witness to the battles long ago that afflicted this peaceful and little visited jewel of old Kirkcudbrightshire (see also **Tristan Stone**).

The Baron's Craig Hotel is a comfortable centre from which to tour this rewarding area south of Dumfries.

Sweetheart Abbey

Map 76, NX 9666

If travelling from the **Mote of Mark** to **Dumfries**, by the A710, you should not fail to visit the lovely rose-red ruins of this last Cistercian house in Scotland. Here, Devorgilla, foundress of Balliol College, Oxford, and builder of the bridge over the Nith at **Dumfries**, is buried with the heart of her husband, John of Balliol, King of Scotland, 1292–96. This story highlights a veritable cult of the heart which is parallel to the symbolism of the Holy Grail, later merged into the more orthodox cult of the *Sacred Heart*.

Goodrich regards **Sweetheart Abbey** as a school of chivalry for Arthur and Gawain.

Loch Arthur

Map 75, NX 9069

Loch Arthur has been known under this name since the earliest written records, the *Kirkgunzeon* charter of 1160. The importance of the Loch was much enhanced by the discovery there of a boat 45 ft. 6 in. long and 4 ft. 10 in. wide at the stern, dating from the Dark Ages. It was hollowed out of a single oak-tree and is the finest canoe (royal barge?) of its type ever to be found in Britain. It is now to be seen at the National Museum of Antiquities in **Edinburgh**. The problem is: What was such a large vessel doing on such a small loch at such an early period? The hypothesis that its use was ceremonial seems at least plausible.

The Loch contains an ancient *crannog* (lake dwelling) and the two highest hills surrounding it in the locality are curiously named Troston (i.e. Tristan) and Lotus. (Odysseus' Isle of the Lotus Eaters bears some resemblance to Avalon.) Mabie Forest to the north-east might suggest a cult of *Mabon* (cf. **Lochmaben** and **Clochmabenstane**).

Access to the lochside can be gained by courtesy of the Loch Arthur Community.

Dumfries
Map 76, NX 9776

It is impossible to travel far in Dumfriesshire without exposing oneself to the traffic bottle-neck of the Nith bridges at **Dumfries** itself. Here are the only two pubs in the world tied to the Broughton Brewery, near **Drumelzier**, where you can be sure (at least in 1989) of finding Merlin Ale on draught as well as in bottles. We were given a great welcome at the New Bazaar in Whitesands, on the east bank of the Nith, almost opposite the Tourist Office, and presented with the Brewery tie and the Merlin pump label.

Lochmaben
Map 77, NY 0882 – 13 miles N.E. of **Dumfries** on A709

Lochmaben seems to have been the major shrine in Britain to the divinely youthful god *Mabon* or *Maponos*. It is mentioned in the Ravenna Cosmography as *locus maponi*. Tolstoy makes a convincing case for **Lochmaben** being the temple where a celebrated sage, like Merlin, a *librarius*, was consulted by the parents of the future St Samson from south-west Wales. They longed to have a child and the priest told the wife, Anna, to sleep in the sacred enclosure where she had a dream, in which she was told by an angel that she would bear a son of great renown. The priest came to her and her husband, Amon, the next morning, already aware of her dream, and prophesied that her son would be unique and 'do great good to many'.

The prophecy was fulfilled in St Samson (d. 565), an important historical figure, and contemporary of Merlin's, who founded the archiepiscopal see of **Dol**. He was also Abbot of Caldey and reformed an Irish monastery. One of the Scilly Isles is named after him, too; so he is a prominent pan-Celtic saint. Tolstoy's interesting suggestion is that Merlin-Lailoken was the successor to the mage of **Lochmaben** who prophesied to Anna and Amon. Whether this be so or not, we are now near the centre of the geographical area where Merlin's presence is well attested.

Just south of the magnificent ruins of the medieval castle, the probable birthplace of Robert the Bruce, is a large circular earthwork which, no doubt, formed the original sacred *temenos*, not far from the junction where four rivers meet to form the *Annan*, affording access to the Solway Firth.

Up the river to the north is the village of St Ann's which in the Celtic world commemorates the old fertility goddess Anu. Down-river is Brydekirk, celebrating Brigit, the goddess of fire and poetry, Christianized as the foster-mother of Christ.

Hoddom

Map 77, NY 1774 or
OS 85 – 168728 (but
not marked on OS
map)

Park by Hoddom Castle
entrance on B727, cross
the bridge over the Annan,
turn immediately right
through a field and soon
you will see ahead of you a
disued graveyard which
contains the ruins of St
Kentigern's chapel.

The old order was changing among the Britons of the North in the sixth century as the dynamic interaction between Merlin-Lailoken and St Kentigern shows (cf. Introduction and **Stobo**). No doubt, Kentigern chose the site of his new Christian foundation at **Hoddom**, not just for its convenient proximity to the river Annan, but because it lay exactly between the two pagan shrines of **Lochmaben** and **Clochmabenstane**, whose glory he thought to eclipse. Here, Merlin came to confront the new order in his *Cernunnos* role of wild man. No doubt, he railed at the monks, interrupting their observances from a rock on the steep wooded flanks of the hill on the other side of the Annan.

There is another old church, dedicated to St Mungo (Kentigern), north of **Hoddom**. Turn left on B723 at Middleshaw past Kirkbank and you will find it in the midst of the Jardine burial ground (**OS 85 – 156729**).

Burnswark

Map 77, NY 1879

We asked Mr A.E. Truckell, former director of the Dumfries Museum, who has taken part in many excavations in the region associated with Merlin-Lailoken, which site – apart from the known ones – he would guess might have been visited by the magus. He responded cannily that the **Burnswark** was a very interesting place, a Roman fort and city, that had survived almost intact until local landowners used it as a quarry for sheep enclosures. It was the major Roman citadel north of **Carlisle**, where all roads met. Mr Truckell pointed out that here, as at so many other Merlin/Arthur sites, further architectural developments took place in the post-Roman/Celtic period, the fifth century. A new building – perhaps one of the few Celtic temples built with hands – was fitted into the old Roman street plan.

We took the car as far as we could and quailed somewhat at the extreme steepness of the grassy glacis which faced us, but, encouraged by the rapid flight of a merlin across our path, we persisted to the summit. It will have been evident from these pages, that hill-forts are not our favourite Merlin sites. After a dozen or so one is inclined to say unfairly: 'When you've seen one, you've seen them all.' **Burnswark** is different: although only earthy outlines remain, it trumpets the grandeur that was Rome. It is a plateau, 920 ft. above the Solway Firth, covering a vast area and commanding a 360-degree strategic view, a dozen miles north of the **Moat of Liddel**. Nobody could pass undetected along the main road between the two strongholds, **Dumbarton** and **Carlisle**, that marked the western extremity of the two great Roman walls.

If you only ever visit one hill-fort site, the relatively unknown **Burnswark** should be your choice. The views and height are unequalled in the British Isles and you will almost certainly have this magnificent panorama to yourself.

Caerlaverock Castle

Map 76, NX 0366 –
S.E. of Dumfries on
B725

Across the treacherous estuary of the Nith from **Sweetheart Abbey** stand the uniquely triangular moated ruins of **Caerlaverock Castle**. The battle of **Arderydd**, where Merlin went mad, was one of the three futile battles of Britain, fought, it was said, over a lark's nest. **Caerlaverock**, the camp of the skylark, is likely to have been that nest. If Gwenddolau had been seeking to extend his territories westward along the Solway, this, the first great obstacle on his route beyond the quicksands of the Nith, would have proved a perilous fort indeed, where, earlier, Lancelot and other heroes proved their worth. According to Goodrich, Arthur was born at **Caerlaverock**, so Merlin's magic might have been wrought for his conception here rather than in Cornish **Tintagel**.

The present castle is late thirteenth century with Renaissance refinements. Some of the details in the carvings and reliefs may refer to its more ancient history. In one a man sits in a tree with a great stag beneath, an image suggestive of Merlin-Lailoken in his wild mode. In another a woman is lifted up out of a boat by an angel. Could this be the mother of Taliesin who, set adrift in a leather bag as a baby, was discovered, probably in the Solway Firth, by Elphin, the son of King Gwyddno? This divine child tells the king:

The prophet Johannes called me Merlin (Merddin),
But now all kings know me as Taliesin.

The Iron Age fort at **Caerlaverock** is down towards the bay beyond the present castle. Like **Lochmaben** it is now a Nature Reserve.

Caerlaverock Castle, the Lark's Nest for which the disastrous battle of Arderydd was fought.

Scotland

Clochmabenstane
Map 77, NY 3267

Turn left at Gretna towards Annan on the A75, left down African Road, opposite Solway Lodge Hotel and, just as you leave the built-up area, take the track by a farm on the left. Park your car at the end and go through the gate opposite the farm to the second field, where you will find the stone.

The **Clochmabenstane**, a megalith, now standing on its own in a field facing the Solway Firth, was once the centre of a stone circle. This has now vanished except for one or two stones still to be discerned under the boundary hedge. Its name suggests that it was part of the cult of the British Apollo, Mabon, the divine patron of the once great kingdom of Rheged, ruled by Urien and his queen, Morgan. That the rites of *Lughnasadh* (Lunasa) in early August, later superseded by the Christian *Lammas* and the feast of the Trans-figuration, were still practised in Britain at the time of Merlin-Lailoken, is proved by St Samson's description of such a ceremony in Cornwall. If Mabon was a god of fertility, as the visit of St Samson's parents to **Lochmaben** suggests, then Gretna Green's fame as the Mecca of eloping couples is a tribute to his abiding power. So is the stone, once 7 ft. high, which now, toppled by the elements, reveals a dual sexual character.

The **Clochmabenstane** is a mere 7 miles down the Esk from the stronghold of Merlin's patron and friend King Gwenddolau. Tolstoy visualizes Merlin as *avatar* of Lugh/Mabon and heir to the chief druids of **Lochmaben,** presiding over the sacred ceremonies on the shores of Solway with the great mountains of Cumbria beyond.

Moat of Liddel/Arderydd
Map 77m NY 4175, not marked; OS map 85 – 402742, marked *Liddel Strength, Motte and Bailey*

Travelling north along the river Esk from Longtown to Canonbie by the A7, take the first road to the right, signposted Kirkandrew, and stop a few yards down by a converted railway station. Follow the dismantled railway track through the gate and across the bridge over the Esk for about half a mile. You could now take the first main path up to the right to Lowmoat Farm and then left to Highmoat Farm, through the farmyard (public footpath) and across two fields until you reach the **Moat of Liddel**; or you can follow

We hope Cumbrians will excuse us for recapturing a few square yards of their border land with Scotland. It was always shifting throughout the centuries and in Merlin's time both sides of the border belonged to Gwyr y Gogledd, the men of the North. **Arderydd** is the vital preliminary of Merlin-Lailoken's adventures in the Forest of Celyddon and belongs naturally to this itinerary.

This is the site of the battle of **Arderydd** (Arthuret), AD573, where Merlin-Lailoken played a notable part, being awarded a gold torque for gallantry. Merlin advised King Gwenddolau to undertake the war which culminated in this fatal battle in which many of those near and dear to him were slain. Like Sweeney at the battle of **Moira**, Merlin succumbed to a strange madness and fled to the woods. Tolstoy, in Chapter 4 of *The Quest for Merlin*, reconstructs the battle of **Arderydd** from all the information that is available.

The battle was exceptionally prolonged, lasting for up to six weeks after the death of Gwenddolau and all 300 of the defenders seem to have been massacred and buried in the Upper Moat orchard. We do not know the identity of the foe, but it may have been Rydderch Hael, Christian king of **Dumbarton**, patron of St Kentigern and Merlin's brother-in-law.

Now much overgrown with trees, thorns and long grass, the earth-walls of the citadel remain formidable after 1½ millennia. Take time to linger and imagine Merlin at the last stand, seeing the skies fall in, and 'numberless, warlike battalions in the heavens like flashing lightning, holdings spears which they brandished furiously at me'.

Hart Fell.

the path further along the river until you see another path up to the right, leading diagonally to the camp. If you are particularly adventurous or ignorant, you will do what we did on our first visit and scramble up the precipitous wooded slopes without a path, immediately under the old fortress where the Liddel water makes a U-turn after its confluence with the Esk. Finally, you can drive almost all the way by taking the first turning left (north) in Longtown on the south side of the bridge, past Netherby Hall, taking the next turning left at the outskirts of the village of Carwinley (Caer Gwenddolau) and then take the next fork right, continuing until you reach Highmoat Farm. Then follow the way through the farmyard to the Moat.

Hart Fell
Map 77, NY 2489; OS 78 – 95118

Leaving Moffat to the north on the A701 Edinburgh Road, take the last fork to the right, Beech Grove, which is a dead-end lane, and follow in the same direction for 2¾ miles. Park outside a tin-roofed hut, with a signpost to the right, just beyond, to **Hart Fell**. The path is not always well defined, but a series of marker-posts on the slopes to the left, above the Auchencat Burn, lead you after about 45 minutes to the cave and spa, the far side of another stream that

It is worth noting that the Liddel immediately below the ancient citadel still forms the border between England and Scotland. Further up the Liddel there is a saddleback hill called Arthur's Seat.

The first time we climbed up **Hart Fell** some years ago, with snow still thick on the ground, we missed the cave completely, though a boy was actually sitting on top of it, and we had to return the next day after consulting the police. Now there is no problem in finding the site, since the tidy-minded authorities have cleaned it up and enclosed it with a fence, which detracts considerably from the wildness of the mad prophet's lair.

The Quest for Merlin, which inspired our own endeavours, presents many convincing arguments for this being Merlin's *fons galabes*.It occurred to Tolstoy that Galabes might well be a corruption of *chalybs*, the iron salts that give the spring its healing properties. We know from the early sources that a healing spring, that could even cure madness (cf. **Barenton**), did play a major role in the denouement of Merlin's forest sojourn, and this may well have been it. The present structure owes much to the munificence of the Marquess of Queensberry who patronized the spa and set his seal on it in 1752. But the spring may well be the one which appeared miraculously while Merlin was conversing with Taliesin and fully restored the prophet's reason. Other authorities, however, have placed the spring flows down the steep flank of **Hart Fell**, below Arthur's Seat. At one point the path rejoins the burn by a precipitous staircase which can be very slippery in wet weather.

near the summit of Broad Law (2756 ft.), the highest mountain in the range, 8 miles north-east of **Hart Fell**.

Hart Fell is the most impressive mountain in the region, and Tolstoy sees it as the *Omphalos* of the North, where Gwenddolau and his druids (no doubt with Merlin at their head) celebrated the festival of *Lughnasadh*. The sacred nature of the mountain is emphasized by its importance as a watershed. Three great rivers, the Tweed, the Clyde and the Annan rise in the vicinity.

Hart Fell is the centre of Wild Merlin's story in the forest of Celyddon that begins with his madness at **Arderydd**, 30 miles to the south-east, and ends with his death – triple like that of Lugh – at **Drumelzier**, 24 miles to the north. Whatever the exact location of Merlin's refuge, there is no gainsaying the bare grandeur of **Hart Fell** Spa and the excitement of the breathless questor, who suddenly sees the grotto at the foot of a mass of tumbled scree and drinks the ferrous waters, the same waters which may have refreshed and healed Merlin, Taliesin, Gwenddydd and their companions.

While in Moffat it is worth visiting the sulphur spring 1½ miles north-east of the town by Well Road, discovered in 1630 and visited by Boswell and Burns. Rather derelict on our first visit, it was completely refurbished in 1987, with the addition of a picnic site, but it still emits a powerful whiff, redolent of Merlin's diabolical origins.

Drumelzier
(Merlin's Grave)
Map 83, NT 1334, off A701 on B712

The name **Drumelzier** may derive from Dunmeller, the hill of Merlin. According to ancient tradition, **Merlin's Grave** is marked by a pile of stones under a thorn-tree where the Powsail Burn flows into the Tweed. It was here, according to *The Life of St Kentigern*, that Merlin-Lailoken met his triple death, as he had prophesied to the saint. The three-fold death links Merlin, though the details vary, to the god Lugh. In the specific case of Merlin-Lailoken, it consisted of stoning by the shepherds of his enemy, King Meldred, falling off a cliff and hanging upside-down from a fisherman's stake till he drowned. The most likely place for his stoning and fall would be the sheer drop between the churchyard and the Powsail Burn. But the topography may have changed somewhat in the past 1400 years. A row of thorn-trees lines the west bank of the Powsail and turns west, parallel to the Tweed. Under one of the oldest hawthorns, next to a holly-tree, may still be found the remains of a cairn which marks Merlin's burial place. As at **Merlin's Tomb** in **Brocéliande**, much has vanished with the passing years, but still, some memorial remains – and some magic. So, we added a stone or two to the pile. This is also the setting for one of the more successful prophecies connected to the Merlin legend, attributed to his Scottish successor from the **Eildons**, Thomas the Rhymer:

> When Tweed and Pausayl meet at Merlin's grave,
> Scotland and England shall one monarch have.

This prediction was fulfilled in 1603 when, during a spate, the Powsail overflowed the cairn towards the Tweed and James VI of Scotland became James I of England, uniting the two monarchies for the first time.

Merlin's name lives on in the nearby Merlindale (**OS 72 – 129341**), the hamlet immediately west of **Drumelzier** across the Tweed bridge, and his legend is recorded in **Stobo Kirk**. Merlin's refuge in his 'sweet apple-tree growing by the river' is believed to have been somewhere between **Drumelzier** and Talla, some 7 miles to the south, on the flank of Broad Law, where an alternative to Merlin's fountain at **Hart Fell** has been situated. Merlin's Ale is brewed a couple of miles away at Broughton (**Map 83, NT 1135**).

Altar Stone
Map 83, NT 1938;
OS 72 – 156359

On B712 turn left towards Dreva before **Stobo** and immediately opposite the first farm on your left in the hedge you will find a large flat stone known as the *Altar Stone*.

Between two Cornish sounding hills, *Trahenna* and *Penvalla*, north of the Tweed, lies, totally hidden and forgotten, this stone on which, according to local tradition, St Kentigern baptized Merlin-Lailoken. It is all the more touching for being so neglected and unassuming, and we had to remove much undergrowth to photograph it.

Stobo Kirk
Map 83, NT 1938

On B712 go past Stobo Castle (now a health farm) towards Peebles until you see a sign to **Stobo Kirk**, 1 mile from Stobo village.

In AD586 St Kentigern evangelized Tweeddale and established his mother-church at **Stobo**, which is dedicated to him under his better-known nickname of Mungo. In this beautiful church is a window showing the baptism of Myrddin by St Kentigern. Just next to the window and near a tombstone engraved with a Grail, is a medieval stone carving of a knight with a sword that seems much more like the wild man with his club. **Stobo** is one of the earliest parishes belonging to the bishopric of **Glasgow**.

Altar Stone, where St Kentigern baptized Merlin.

Stobo Kirk. The window depicts the baptism of Merlin.

KENTIGERN MYRDAIN

Three miles to the east is Cademuir Hill, scene of Arthur's seventh great battle where there once stood a cromlech known as Arthur's Oven (see **Arthur's O'On**).

The Eildon Hills
Map 84, NT 5532

The Eildon Hills are unquestionably the major centre of magic, prophecy and poetry in Scotland. Its principal direct connection with the Merlin trail lies in the local legend of *Canonbie Dick*, recounted in Reginald Scott's *Discovery of Witchcraft* (1665). (Sir Walter Scott, himself, the local genius, who more than anyone else preserved the spirit of old Scotland, planned to write a novel about it.) In the tale, a horse-coper named Dick, from Canonbie, the nearest town to **Arderydd**, scene of Merlin's flight into madness, is riding over Bowden Moor, just south of the **Eildons**, with a pair of horses which he had unsuccessfully taken to market. He encounters an old man who offers him antique coins for the horses and arranges to buy more. At one point the old man leads him up to a well-known resort of witches, a rocky outcrop of the **Eildons** known as the *Lucken Hare*, deposited there by the familiar spirit of the famous local magician, Michael Scot. Dick follows the old man into a subterranean passage, where he sees King Arthur and his knights asleep. Here the story follows a form familiar from many other such (cf. **Alderley Edge**). Dick blows a horn, waking all the knights and draws a sword to protect himself from them. The old man, who now reveals himself as Thomas the Rhymer of Erceldoune, informs him that he has carried out these two actions in the wrong order. Had he drawn the sword first, he would have been king of all Britain. The old man in these stories is usually Merlin himself, although he is sometimes identified with a later, local figure, or simply called the wizard.

Thomas the Rhymer (1220?–1297?) was a historical figure and prophet, who foretold the happening at **Drumelzier**, which synchronized with the advent of the Scots King, James VI, to the throne of England. Thomas was himself the subject of a Merlinesque story:

> **True Thomas lay on Huntlie bank;**
> **A ferlie he spied wi' his e'e;**
> **And there he saw a ladye bright**
> **Come riding down by the Eildon Tree.**

The fairy who came to him revealed herself as the Queen of Elfland and they became lovers. She led him into her underground realm beneath the **Eildons** and introduced him to an Avalon of fruits and flowers. After three years, which seemed to him like three days, she returned him to the everyday world, having taught him the arts of prophecy.

In this version of the story a Christian, moralizing element is present: the queen becomes hideous after sex, the fruits of fairyland are not to be eaten, paths lead to hell or purgatory, in contrast to many more positive accounts of Merlin's story with Vivian. On the other hand, a more primitive attitude prevails in that here it is the Morgan/Vivian character who initiates and instructs the man.

Thus Thomas the Rhymer, like Melerius (see **Caerleon**) or Eon de l'Etoile (see **Barenton**), is clearly a latter-day Merlin figure. He is not the only one to walk into the pages of history from the **Eildons**. Michael Scot (1175?–1234?), MA Oxon, Ph.D. Paris, was the greatest magician of his age and astrologer-in-chief to Stupor Mundi, the Holy Roman Emperor Frederick II of Hohenstaufen, in his court at Palermo. It was he, according to legend, who split Mount Eildon, originally one, into its present triple-toothed outline. He studied magic – which would have included astrology, alchemy and the cabbala – at the Mecca of medieval occultists, Toledo. No doubt it was his influence which led Frederick II to have the prophecies of Merlin translated from Latin into the vulgar tongue. Wolfram von Eschenbach was writing his Parzival at the same period. Was Michael perhaps the inspiration for his original character, Klingsor, whose castle he placed in Sicily?

Finally, there is Sir Walter Scott (1771–1832), known to his contemporaries as the Wizard of the North. Scott's View, along with his great house, Abbotsford, are important goals of pilgrimage for any visitor to the area. Other important sites are the Eildon Stone (**OS 73 563336**), which was erected to mark the spot where Thomas the Rhymer met the Fairy Queen and the *Lucken Hare* where she led him.

Fast Castle
Map 85 NT 8772 – 2.3 miles off A1107, signposted

Leave your car beyond the cottages at Dowlaw Farm. Approx. 15 minutes' walk down to the castle on a rough path.

This is where Goodrich visualizes Merlin in his Northumbrian retreat. Here he could have stayed with his old friend and chronicler, Blaise, perhaps his old grey wolf, since *bleiz* means wolf in old British. This notion gained some support from Sir Walter Scott's *The Bride of Lammermoor* in which **Fast Castle** is called *Wolf's Crag*. This site, like several others connected with Merlin, is said to conceal a treasure.

Strathclyde, Central and Lothian

Greenan Castle
Map 81, NS 3320; OS map 70 – 312192 – off A719, S. of Ayr direction Greenan

Much publicity has been given recently to Goodrich's claim, apparently supported by *Burke's Peerage*, to have discovered Camelot at the ruined **Greenan Castle**, 2½ miles south-east of the town centre. The gaunt outline of the remaining tower is a romantic site, especially in the sunset. But to get close to it, whether along the beach and up the cliff or through very private property from Greenan Farm, is no easy matter. De'il's Dyke lies out to sea just west of the castle and in the distance looms the unmistakable cone of Ailsa Craig where Sweeney spent six weeks. The present incumbent to the Barony of **Greenan** lives in Indiana, no doubt assisting Jones with his inquiries about the Holy Grail.

Glasgow Cathedral

St Kentigern built the first church on this site, and the lower church was designed to contain his tomb. He is the patron saint of the city and befriended Merlin-Lailoken on the day of his death (see **Drumelzier**).

Dumbarton
Map 87 NS 3975

It is worth approaching Dumbarton on the M8 via Erskine Bridge to get the most dramatic views of Dumbarton Rock across the waters of the Clyde.

Dumbarton, *Dun Breatann*, the fortress of the Britons, was the capital of the Britons of the North until late in the eleventh century. It was also known as *Alclud*, the Clyde Rock, which describes perfectly its dominating position over all shipping up and down the estuary and all armies proceeding along its north shore.

At the time of the battle of **Arderydd** it was the capital of Rhydderch Hael and his queen, Gwenddydd, Merlin's sister. Rhydderch, patron of St Kentigern, was the defender of the faith in Strathclyde and the presumed victor of **Arderydd**. Merlin spent two sojourns during his madness at Rhydderch's court. So, as you climb the steep steps of the citadel, spare a thought for the prophet imprisoned there, yearning for the friendly trees and beasts of Celyddon.

During Merlin's captivity at **Dumbarton**, he remained quite dumb and unresponsive. One day, Rhydderch removed a leaf from Queen Gwenddydd's hair, at which Merlin burst out laughing. He agreed to answer Rhydderch's questioning on condition that he be free to return to his life in the forest. Gwenddydd, he claimed, picked up the leaf while lying with her lover in some woody glade. She persuaded Rhydderch to put Merlin's prophetic powers to the test in order to be exonerated from her adultery by discrediting him. She introduced a youth in three different disguises and asked Merlin to predict the death of these supposedly separate individuals. The three deaths foretold by Merlin correspond to the triple death that he himself would one day suffer (see **Drumelzier**). The youth, too, fulfilled the prophecy and died this triple death shortly after Merlin returned to Celyddon.

During his second internment in **Dumbarton** Merlin's laughter again secured his release when he correctly prophesied the death of a youth who had just bought a new pair of shoes, and the existence of a hidden treasure beneath a seated beggar who was bewailing his lot.

Dumbarton, from across the Clyde, is still magnificent and so is the ascent of the twin-peaked rock itself, but, alas, urban Clydeside has set its mark on the approaches to the mighty fortress.

At Dumbuck, just north of **Dumbarton** (**OS 64 – 425745**), there is a legend of a sleeping hero awaiting the right moment to return and reunite the three kingdoms.

Loch Lomond

The road from **Dumbarton** to **Stirling** passes the southern tip of the queen of Scottish lochs, scene of the northernmost of Arthur's victories. Ben Arthur, The Cobbler, is a striking mountain in the Argyll National Forest Park, 10 miles west of Tarbet, three-quarters of the way up the Loch, in the heartland of Clan MacArthur, which claims descent from Arthur's only surviving son, Smervie.

Stirling
Map 87, NS 7993

The literary tradition linking **Stirling** with Arthur's Round Table is a venerable one, dating, as Geoffrey Ashe states, to William of Worcester in the fifteenth century and Sir David Lyndsay (1490–1555), poet, *Lyon King of Arms* and tutor to the future James V. Such references thus antedate the royal garden, known as the King's Knot, which was not constructed until 1627.

Admittedly, it was fashionable during the whole of the Middle Ages to construct Round Tables, whether of wood (cf. **Winchester**) or earth (cf. **Penrith**) – the latter for use of tournaments and pageants – as well as associating Roman constructions with Merlin's famous invention (cf. **Caerleon**). Goodrich makes out a good case for the **Stirling** area being a major Arthurian centre (cf. **Arthur's O'On**).

The King's Knot today is still a strange and mysterious grassy shape in a public park below the castle walls, like a sand-mould imprinted by some giant hand. Alas, that hand cannot chastise those who today see it as a convenient dumping ground for garbage.

Here we are at the centre of Scottish history, the key to Scotland, its cockpit and the gateway to the Highlands. Here, at the bridge across the Forth, Wallace won his greatest victory. Here, Bruce liberated Scotland from the Sassenach yoke on the field of Bannockburn. The ancient church of St Ninian near the scene of the battle is, for Goodrich, the key to the mysteries of Arthur and Lancelot.

Arthur's O'On (Stenhousemuir)
Map 88, NS 8783

We had read in the London newspapers early in 1989 of a *Rotunda*, located on the banks of the Carron river, near **Stirling**, that Goodrich and Robert Mitchell considered to be King Arthur's Round Table. So, in the hope of stumbling over it, we travelled cross-country from **Stirling** to Carron Bridge and began to work our way down-river in the general direction of Camelon (*Camlann*?) – an outpost on the Antonine Wall – and the Carron Iron Works. A telephone call to Adrian Malloney of the *Falkirk Herald* put us on the right track. **Arthur's O'On**, a dome-shaped structure, 20 ft. by 20 ft., with an opening to the heavens like the Pantheon, existed until 1743, when it was destroyed to repair the mill-dam on the Carron River. Until then it had been considered the most complete and best preserved Roman building in Great Britain, and was visited, described and discussed by numerous antiquaries. Here, Merlin would have had a fine observatory from which to plot the path of the planets.

Sections of the Round Table, measuring 4½ ft. by 1 ft., are now kept in the back-garden of a house in Adam Street, Stenhousemuir. Street names near by include Castle Drive and Arthur's Drive.

Another Arthur's Oven was an almost perfect cromlech at Cademuir, which is the Welsh for great battle, just south-west of Peebles, the scene of Arthur's seventh victory, where the Manor Water enters the Tweed near **Stobo**. It, too, was destroyed – by Sir Walter Scott's father, of all people – for use in road building and construction work.

Edinburgh
Map 89, NT 2573

Edinburgh was already an important centre, thanks to its Castle Rock overlooking the Forth, when it was captured by the Northumbrians in AD638, who called it after Edwin, their late great king. Originally it was *Duneadain*, *Dun Eideann*, 'the fort on the slope'. In Tolkien's *The Lord of the Rings*, the men of the west, who still survive in the northern kingdom under the leadership of the Once and Future King, *Aragorn*, are called the *Dunedain*.

Goodrich has put forward the provocative proposal that the Calton

Hill – and not **Stonehenge** – with its wonderful views over the city, Holyroodhouse and Arthur's Seat in the background, was the setting for Merlin's memorial to the Celtic chieftains, treacherously murdered by Hengist. Curiously, it was to become the site of the twelve-columned portico of the national monument, commemorating Scots who died in the Napoleonic wars, an unfinished Parthenon, which is now one of the landmarks of **Edinburgh**.

If Arthur was truly a king of Scotland, this would confirm the proud boast of Clan MacArthur that they are descended from Smervie the Great, his only surviving son. There is a saying in the Western Highlands: 'There is nothing older, unless the hills, MacArthur, and the Devil'.

North Berwick
Map 89, NT 5585

According to Goodrich, drawing from various sources, especially the *Prose Lancelot*, **North Berwick** is Benoïc whose king and queen – Ban and Helen – were the parents of Sir Lancelot. Merlin and the Lady of the Lake visited them by boat when the child was one year old and agreed that he was the most beautiful creature in the world. Benoïc was besieged by King Claudas, and the royal family were forced to flee with their infant son. Ban died of a heart attack on Berwick Law, AD612 – while looking down on his captured and burning palace – and Helen, herself a descendant of the first Grail-bearer, Joseph of Arimathea, and daughter of the Grail-King Pelles, climbed the volcanic hill to be with her husband, leaving her son by the roadside. There the Lady of the Lake found him and bore him away to her castle (cf. **Comper**), where she raised him to become the best knight in the world.

Traprain Law, 6 miles to the south, is the Dunpeldyr of Mary Stewart's *The Last Enchantment* and the site of an excavation which revealed a superb table service and silver christening spoons, demonstrating the high standard of living of Dark Age chieftains.

Brittany

Introduction

Brittany, Little Britain or Armorica, a Gallic land, which had maintained something of its language and traditions under the Roman Empire, was occupied by waves of immigrants from Devon, Cornwall and Wales from as early as the fourth century. They imposed their British tongue and customs on their new homeland. If there is one tradition that seems specifically Breton it is the major emphasis accorded to the cult of Ankou – death and the dead. Morgan, who is the Great Queen of the Otherworld, is also particularly well established the length of the Breton sea-board. Aurelius Ambrosius and Uther Pendragon took refuge in Brittany and gathered their expeditionary force there for the defeat of Vortigern and the reconquest of Britain. Mary Stewart, plausibly, has Merlin take the infant Arthur to Brittany as his first refuge.

Metric measures have been given in this chapter to tie in with the European maps.

North Brittany

Mont St Michel and Tombelaine
Map 230, fold 13

These two islets are situated at the west of the Bay of Avranches, which until the seventh century contained many towns and villages in the midst of the Forest of Sessiacum. This forest was sacred to Sessia, an underworld goddess, like Persephone, of seeds, grains and fertility. It is also one of the reputed sites of Merlin's tomb.

Merlin himself was, according to the legend recounted by Rabelais, indirectly responsible for the creation of the two isles. Wishing to arrange the conception of a gigantic champion – the future Gargantua – who would come to the aid of King Arthur, he first created his parents. Taking the bones of two whales, he sprinkled them with Lancelot's blood and Guinevere's nail-clippings before pulverizing them with heat and hammer-blows and forming the

Brittany

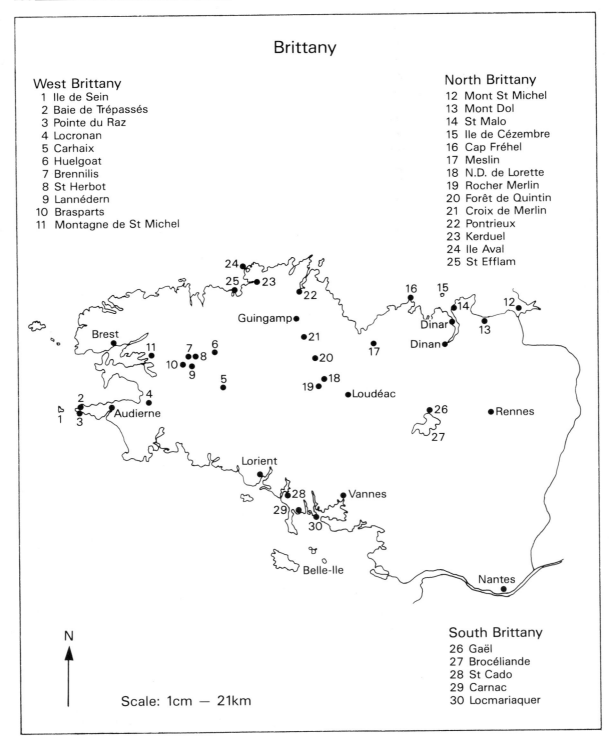

West Brittany
1 Ile de Sein
2 Baie de Trépassés
3 Pointe du Raz
4 Locronan
5 Carhaix
6 Huelgoat
7 Brennilis
8 St Herbot
9 Lannédern
10 Brasparts
11 Montagne de St Michel

North Brittany
12 Mont St Michel
13 Mont Dol
14 St Malo
15 Ile de Cézembre
16 Cap Fréhel
17 Meslin
18 N.D. de Lorette
19 Rocher Merlin
20 Forêt de Quintin
21 Croix de Merlin
22 Pontrieux
23 Kerduel
24 Ile Aval
25 St Efflam

South Brittany
26 Gaël
27 Brocéliande
28 St Cado
29 Carnac
30 Locmariaquer

N

Scale: 1cm — 21km

future parents, Gargamelle and Grant-Gousier. Counselled by Merlin each carried a great rock from the east to demonstrate their strength to Arthur. After a quarrel with the Bretons, Grant-Gousier put his stone down near the coast and it became **Mont St Michel**. Gargamelle placed hers somewhat further where it is now known as **Tombelaine**. They both died of a fever and Merlin took the orphaned Gargantua off to Arthur's court.

Another legend relates that both islands, as well as **Mont Dol**, were placed by Gargantua himself. The twelfth-century Roman de Brut tells how a Spanish giant called Dinabuc abducted and raped Helen, the daughter of the king of Brittany. She was avenged by King Arthur, but **Tombelaine** still commemorates the place of her martyrdom. **Tombelaine**, no doubt the original name of **Mont St Michel** itself, is the tomb or mount of Belen, the shining god of the Celts, who, as so often, is displaced by St Michael whose gilded form commands La Merveille and its great basilica.

The Christian cult dates from the eighth century when St Aubert brought back a piece of the archangel Michael's cloak from Monte St Angelo on the Gargano Peninsula. The preface *garg* usually denotes the jaws of hell where St Michael consigns the dragon to the underworld (cf. **Mont St Michel de Brasparts**, **St Michael's Mount** in Cornwall, the Tor at **Glastonbury**, Skellig Michael on the Dingle Peninsula and **Carnac**). For a long time the forces of Christianity and Paganism coexisted uneasily on the holy isle and its surroundings.

Tombelaine, like the **Isle de Sein**, was the home of a college of druidessses, who, like their sisters on the **Isle de Sein**, calmed storms with the help of a youth who had come to them for his sexual initiation and who shot arrows into the waves at their behest. The druidic cult in these parts did not die out until the great flood of AD709.

To the north of **Tombelaine**, a short distance inland from the sea, is the village of St Michel-des-Loups (St Michael of the Wolves) with its nearby cross of St Blaise (bleiz = wolf), preserving into the Christian era the necessary proximity of the celestial and infernal deities which Merlin incarnated in his mythical life.

Mont Dol
Map 230, fold 12 – 5 km N. of **Dol**

Mont Dol is indirectly connected to the Merlin tradition as the chief shrine of Taranis or Sucellus, the Gallic equivalent of the Dagda, lord of great knowledge and patron of druids. He resembles Merlin in his form of uncouth wild man and, like Merlin, is a harpist and shape-changer whose cauldron is the earliest prototype of the Holy Grail. In the Christian era he becomes the oafish giant Gargantua and, eventually, the Devil. As Gargantua (cf. **Mont St Michel**) he experiences a pain in his foot while walking in the area and picks three pebbles out of his sandals which he tosses away to form **Mont Dol**, **Mont St Michel** and **Tombelaine**. As the Devil, he had either a great battle here with the Archangel Michael or a competition to see who could leap the furthest. In any case he has left his imprint on various rocks to be found on the mount in the form of a seat, a footprint and claw-marks. In yet another conflict with the archangel he agrees to exchange the abbey of **Mont St Michel**, which, curiously enough he has built himself, for a crystal palace constructed by St Michael on **Mont Dol**. As usual, the Devil gets the worst of the bargain and the glass castle, reminiscent of Arianrhod's and Vivian's, turned out to be of ice and melted, leaving the pond on the plateau which can be seen to this day and has never been known to dry up.

Champp-Dolent
Map 230, fold 12, marked *Menhir de Champ-Dolent*

In the struggles between Christianity and the old religion, Taranis/Satan also had problems with St Samson (cf. **Lochmaben**), the strong man of Breton Christianity. Enraged by the saint's efforts to build his cathedral at **Dol** he hurled a great stone at it, which knocked

Champ Dolent, the stone hurled by the Devil at St Samson.

off one of its towers and landed at Champ-Dolent where it stands now, 9 m (29ft.) high, one of the finest menhirs in Brittany.

When we went there it had lost the cross which for centuries surmounted it – the revenge of Taranis? The menhir is sinking into the earth by 1 in. per century and its final disappearance will coincide with the end of the world.

Another legend concerning the stone was that it dropped from heaven to put an end to a furious battle between two brothers. Are these the gods of light and darkness who ever turn the cosmic wheel that is the symbol of Taranis, or are they the *frères-ennemis* of Celtic paganism and Christianity?

Between Taranis and the final establishment of Christianity two other gods were worshipped on **Mont Dol**. One was the bull-god Mithras, a model of whose altar can be seen in the Mairie (town hall) at **Dol**. The other god of **Mont Dol** is the Teutonic god of wisdom, Wotan, in whose honour the site was renamed Godebourg and who has much in common with his enemy-brother Merlin. His spring, which once healed battle wounds, is now imprisoned in a concrete block. One final Merlinesque element is to be found in the ancient trees whose contorted forms lead the seeker close to the heart of a still living nature cult, especially if they be embraced and listened to.

In the village church at the foot of the hill is a fresco showing demons turning a human wheel and feeding their victims into the maw of death, represented as a great wolf. More cheerfully, at the outskirts of the village at *Au Pied du Mont*, you can refresh yourself with excellent *crêpes salées*, home-made cider and, if you are lucky, other liquid *spécialités de la maison* to accompany your coffee. Their home-made pork in cider is a feast well worthy of Merlin.

St Malo
Map 230, fold 11

Xavier de Langlais in *Le Roman du Roi Arthur*, a reconstruction of the Merlin/Arthur legends from ancient and medieval texts, has Merlin disembark at **St Malo** with his friends King Ban and King Bohor *en route* to **Brocéliande** and the tender bonds of Vivian.

Dinard
Map 230, fold 11

Dinard is 'the hill of the bear' or 'of Arthur'. Morgan, his sister, goddess of waters, has left her imprint on many of the place-names in the vicinity such as Le Château de la Goule aux Fées, a cave to the west of St Enogat, and, specifically, in one of the inlets under the Promenade du Clair de Lune.

Ile de Cézembre
Map 230, fold 11

20 minutes by ferry due N. from Dinard

In his book *Le Testament de Merlin* Théophile Briant makes the **Ile de Cézembre** Merlin's place of initiation. There dwells the king of the serpents amid the wisest and most terrifying creatures on earth; there, from a great cliff, Merlin underwent his heavenly assumption; there, perhaps, he still lies at the entrance to a great cave. Barinthus/Brendan, the great navigator, knew the island well.

Cap Fréhel
Map 230, fold 10

Meslin
Map 230, fold 23

Le Rocher Merlin and Notre Dame de Lorette
Map 230, fold 22.
Map: Carte Institut Géographique National, Série Bleue – Pontivy – 0818 est. 210–1073 (helpful for **Le Rocher Merlin**), 500 m from Lohan on the GR371 off D69

Travelling S.W. on the D35 from Uzel to Mur de Bretagne take the first turning to the right after Le Quillio which is signposted **N.D. de Lorette**, and, where the road bends sharply right up-hill, carry straight on for approx. another 100 m until you come to a group of farm buildings and the road becomes a track. Across the field on your right you will see a large rocky outcrop.

Briant (see **Ile de Cézembre**) makes Merlin leave his pupil here near the strange rocks of La Fauconnière, which means the female falconer, to undertake the first part of the great initiation.

Bellamy mentions a number of places in Brittany with names that may point to a connection with Merlin: the village of Merlin in Plumergat (Morbihan), the hamlet of Meslin in Pleugriffet (Morbihan) and another of the same name between Lamballe and Moncontour (Côte du Nord). This last seemed the most promising, being between **Mont St Michel** and **Le Rocher Merlin**, but the parish priest, who had lived for 70 years in the area, knew nothing of any Merlin tradition, though Bellamy, drawing on a number of nineteenth-century writers, seems to favour such a derivation. It is noteworthy that 6 km to the south-west is the parish of St Blaise.

The **Rocher Merlin**, now thoroughly overgrown and difficult to reach, contains, hidden by the undergrowth, a small cave some 2 m deep, known as *La Maison de Merlin*. This was a revolving home, like Arianrhod's castle, which enabled Merlin in his exiguous retreat to face always away from the wind. If it should happen to blow from all four quarters at once, he simply retracted his grotto underground. From here he taught the local inhabitants agriculture and the craft of alloying metals. He evidently assumed his giant form since he placed his feet on two rocks divided by a valley, to drink from the pond of Le Roz.

A nineteenth-century photograph shows a great natural vault formed by a dragon-shaped stone. From the base of the rock to the summit measures 9 m and the arch, covering the 7 m wide entrance, has a thickness of 3.3 m.

We parked our car by the end of the road where a thorny footpath led uphill to the right. Various dogs appeared and then two delightful children, Arnoud, aged about six and his little sister. They, and the dogs, led us on an extremely hazardous and prickly rock-climbing adventure to the top of the outcrop. Coming down was even trickier. This is not an ascent to be undertaken lightly, especially in wet weather.

Many impressive rock formations form a ridgeway between **Le Rocher Merlin** and the summit of **Notre Dame de Lorette**, known as the church of the Romans, comprising 33 stones. It has been much excavated and was believed, as late as the nineteenth century, to conceal a buried treasure. Do not fail to visit the sacred well, which heals cripples, at the foot of the drive leading up to the church. As at the **Fontaine de Barenton**, the pagan custom of silvering the waters with pins or coins has been preserved. This whole area exudes a strange otherworldly atmosphere that seems as ancient as the spring and rocks themselves. The magician Eon de l'Etoile (see **Barenton**) was born in nearby Loudéac.

The Forest of Quintin/Forêt de Lorge
Map 230, fold 22/23

The nineteenth-century historian of northern Brittany, M. Habasque, fell asleep one day in the glades of the **Forêt de Lorge** near the swineherd's spring in what was in the Middle Ages still part of **Brocéliande**. He dreamt of meeting Merlin in the depth of a crystalline cave. By his side was Vivian and the three of them conversed for a long time about King Arthur's knights and the affairs of the day. At the end of the dream Merlin forbade M. Habasque to divulge secrets he had learnt, but told him to publish that, more fortunate than Sir Gawain, he had seen both Merlin and Vivian. This dream encounter cannot be pinned down in geographical terms today, but the **Forêt de Lorge** or de l'Hermitage is still wonderful despite the ravages of the great storm of 1987 and its heart is the small bourg to the north of the present village, with a large church, a square and roads leading to a mysterious castle built with stones from Quintin. Between Quintin and the Château de Lorge the village of St. Brandan evokes the memory of the great Celtic voyager to the blessed isles and Merlin's companion on the voyage to *Avalon*. According to some authorities Merlin's tomb is somewhere in the forest.

Croix de Merlin
Map 230, fold 22

Turn off D7 at Boquého on to D24 and where you see the sign on your right to Manoir de Kermedret, opposite a house called Bellevue, you will see the cross.

In an old French Chronicle by Jean Cabaret d'Orville it is stated that in the life of Louis III, Duke of Bourbon, there was a battle at la Croix Malchast (Malchalt) where Merlin performed his wonders. Merlin's wonders included prophecies about the battle which took place there in 1394, when the constable of Clisson was advancing towards Quintin, and about the battle between the Duc de Mercoeur and the prince de Dombes in 1591.

It is possible that the Merlin monument, known today as the Croix de St Yves, was originally on the summit of Marc'hallac'h, a short distance to the west, and has now been incorporated into the present Christian cross restored in 1836.

The cross has suffered much from the ravages of time and weather. At the four corners of the base are carvings of four grotesque faces, more likely the winds than the evangelists.

Pontrieux
Map 230, fold 7

Ariosto in his *Orlando Furioso* places the tomb of Merlin in a wood near **Pontrieux**:

> ... verso le selve, prossime al Pontiero
> Dove la vocal tomba di Merlino.

The castle of La Roche-Jagu on the wooded banks of the Trieux sounds a promising candidate for the site, but one should point out that some scholars consider Ariosto's Pontiero to be not **Pontrieux** but Poitiers, Eleanor of Aquitaine's capital and that of the province (Poitou) which claims to be Merlin's birthplace as well as the home of his daughter Mélusine.

Kerduel
Map 230, fold 6

c. 5 km N.W. of Lannion towards Pleumeur-Bodou and the **Ile Aval**, take the drive through the large gates on the right. Grounds only open to the public June, July and August.

Situated between an aerodrome and a space station lies Brittany's answer to the mystery of the location of Carduel (see **Caerwent**) where Merlin founded the Round Table.

We came to the Trégor Peninsula in search of the **Ile Aval**, but were intrigued to see on the map a place called **Kerduel** not far away. The day before, we had bought Michel Rio's *Merlin*, hot from the press, in which he places the whole drama of the passing of Arthur in Trégor. Could this be the palace on the lake of Diana, home of Vivian? We could not resist the challenge of investigation.

Since it was probably private property we did not expect to get very far and stopped the car half-way down the drive for a photo-opportunity. There, on our right, through the trees, stood a fine castle and chapel, perfectly mirrored in a lake. The vision compelled us to continue. As we arrived in the courtyard someone was getting out of a car. This turned out to be the present Lady of the Lake, the Comtesse de Champagny de Kerduel, whose family have lived here since the thirteenth century. She very graciously showed us round her château, parts of which date back to the Roman period, and confirmed the tradition from which Rio derived his story. Exploring the grounds we found next to a second, funerary chapel, a magnificent old covered well which, until the hurricane of 1987, had been sheltered by the oldest and grandest oak-tree on the estate. Rio makes the Welsh Carduel the home of the Round Table and the Breton Kerduel the home of Vivian.

Between **Kerduel** and the **Ile Aval** are three features of some interest. The first, to the west of the D21 at Pleumeur-Bodou is the sacred wood which Rio calls the Bois en Val, Merlin's refuge, though little magic remains today. According to the early thirteenth-century romance *Lancelot of the Lake*: 'The forest, where the lake was, was the smallest forest in Gaul and Brittany, for it was no more than ten English leagues long and six or seven wide, and it was called the Wood in the Valley'. The second is the remarkable 8 m high Christianized menhir of St Duzec, situated outside Penvern. The third was a stone 2.1 m × 0.7 m × 2.2 m; covered in little carved crosses which no one could ever count exactly, known as the tomb of Arthur or of King Grallon or of the King of the Trigoz, a group of rocks north-west of the **Isle Aval**. Bellamy saw this tombstone in the late nineteenth century on the side of the road and suspected that it would soon be used as raw material for the new highway.

Ile Aval
Michelin map 230, fold 6. Better still, Collection Rivages 19, La Côte de Granit Rose, obtainable from

This is Brittany's own Isle of Avalon, which contains a standing stone – all that remains of its tomb of Arthur. Although the tradition is not ancient, other sites in the area (see **Kerduel** and **St Efflam**) lend support to this legend.

Michel Rio in his novel *Merlin* describes how the magician constructed a great mausoleum for the king whose body he had borne

local bookshop at Trébeurden

1 km north of Trébeurden on N786D, take the first turning on left at Penvern to Ile Grande; turn right at T-junction, leave your car in the first beach car park on your right.

to this island where Morgan ruled. There are many isles off the Breton coast and many commemorations of Morgan in image and toponymy, but islands like **Aval**, **St Michael's Mount**, **Mont St Michel** and Lindisfarne, which can be reached on foot at certain times, are particularly appropriate symbols of that Celtic Otherworld, which is both remote and near at hand. However tenuous the links with the historical Arthur may be, it is significant that this is the only true island in the whole Arthurian canon to bear the time-honoured name of Aval – Apple-Isle.

It was half an hour before low tide and, as there was still a certain amount of water between the islands, we walked across barefoot, an agreeable experience even in March. The passage across was marked by two lines of weed-covered stones, as though there had once been a highway to the resting-place of the great king. As we crossed we had the curious impression of being under sea level as we watched the huge waves breaking over the line of rocks to the west of us. Once across, not realizing that the island was private, we climbed over a fence and began to explore it. The most important feature is, of course, the megalith at the north end of a square grassy field enclosed with dry-stone walls. At one corner of the wall stands a cross, a sign of the period of transition from paganism to Christianity over which Arthur reigned. This, quite obviously, to judge by the numbers of fallen menhirs – there is also a double alignment in the vicinity – was once an important site.

Just next to the field is a covered well whose water lies deep – the stone we dropped into it took five seconds to reach bottom.

Eventually the present owner of the island discovered us and asked us to leave. Until recently it was owned by cousins of the Champagny family of **Kerduel**.

Ile Aval, Brittany's Isle of Avalon, one of King Arthur's final resting-places.

If you have time before or after the crossing you might enjoy a stop at La Balise, where we were given a warm welcome, two dozen oysters and a good Muscadet at the bar, as the whole restaurant was full of politicians celebrating the local elections.

To the west of the causeway from Penvern, just as you reach the Ile Grande, is the remarkable megalithic *allée couverte* called le Lias. It faces the Isle of Avalon and is reputed to be the entrance hall to the fairy place where Arthur still resides.

St Efflam
Map 230, fold 6

At the western extremity of the Lieu de Grève on the D786 turn right on the small unmarked road along the shore at the end of the bay (do not go up the hill in the direction of Plestin-les-Grèves). You will see the chapel on the hill to your left with a path leading up to it. Park there and climb the steps along which, to the right, is the domed well-house of **St Efflam**. The renovated chapel stands just above.

History relates that the Irish hermit, Efflam, landed at the Grand Rocher in the Lieu de Grève with seven companions in AD470 and made his home by the spring until his death in AD512. The church of Plestin-les-Grèves contains his tomb. Myth makes Efflam the brother-in-law or cousin of King Arthur. On his arrival in Armorica, Efflam found Arthur battling against a huge dragon and parched with thirst. Efflam not only produced water from the hillside with his staff but banished the dragon, which leapt into the waves either from the Grand Rocher or the Roche Rouge, visible at low tide 500 m north-east in the bay. Efflam's wife, Enora, whom he had abandoned on their wedding night after reading her *The Life of St Alexis,*, came and joined him, setting up her own hermitage near by. In the church of Plestin-les-Grèves an interesting image at the side of the tomb of St Efflam shows a dragon lying on its back with a crowned figure holdings its tail and piercing its belly, while, at the head, stands a naked wild man holding a skull and a knobkerry.

South Brittany

A dark forest, as Dante noted, is a good place to get lost and to find oneself again. The Forest of **Brocéliande** is such a forest and does not yield its secrets easily. It covers a large area, some 16 km by 8 km, much of it private, criss-crossed with roads and tracks, scantily signposted. The only town of any importance is Paimpont, which, having an hotel and tourist office, is one obvious base for exploration.

Brocéliande
Map 230, fold 38/39

Brocéliande has been for eight centuries the most important centre of the Merlin tradition in France. During the period of Arthur and Merlin (early sixth century) emigration from Britain to Brittany was at its height, partly owing to the Saxon inroads into the mother island. It is not improbable that an important religious leader from Britain – a Merlin – would have re-established a religious school for the colonists on an old sacred site and carried out periodic visitations. According to legend, Merlin saw Vivian, his enchantress, at **Barenton** four times in sixteen years and now abides with her for ever in **Brocéliande**.

Prof. Anatole Le Braz describes a meeting of Vivian with an old wood-gatherer near the Pas-du-Houx in 1910. She blessed Vivian as the saintly 'Good Lady of the Forest' who saved her husband from the guns of gamekeepers by hiding him in a thick mist and murmuring in his ear: 'Escape, my son, the spirit of Vivian will watch over you until you have crawled out of the forest.'

Barenton was always there and Breton soldiers at the battle of Hastings boasted of its virtues. Certainly, given the constant comings and goings from earliest times between Great Britain and Little Britain, the legends of Arthur, Merlin, Morgan and Vivian were part of the Breton heritage. Although it is not always clear which legends originated on which side of the channel, Arthur and Merlin found a place in **Brocéliande** in the late eleventh century, when Raoul de Gaël, the lord of the region, returned from Britain where William the Conqueror had made him, for a time, king of East Anglia. It is noteworthy that Breckland, in the heart of East Anglia, is a doublet of **Brocéliande** (Bréchéliande – swampy land).

Versed in the lore of the Celtic bards in Britain and eager to enhance the prestige of his own family and domaine, he implanted the Arthurian legends in **Brocéliande**, thereby enriching un-wittingly the culture of Western Europe.

Tréhorenteuc

4 km E. of Néant-sur-Yvel on the D154.

Tréhorenteuc, the gateway to the **Val-sans-Retour**, is a good place to prepare yourself for the exploration of **Brocéliande**. This is thanks in part to its geographical situation, but mainly to the work of its remarkable parish priest, the Abbé Gillard. Between 1942 and 1962 he devoted himself to the restoration of the ancient church and to the production of twenty pamphlets, available in the village, mainly dedicated to the mysteries of **Brocéliande**. The original church was built in the seventh century to counteract the influence of the druids

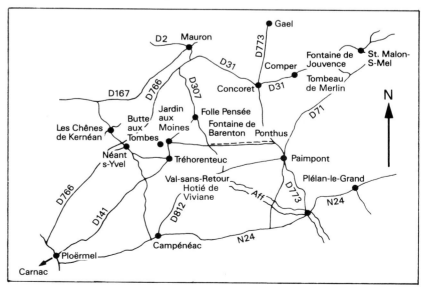

The Brocéliande area with its wealth of sites.

who still flourished by the **Jardin-aux-Moines**.

The church is unique in the symbolism of its stained glass, paintings and stations of the Cross – all the legends of **Brocéliande** are depicted here. Where else will you find the Grail banquet at the Round Table juxtaposed with Christ's Last Supper, or see a seductive Morgan, all in red, looking on as Jesus falls beneath the weight of the Cross? Few can ever have done more than the Abbé Gillard to harmonize the legend of Arthur, Merlin, the Round Table and the Grail with traditional Christian teaching.

If the church is shut, the key can be obtained from the sacristan, whose house is the second on the right in the courtyard behind the church, just off the main street. To obtain postcards and guidebooks, enquire at the second café on the left at the crossroads.

Le Val-Sans-Retour (Valley of No Return/ Perilous Valley/ Valley of False Lovers)

The **Val-sans-Retour** is located just outside **Tréhorenteuc**. This hidden, vulva-cleft of a valley is literally a place of enchantment.

The legend tells us that when Morgan le Fay, who had learnt her magic from Merlin, was betrayed by her lover, Guyomard, Guinevere's cousin, she avenged herself by imprisoning her rival in a block of ice up to her waist and in a brazier from her belt to her head. She also cast a spell on the **Val-sans-Retour** with a deceptive wall of mist, apparently solid on the inside. This wall crept up behind any intruder, and if he was an unfaithful lover he would be trapped for ever. She turned the valley into an earthly paradise, offering her victims all manner of joys, pleasures and distractions. They began to see their enchanted world as the only reality and the world outside the valley as terrifyingly dangerous, beset by murderous creatures, so that in time they lost all desire to escape. They lived happily in this imaginary world where everything was possible if only one wished for it. But eventually, in the course of time, the captives lost their taste for this garden of worldly delights, and in the eighteenth year of the enchantment Lancelot, faithful to Guinevere, crossed the threshold of the **Val**, fought off the illusory dragons and giants, walked through the non-existing waters and fires, which seemed to surround the valley, and set the lovers free. The spell was broken when the last of them rejoined society. The legend, however, warns us still to visit the **Val-sans-Retour** only with clean hands and a pure heart.

We had an unusual experience here. From the car park outside **Tréhorenteuc** we followed the signs to **Le Val-sans-Retour**, a wide path leading gently upward with woodland to the right. After we had walked for approximately one mile, we were beginning to wonder whether we had missed a turn. Occasionally we saw a little white or red and yellow ribbon tied to a bush, the only sign that we might just still be on the right track. Eventually, we thought that we had gone quite far enough as we were sure that the valley was down there somewhere. So when we saw a small blue and red paint-mark on a rock at the beginning of a path to the right, we took it, although we still had no idea where it might be leading us. Then we heard running water. From now on it was easy, we simply followed the sound of water until we actually came upon the small stream. By this time we were in thick woodland with high banks on both sides of the stream. It was getting late and dark and we walked faster, running whenever the path straightened a little, hoping to leave the **Valley of no Return** before nightfall. Our goal was the mysterious lake at the end of the valley.

Finally, after what seemed like another hour's walk, there was the lake, the *Mirror of the Fairies*, overhung by trees, perfectly still and about a quarter of its surface covered with small white flowers. The timeless atmosphere of this enchanted place enveloped us and we sat down to rest before our long walk back. Three hikers suddenly appeared out of the woods and we asked them if they knew the quickest way back to the car-park of **Tréhorenteuc**: 'Just down the path, about three minutes.' We had come full circle, a good two hours' walk. But the **Val-sans-Retour** is not just a valley and a lake but a state of mind – an archetypal experience. It, above all Merlin sites, demands that the seeker be lost, frustrated, unsure of the way, in and out, if this sacred place is to reveal its magic.

The Rock of the False Lovers (Le Rocher des Faux Amants)

Two years later, with the benefit of experience, we approached the **Val-sans-Retour** the easy way and went off in search of **The Rock of the False Lovers**, situated on the crest to the east, overlooking the lake and which we had missed on our first visit. At the **Tréhorenteuc** end of the lake, near Lancelot's plank-bridge, take the steep path up the hill, following the marks of red and white stripes and yellow circles. Continue until you come across this unmistakable twin-rock formation. The **False Lovers** are none other than Guyomard and his lovely sweetheart, caught in *flagrante delicto* by Morgan, who condemned them with a familiar druidic spell, to live

Rock of False Lovers, the petrified victims of the jealous Morgan's revenge.

in perpetual petrifaction, side by side, unable to communicate. From here there is a unique view of the Fairies' Mirror, the point where the two worlds reflect each other.

Jardin aux Moines
(The Garden of the Monks)

300 m S.W. of the intersection of D141 and the Néant-sur-Yvel/le Pertuis Néanti road. If you come from **Tréhorenteuc** or from Néant-sur-Yvel look for the 'Camping' sign just before you reach the crossroads and park your car there.

The **Jardin aux Moines**, situated in a birch thicket, was excavated in 1983 and 1984 by M. Briard. The site has always been well known as a sacred pagan centre and burial ground. It is a remarkable structure, 25 m long by 5–6 m wide, surrounded by stones, some of which, as at **Stonehenge**, have been brought from afar. At the far end a transversal line of stones creates what seems to be a smaller, second chamber. The monument dates back to at least 3000BC but has become involved in the story of Merlin. One local tradition regards this site as commemorating the triumph of Merlin over Vortigern. This is suggested by the alternating red and white stones representing the warring dragons. The Christian explanation is that St Méen, on a visitation and finding a group of gluttonous monks at table here, turned them into these stones.

There are some twenty further monuments in the maze-like Butte aux Tombes (Hill of the Tombs) which comprises the whole surrounding area, but which have not yet been excavated.

The Fountain of Barenton

At the end of the village, park your car and follow the path into the woods. At the next crossing of paths turn right. This is the ligne de **Barenton**. From now on you will get the sense of climbing and in a wet season the waters from the spring come to meet you all the way, foaming with the natural detritus of vegetable matter. Cross a wide forest track and continue on the other side where you note a group of hollies at the beginning of the path, guarding the lower approaches to the spring. Follow the stream

To reach the **Fountain of Barenton** you should first go to Folle Pensée. Whatever its name means, *mad thought* or *madman cured*, Folle Pensée is a beautiful little village, some of whose houses are said to have been built with stone from the chapel of **Barenton** – le Moinet – which was destroyed in 1148 after the arrest of Eon de l'Etoile. Bellamy describes three stones, near the village, called *Les roches du Champ Morgan*. Today they have disappeared but their memory testifies to the presence of Morgan le Fay.

A hill, a tree, a spring, a stone – such is the stuff of the Celtic mysteries. Here, at the sacred heart of **Brocéliande**, all play their part. **Barenton**, like Merlin himself, has many spellings, all of which lead us back to the age of the druids. As Belenton, it is the mount of Belen, warrior god of the golden hair, who makes the corn and wine grow and yield fruit in due season, and shows his displeasure in the thunderstorm. In that case it might also be Bar-en-Tun, the hill of the storm, at 255 m the highest peak in the forest, a druidic observatory that would be dear to Merlin's heart, whence storms and stars could be observed, and the fate of kings predicted. Another etymology is Baren-Ton, the hill of the tribunal – of priests and druids. To jump ahead for a moment to the Christian era, St Barenton was a disciple of St Brendan the Navigator, probably the same ferryman of souls who, as Barinthus, transported the body of Arthur, accompanied by Merlin and Taliesin, to Avalon. The Recteur of **Tréhorenteuc** is certain that near the spring of **Barenton** there stood a druidic school where they taught a course lasting twenty years, comprising – apart or stream-bed until you see on your left a red arrow, a red E and then a blue mark on a stone and once again note the hollies. Here you turn left and in a short while you will be at the fountain.

from reading and writing ogham – religion, law, history, poetry, medicine, astrology and music. That it was served by druidesses seems clear from the legends surrounding it, for it has always been associated with fairies and beautiful maidens, as well as healing and rain-making powers. Already, at the battle of Hastings, the Conqueror's Breton contingent boasted of the fountain's magic. In the middle of the twelfth century Robert Wace, the first writer (along with Marie de France) to introduce Celtic material into French literature, made the arduous pilgrimage to **Barenton** and described it in his poem *Le Roman de Rou*.

No less than fourteen Arthurian romances attest to the mysteries of **Barenton**. Merlin, in the guise of a handsome young student, found his Vivian here and wooed her with his wonders, which included the conjuring up of knights and ladies to dance for her. Here the Black Knight, guardian of the spring – and no doubt of the priestesses – fought to the death with any stranger who dared to encroach on the sacred precincts. Here, in 1145, a heretical priest-wizard, Eon de l'Etoile, established a new religious order, in some ways not far removed from the merry paganism of old. This Gnostic mixture of Robin Hood and Friar Tuck, a true successor to Merlin, encountered us on our way from Concoret to Folle Pensée, in the form of one of his totem-birds, the sparrowhawk. He flew along beside us, about six inches above the road, keeping exact pace with the car for more than a kilometre. One of Eon's sparrowhawks seized a man in its talons and killed him by dropping him from a great height on to a rock.

As late as 1835 the parish priest of Concoret led his flock to **Barenton** during a severe drought to bless the fountain and shake Merlin's rain-stone (already in 1577 called by Roch le Baillif *le perron de Merlin*). Their prayers were answered and heavy showers ensued. Until quite recently the girls of the surrounding countryside came to awaken the fairy by dropping pins into the water to enlist her aid in finding a husband. The young men would gaze into the still surface of the fountain by moonlight to espy, if they might, the face of the true love who awaited them in their future. To come upon **Barenton** is still a delight and a surprise, though none of the great old oaks which once surrounded it has survived the exigencies of commercial forestry. Nevertheless, the clump of seven trees – oak, pine and the shamanistic silver birch – which overlook the fountain, will, if spared, one day be impressive. Even today one can sit and meditate on two cunningly placed stones which over the years have become one with the tangled roots of twin oaks. The fountain itself is clear and free from undergrowth and weeds. The stones forming the basin are in good condition, as is Merlin's stone, plain to see between the fountain and the clump of trees. The first time we visited it there was a young student, a romantic refugee from the Sixties, sitting on it in deep stillness with a book in his hands. On that occasion we observed the bubbles in the fountain, but stayed only a short time, boldly pouring some water on *le perron*, braving the rain-gods, after the student, disturbed from his reverie, had sauntered off further into the forest. Within five minutes it was raining quite hard and we had the wet walk we deserved back to the car.

On the next occasion we had leisure to play with the fairy and she with us. When you arrive at **Barenton** the water is generally quite still within its basin. But touch the surface, as we did, with our knobbly path-finding staff, called Merlin many years before this book was thought of, or with the 100-year-old blackthorn stick from County Cork, and at once the dance of the bubbles begins in response to the stimulus. On our third visit we were accompanied by two women from Paris who were mysteriously drawn to settle in **Brocéliande** and seemed to us to re-establish a certain continuity with the fairy druidesses of yore. Yore in **Brocéliande** is not so distant as might be imagined if traditions of the survival of *white ladies* in the forest up to the time of the Revolution are to be believed. Under the guidance of the senior 'druidess' we performed a Merlin apple ritual. She cut an apple into three transversal segments revealing the pentagram at the core of the fruit. The middle segment was divided into five portions; each of us ate one and the fifth was thrown into the fountain. Never did we see it bubble so merrily, nor did so many little frogs, newts and fishes appear.

In the neighbourhood, thanks to the 1987 hurricane, which revealed them, you will find, if you search, a few remnants of dressed stones from the early college or its Christian successor, covered in silver-grey clay. A group of healers from Paris claim that this clay possesses healing and protective qualities. That the magic of the fountain of Barenton still continues is evidenced by another recent experience. One of our guides, on *Lugnasadh*, the first of August, the feast of the marriage of sun and earth, saw the sun and full moon, as well as a third inexplicable light reflected in the fountain.

Camp du Tournoi (Field of the Tournament)
Between **Barenton** and **Ponthus**, 300–400 m east of the fountain, below the escarpment which leads up to the junction of six paths, lies the *Champ de Bataille*, otherwise known as *Camp du Tournoi*. In Bellamy's time the field was surrounded by a bank 1 m high above a ditch 1 m wide. In it a man-made pit, 6 m × 4 m × 2 m, was known as Merlin's tomb. This site is no longer clearly discernible, but it was here, no doubt, that Ponthus, or the Black Knight, challenged all intruders and that Merlin made the dancing floor for his knights and ladies in order to amuse Vivian.

L'Abreuvoir de Merlin (The alternative Barenton)
Our companions, the modern druidesses, led us, although even they

Retrace your steps to where you last turned left towards the fountain of **Barenton**, about 40m, turn left here and walk on this less used track until you can see the hollies in the wood to your right. Continue in the direction of the path from the hollies until you reach l'Abreuvoir.

had some difficulty in finding it, to this wild untended, sister of **Barenton**, known to few, which they think of as the spring where Merlin, especially in his animal form of stag, wolf or boar, went to quench his thirst. Surrounding holly-trees hint that the site is not without significance. This is the spring of the wild man and the animals, perhaps how the real **Barenton** looked in its years of neglect and disrepair. When we cleared away the fallen branches and weeds its natural shape was revealed, remarkably like its civilized twin, just a few hundred yards away. Both are cold and yet they boil.

Ponthus

While visiting **Barenton** do not shirk the challenge of seeking the forest's greatest and most elusive treasure, le Hêtre (beech) **Ponthus**. We felt Merlin's presence more powerfully here than at any other site in **Brocéliande**. Even locals often have difficulty in finding it and rudimentary infantry map-reading skills proved of little avail.

The local guide of the Syndicats d'Initiative de Brocéliande suggests returning to Folle Pensée where you take the road towards Paimpont, which rises steeply, until you arrive at crossroads called *des Maffrais*. Park your car there and continue on foot by a path to the left. Go over the crossroads of Ponthus where six paths meet and continue straight on for 500 m towards Ville-d'Anet, then take a smaller path to the left. After 800 m you will see on your left the tree which marks the site of the castle of Ponthus.

As soon as you see it you will know it. To begin with, it is huge, totally dwarfing its mean entourage of official fir-trees and is suffused with an uncanny, green, luminous glow. The mayor of Néant says that it is suffering from the 'maladie des sapins', a sickness caught from the surrounding conifers, but to us it seemed like a blessed greenness of the god of vegetation himself. It was already ancient and mighty when Bellamy described it in the 1880s, though it is clearly younger than the castle of Ponthus on whose ruins it stands. We saw it on a cold spring day with snow on the ground and more flurries in the air. Suddenly a shaft of sunlight conjured up its inner radiance, like Belen greeting Cernunnos. Treat it as a living, responsible, godlike being, press against it and draw sustenance from its strength and you will know what the word numinous means. Once the forest was full of such green giants.

Who was Ponthus, the scattered remains of whose castle lie all around, covered in moss, almost indistinguishable from the roots of the trees which bestride them? Clearly an important figure, since Paimpont, the present name of both the forest and its only town are, according to some etymologies, named for him – Pen-Ponthi. According to the legend he was a prince of Galicia, shipwrecked on the coast of Morbihan, who after many adventures, married the fair Sidoine, daughter of the Lord of Gaël.

Ponthus provides interesting, if legendary, evidence of the links between **Brittany** and **Galicia**. The descendants of Ponthus and Sidoine held the castle until its destruction in 1372, when Comper also fell. Its last chatelaine, who longed to have a child, tempted the fates by crying out: 'I want one, whether it comes from God or the devil!' She brought forth a son as dark and hairy as Merlin. It is said that a week after his birth the castle – like Vortigern's – collapsed, killing all the inhabitants.

Comper (Vivian's Birthplace and Arthur's Oak)

On D31, 2 km E. of Concoret (Kon-Korred – valley of fairies or druids). The grounds of the Château de Comper are open every day except Tuesday and Friday.

The Château de Comper, the only one of the five ancient castles of **Brocéliande** still standing, was built on Gallo-Roman foundations and destroyed and rebuilt many times.

Under the lake, Merlin, in an attempt to win her heart, created an invisible castle for Vivian, which was to become his enchanted prison. One legend tells us that Vivian appeared at the court of King Arthur in pursuit of a white hart. After a series of adventures in which her favourite hound was kidnapped by one knight and Vivian herself by another, Merlin organized a successful rescue operation and fell in love with her. She was only fifteen and found his advances repugnant. Nevertheless, she promised him her hand in order to elicit the secrets of his magic. They returned to her own land of Brittany where he showed her the lake of Diana. There the goddess had once betrayed her lover Faunus, and sealed him in a tomb. When she told her new love, Felix, what she had done to free herself for him, he beheaded her and cast her body into the lake of **Comper**. When Vivian heard of Diana's underwater palace she wanted one too and persuaded Merlin to grant her this favour. In another version of the story the goddess Diana comes even closer to the world of the Breton romances. She protected King Ban, the father of Lancelot, and also the handsome young Lord of **Brocéliande**, Dyonas. He was given this name by the daughter of Diana, 'the siren or queen of Sicily'. He married the niece of the Duke of Burgundy by whom he had one child, Vivian, born in the château. Diana, her godmother, whom she resembled in many respects, promised her the wisest man in the world as her husband and prophesied that she would become an even greater fairy than herself. Merlin went to see this beautiful

Entrance to the Birthplace of Vivian, Merlin's beloved Lady of the Lake.

maiden in the forest of **Brocéliande** and they fell in love. Diana performed the marriage ceremony and received their vows. Vivian then put a spell on her castle so that no one could enter or leave the hawthorn hedge surrounding the park, to keep Merlin always with her. Nevertheless, she permitted Gawain, who had been sent in search of Merlin by King Arthur, to speak to him and served them an excellent lunch in a grotto, promising Gawain that he might return from time to time.

A famous story about Vivian, who is also the Lady of the Lake, concerns Sir Lancelot. One day his parents, King Ban and Queen Helen, were driven with the baby son from the castle of Benoïc (cf. **North Berwick**). Watching his stronghold go up in flames, Ban suffered a heart attack and Helen rushed to his assistance, leaving the baby Lancelot on the deserted roadside. The Lady of the Lake, who loved the boy, picked him up and dived with him to her underwater palace near where the river still flows into the southern end of the mere of **Comper**. There she raised him to be the best knight in the world.

In the castle grounds take the path to the left, between the lake and the building. As you pass the overflow from the lake, turn left, and immediately in front of you is one of the secret treasures of **Brocéliande**, an ancient, majestic oak, growing out of a great wall of living rock. The tree is known for its vibrant healing qualities and is reputed to be the tomb of Arthur. Through the grove lies another lake, hidden and even more mysterious than its larger sister.

To gain another impression of the lake and the castle drive south on a small road along the walls of the estate and take the next turn to the left until you see Vivian's lake on your left. Park at the end of the field and walk down to the lake (the footpath which we took in 1986 was totally covered by brambles and blocked with barbed wire when we returned in 1988). From here you can see the castle in the distance, and where the river snakes into the lake, below the pine woods, we saw thirty goldfinches alighting on the sedge, while a viper rustled through the dry grass.

Tombeau de Merlin and la Fontaine de Jouvence (Merlin's Tomb and the Fountain of Youth)

If you are coming from **Comper** continue on the D31 towards St Malon for approximately 4 km, turn

Immediately on your left, beneath an old holly-tree stands all that remains of the once splendid dolmen that was Merlin's Tomb, where he lies under the spell of Vivian, surrounded by nine magic circles. At one time the tomb of Vivian was also reputed to be no more than a rifle shot away. The decline of Merlin's Tomb set in during the Revolution at the hands of treasure-seekers who dug beneath the stones. But a photograph of 1889 shows six megaliths up to 1.50 m in height and 1.60 m in width on one side of the *allée couverte* and four stones on the other with some roof slabs still in situ. By 1892 all had been overturned and two years later there was nothing left but the relatively meagre remains visible today.

Whether oral tradition already associated the site with Merlin right towards la Ville Guichais and look for a sign to *Le Tombeau* on your left.

If you are coming from Paimpont on the D71 direction St Malon, after about 8 km, before reaching La Ville Moisan, follow signpost to La Sangle. You will notice on your right a handsome house on a large lake. Take the next turning on the right and park off the road. Follow the track (yellow arrow) through the trees to a field.

before the early nineteenth century or not, it, and the nearby Fountain of Youth, formed a highly important druidic shrine on the emplacement of a neolithic temenos. It is possible that the village of St Malon-sur-Mel in the vicinity may have evoked echoes of Merlin, of whose name there are so many variant spellings.

Now follow the secret druid way from death to eternal youth across the field, opposite the tomb. Climb over an earth parapet and turn left along the fence, where you should see a yellow arrow, and continue round a bend to the right. After a short distance and just before the

Merlin's Tomb. All that remains of the great stone avenue, destroyed by treasure hunters.

sign 'Attention Vipères' on a tree, turn right and you will find the Fountain of Youth.

The fountain of the goddess Juventa has, like Merlin's tomb, sadly fallen from its former glory. Once it was a *Jaouanc*, a natural baptismal font of the pagan, Celtic world where, at midsummer, during an all-night ritual, fires were lit and children led to the spring, after which their sex was noted in a register and they became members of the community. The Christian monks later built a chapel in the vicinity to St Jouan (Jean), our John the Baptist, whose feast, 24th June, is still celebrated with fire and water in many parts of Europe. The fountain is reputed never to dry up and Bellamy noted in the last century that even the oldest inhabitants of the hamlet, now called Les Landelles – within whose parish the fountain stands – look no more than 35 years of age.

An earlier writer describes its setting on a hillside surrounded by colossal stones and an oak grove. A small spiral staircase carved in the rock once led to the summit. But all that is visible now, through the fence protecting a very private estate, is a mass of moss-covered tumbled stones on top of the hillock. The fountain itself, overhung and stagnant when we visited it in 1986, is now clean, clear and more inviting to the would-be imbiber of eternal youth. A few yards further down the path, the sign warning travellers to beware of the vipers is the only remaining souvenir of the serpent priests and priestesses of antiquity. But the nearest hamlet to the east, la Ville Guyomard, still bears witness to the presence in these parts of Morgan's lover (cf. **Val-sans-Retour**).

Pont du Secret

Near the crossing of N24 and the road to Forges de Paimpont, about 2½ km W. of Plélan-le-Grand, look for the Auberge du Pont du Secret and park there.

At first glance the modernized and reinforced bridge on the N24 is hardly the place for a romantic tryst, but strengthen the imagination with a glass of the Inn's excellent old Calvados and you will see Lancelot and Guinevere in two trees which have grown together over the centuries to form an arch over the path leading down to the river Aff. This is a clear trout-stream whose water-meadows in spring are a mass of primroses, celandines, anemones and wild crocuses. We were blessed by the sudden flash of a kingfisher that summoned up for us the sovereign of the Grail.

It was here that Lancelot and Guinevere met secretly to exchange their vows of love. A Christian legend has it that Christ appeared to them in the form of a white hart with a golden collar to bring them to an awareness of their sin. But we should bear in mind that the stag in **Brocéliande** is, above all, the animal of the non-moralistic Merlin, whose prophetic vision would, however, have foreseen the damage to the Round Table that these amours would wreak.

Insignificant as this site may be, the secret meetings of Lancelot and Guinevere were not, and, as a consequence, much turbulent water was to flow under the bridge.

Hotié de Viviane (Vivian's Hostel and Tomb of the Druids)

Off D40 at Le Chatenay, direction Beauvais, take the second turning on the left. When you have passed the last group of houses (La Touche Guérin) on your right, you will find one more with double wooden gates. Just there is a fork in the road and you take the right-hand track; keep to the right until you reach the end of the track and come to a field with a rocky crest above it up a short, steep path, between two oak-trees. The first time we came here we thought that this naturally serrated crest *was* the **Hotié**. It is not. Pursue the path a bit further to the left down the other side of the peak until you come upon the arrangement of stones that is the **Hotié de Viviane**.

There are many tombs of Merlin in the West. In the Forest of **Brocéliande** two départements lay claim to it. The **Hotié de Viviane** is Morbihan's answer to the better known **Tombeau de Merlin** in Ille-et-Vilaine north of Paimpont. It is a most remarkable megalithic monument which was excavated in 1982/3. The central tomb measures 2.9 m × 1.6 m and is enclosed by stone slabs of 1.4 m–1.6 m high. The unique feature of this site is the surround of carefully arranged smaller stones, forming an ellipse 12 m × 10.5 m, pointing outward at an angle of 45 degrees. With a little imagination one may see here the nine circles traced by Vivian's magic round the tomb of Merlin. From archaeological evidence this was the burial place of some important neolithic chieftain from the period 3000–2500BC. Be that as it may, Merlin is probably here to stay and the red rocky outcrop a little further up the path offers the finest views imaginable over the **Val-sans-Retour,** the whole Forest of **Brocéliande** and the flatter lands leading south to the Gulf of Morbihan. Gorse and broom are plentiful throughout Brittany but nowhere more splendid than here. Some damage has been done to the site already by picnickers dislodging stones for their barbecues.

This is the second most difficult site, after Ponthus, to find in the whole treasure hunt of **Brocéliande**, but is well worth the effort.

Hotié de Viviane, the guest house of Vivian and Merlin's prison of love.

Les Chênes de Kernéan

Take the D134 north from Néant-sur-Yvel to le Bois-de-la-Roche; keep going left through the village towards Guilliers on the D167. At the first left turn you will see in about 2 km a chapel. Leave the car and enter the grove of oaks.

So much of the ancient hardwood forest, which once covered the whole of Brittany, has now been cleared or replaced by conifers that **les Chênes de Kernéan** merit a short detour from the **Brocéliande** circuit. Nowhere captures the extraordinary sylvan magic more than this grove, many centuries old, of gnarled druidic hollow oaks, which miraculously still put out their leaves each spring.

Gaël
Map 230, fold 10

In his *Tristan le Voyageur ou la France au XIme Siècle* (Paris 1825), Marchangy refers to the ruins of the château of **Gaël** as the sumptuous former residence of King Arthur. In Villemarqué's *Myrdhin*, Merlin visits his friend King Ban the Blessed in his palace of **Gaël** to summon him to Arthur's assistance on the battlefield of Salisbury.

The quiet little town of **Gaël**, which once possessed a druidic well that cured rabies, shows no signs today of its former greatness as the residence of King Judicael and the capital of the two Dumnonias of Devon and Brittany. It does boast, however, a friendly crêperie with a welcome throughout the day.

Carnac
Map 230, fold 35/49 – 13 km S.W. of Auray

Although there are no specific Merlin locations in the Vannes/Morbihan area, Mary Stewart in *The Crystal Cave*, no doubt with reason, places many of the young Merlin's Breton adventures in this part of southern Brittany, some 50 km south-west of **Brocéliande**. It is also worth noting, in connection with Merlin, that the patron of the church is St Cornély, a Christianized successor to the god Cernunnos, as well as to the bull rites of Mithras, which Mary Stewart also places here. If Merlin had come to these parts he would understandably have visited **Carnac**, the 'Celtic Jerusalem' and prehistoric capital of the neolithic age, which was the ancient high place of Cernunnos and a great druidic centre of Gaul. With its 5000 menhirs, the **Carnac** alignments, some over 1 km in length, are an overwhelmingly impressive site. A visit to **Carnac** and to the dolmens of Locmariaquer, overlooking the *little sea*, Morbihan, offer an experience of a civilization that was wholly other.

Carnac has its own **Mont St Michel** and entrance to the underworld, with a remarkable neolithic temple beneath its chapel, on top of the tumulus, just to the north of the D781 on the eastern outskirts of the town.

St Cado
Map 230, fold 35

St Cado, who visited Merlin in his madness, came to Morbihan from Wales and established an island hermitage, linked to the mainland by a causeway, which he tricked Satan into building for him. St Cado's stone-bed is noted for healing deafness.

West Brittany

Ile de Sein
Map 230, fold 15/16

For the Ile de Sein take the ferry (1½ hours) from Audierne, 35 km W. of **Quimper** by D784. Ferry times vary according to seasons. Consult *Michelin Green Guide* or any tourist office.

The connection between Merlin and the cult of the dead is strongly reinforced in this peninsula of **Cornouaille**. Some French writers have claimed that his birthplace was the **Ile de Sein**. Certainly it was famous from the first century as the site of a Gallic oracle served by nine priestesses. Their exceptional powers included the ability to influence the weather, change their shapes at will, healing and prophecy. Pomponius Mela refers to their everlasting virginity, while Posidonius stresses the Dionysian aspects of their rites. In the Celtic world these were not necessarily contradictories since *virgin* merely implied belonging to no man.

The **Ile de Sein** is a strange flat snake of an island, 1.8 km long with an average height above sea-level of 1.50 m. It has even been known to disappear beneath the waves. The channel between it and the **Pointe du Raz** is one of the most treacherous on the Breton coast, hence it is the land *par excellence* of Ankou, the personification of death, and his troop of wandering souls, the *Anaon*.

Pointe du Raz
Map 230, fold 16

The **Pointe du Raz** is 15 km W. of Audierne by the D784. This passes through Plogoff where an Arthurian connection links the church of St Ke to Sir Kay the Seneschal who, according to legend, took holy orders after the battle of Camlann and ended his days here as bishop. One of his squires was Ronan (cf. **Locronan**).

It is worth parking your car at the **Pointe du Raz** and walking as far as you can down towards the unquiet rocks of the *Hell of Plogoff*, one of the most westerly bastions of the European mainland. As at **Land's End**, in the other Cornwall, there is a large complex of shops and cafés. On a clear day you will see the **Ile de Sein** out in the ocean beyond the lighthouse.

Baie des Trépassés (Bay of the Dead)
Map 230, fold 16

From the **Pointe du Raz** go back 3 km past **Lescoff** and turn left down to the **Baie des Trépassés** where there is an hotel and car park.

Here is one of the sites of the legendary city of *Is*, lost forever, like its Cornish counterpart of *Lyonesse*, beneath the water. The lake of *Lawal* across the road from the hotel may cover parts of its remains. While *Lyonesse* foundered at the behest of Merlin, the engulfing of *Is* was brought about by *Dahud-Ahès*, an ancient Breton goddess, in her spirit of independence against her father, the King, and the new religion. She was 'in league with the Devil' and opened the floodgates that guarded the city. Its submersion – and hers – symbolizes that of the old Celtic cult of Morgan. In that, death was an adventure not to be feared since it led inevitably to rebirth. Both *Is* and *Dahud* have since been seen under the waves by fishermen and it is said that one day they will re-emerge. A second evangelization of Brittany in the seventeenth century literally put the fear of God into its inhabitants so that the **Baie des Trépassés**, once a point of departure for a western *Avalon*, became the final stage of a voyage to eternal damnation.

Morgan's Rock guarding the northern entrance to the Baie des Trépassés, looks south towards the Ile de Sein, Merlin's Breton birthplace.

Rocher de Morgan
Map 230, fold 16

Continue north, about 2 km leaving **Trouguerl** with its wall of *Is*) on your right to where the road ends at the church of **St They**, just short of the **Pointe du Van**. Follow the path to the left from the car park down to the church.

Locronan (The Parish of Ronan)
Map 230, fold 18

17 km N.W. of **Quimper** by the D39, 10 km E. of Douarnenez by D7.

Going a little further towards the cliffs you will see, if you look right, the **Rocher de Morgan**, the true Queen of Brittany and its seas, with the **Ile de Sein** in the distance. Turn your back on the rock and follow the coastal path the other side of the church to the covered fontaine de St They. There is the statue of a saint in one niche and, until a few years ago, the other contained a stone, apparently also revered, showing that the old practices of Morgan's people have not wholly faded away.

We have included **Locronan**, the most beautiful small town in Brittany, with its magnificent church of St Ronan, in the itinerary for two reasons: the first is that it offers a good example of a Christianized druidic cult, and the second that a St Ronan plays an important part in the story of Sweeney, the Irish Merlin. There are four different St Ronans, from the northern Hebrides to the Bay of Douarnenez, and little is known of any of them. Recurring themes common to them all include long sea-voyages and trouble with women and the Devil, i.e. the old religion. The date of this Ronan is uncertain, though if he was the same offended cleric who cursed Sweeney and caused his madness, he would date from the seventh century. This is a more likely period for him to have found pagan practices in full swing here than the ninth century, as suggested in the local guide. One thing that is certain is the existence of a fertility cult whose focus, the Gazak Ven or Stone Mare (of Epona, Rhiannon or Macha), can still be seen on the moors part-way along the route of the Christian procession, the *Troménie*, near where the pilgrimage route crosses the road to **Quimper**. The Stone Mare was later renamed St Ronan's Chair and considered to be the boat which brought him from Ireland. To sit in its saddle is a cure for barrenness (cf. **Lochmaben**).

Carhaix
Map 230, fold 20

According to Xavier de l'Anglais, **Carhaix** is the capital of Carmelide, where Arthur met and fell in love with Guinevere, and Merlin, bearing the dragon banner, brought victory to Leodagan and Arthur (cf. **Carmel Head**).

This was, no doubt, near Châteauneuf-du-Faou – with the additional assistance of the Madonna of the Oak-Tree, Notre Dame du Crann. It is also reputedly the city of Ahès, the ancient goddess, diabolized by the Christians at the **Baie des Trépassés** and **Huelgoat**.

It was in the sixth century the stronghold of a Breton Bluebeard, Comorre, who murdered five wives. These were avenged by his son, Trémeur, restored to life by St Gildas, after decapitation, whose cult still lives on in **Carhaix** and whose life offers certain parallels to that of St Mylor (Melor) of Amesbury (cf. **Stonehenge**).

The village of Clédeu-Poher, south-east of **Carhaix** on the N164, has an interesting calvary with images of the Holy Grail. In the *Guide de la Bretagne* the heading for this entry is 'Birth of the Holy Grail'. Those who have read the *Holy Blood and the Holy Grail* may be interested to note that this is the homeland of Alain Poher, former President of France and President of the French Senate, considered by the Prieuré de Sion as being, through the Holy Blood of Mary Magdalen, 'a true pretender to the throne of France'.

Huelgoat
Map 230, fold 19
Leave **Carhaix** by the D764 and take the first turning to the right outside the town, northwards along the River Argent, through Poullaouen. If it happens to be lunchtime stop at the admirable *belle époque* Auberge de la Truite, at the former station of Locmaria-Berrien. Then, before you reach the town of **Huelgoat**, park in the first public car park on your right.

Huelgoat, meaning high wood, is the western-most bastion of the great forest of **Brocéliande**. As Markale points out, it is not impossible that Merlin and Vivian dwell here under a great rock, rather than in the forest of Paimpont, though there are no clearly defined Merlin sites at **Huelgoat**. If, however, you cross the road from the car-park and walk south-east above the River Argent, you will soon come across Huelgoat's crueller version of the **Val-sans-Retour**. There is an opening in the wall and a steep staircase leads down to the *Gouffre* where the 'silver' river goes underground. Above is a menacing crag with a sinister legend. The Breton goddess who goes under many names, Morgan, Vivian, Mélusine, is here called Ahès or Dahud.

This eminence was her castle whither, in her unquenchable thirst for lovers, she lured them for a night, only to push them each morning to their death into the swirling cataract beneath, where a black man was waiting to conduct them into the underworld. As elsewhere in

Huelgoat, there is an amazing chaos of tumbled rocks where the Argent re-emerges.

Arthur's Cave

Retrace your steps to the car-park. You now have a choice, depending on how much time is available to you. You should at least visit _Arthur's Cave_, taking the second path to the right across the stream Clair Ruisseau. Follow the signpost to _Grotte d'Artus_. This is one of the many sites where Arthur and his knights are said to be sleeping, awaiting the day when he will rise again to set the Celtic peoples free.

Arthur's Camp

If you wish to visit _Arthur's Camp_ (Le camp d'Artus) retrace your steps, take the first right and the second right and follow the up-hill path to the great hill-fort. You could go on from _Arthur's Cave_ and visit the _Mare aux Sangliers_ (the wild Boar's pool), which sadly, in the hurricane of 1987, lost the great trees that once gave shade to its beasts, though one stump clings octopus-like to a great stone from which its roots are almost indistinguishable. It is worth recalling that the wild boar – le solitaire – is a symbol of the druid and one of Merlin's totem animals. Now comes the adventure: retrace your steps some 30 yds. and then take the _grand escalier_, a staircase which climbs steeply to the path leading to _Arthur's Camp_ on the right. Here a word of warning is necessary: because of the devastation in 1987 of this greatest and most evocative of the Breton forests, the _grand escalier_ was almost impassable in 1988, so great was the number of fallen trees. But the greatest tragedy is _Arthur's Camp_ where hardly a tree remains standing within the elliptical enclosure, 1200 m × 350 m. Walking within the perimeter, off the path, was virtually impossible, but it is still worth pursuing your way to the far end to climb the mighty ramparts, like those at **Cadbury**, which protected the stronghold. It was first constructed in the Gallo-Roman period during the first century BC, was taken over by the Romans and, as at many Arthurian sites, was inhabited again after their departure. Certainly there is an Arthurian tradition in the area (cf. **Carhaix**).

Chaos du Moulin

Stones, unlike trees, are not subject to hurricanes or other changes and chances of this fleeting world. Before leaving **Huelgoat** you should not fail to visit the amazing _Chaos_. You can take either of two paths to the west: _le Sentier des Amoureux_ or the _Allée Violette_. Alternatively you can drive into town, turn right by the lake and park there. Across the main road is the entrance to the _Chaos_, a whole valley of boulders tossed higgledy-piggledy as though by some giant. This giant was the Gawr or Gargantua, an _alter ego_ of Merlin in his guise of wild man. As forests go, this, even more than Paimpont/ **Brocéliande**, is an altered state of consciousness.

Grotte du Diable

An important site to visit is the *Grotte du Diable* which had a curious, hallucinatory effect on us. The crepuscular greenery inside the grotto, the extreme depth of this secret world and the roar of the underground River Argent would have made a most dramatic sojourning place for Merlin, the Devil's son.

The child in all of us could hardly fail to be fascinated by the challenge of scrambling among the surrounding rocks and finding appropriate names for their tormented forms. As we were leaving this mouth of hell, a black cat crossed our path into the devil's underworld where there can be little in the way of feline delights. One of the curious features about this area is that you do not know which are rocks and which are roots – they merge into one another so easily.

It is, no doubt, just a coincidence that the forest and parish immediately to the east of **Huelgoat** are dedicated to St Ambroise, the French for Merlin's name, Emrys (cf. **Stonehenge**).

Brennilis
Map 230, fold 19

Brennilis signifies the marsh of Hell and this village forms a bridge of transition to the other world. At the western extreme of Brittany the forestland, Argoat, which ends at **Huelgoat**, is separated from Armor, the seacoast, by a spectral no-man's-land, containing its own underworld and leading on to the lost cities and islands of dead souls beyond.

If the church is shut, turn right beyond it and drive to the end of the narrow lane, keeping to your right. The last house on the left is the presbytery, marked by a cross, where, with any luck, you will find the recteur, who graciously showed us round his church. It is indeed worth the trouble to visit this large church at the entrance to Hell. In the Sanctuary, to emphasize the pagan connection, are wooden carvings of the sibyls of antiquity. Our Lady of Brennilis, of whom there are two statues, has a unique feature of a plait down her back that turns into the tail of the mermaid – Lilith, Marie-Morgane, the ancient Celtic goddess of water on whom she stands. Another unusual feature is the stained-glass window depicting St Anne (the Celtic goddess Anu in her Christianized form) with the Virgin Mary in her womb.

Yeun Elez

To reach Hell, *Yeun Elez*, take the first turning on the right south out of the village to the suitably situated nuclear power station and keep going right to the end of the road. There you will find a recently constructed reservoir which, dark and sinister, does nothing to detract from the region's reputation. It is not unlike **Dozmary Pool** in Cornwall, but is surrounded by treacherous black quicksands. From this place of the dragon one looks west to the **Montagne St Michel**, Belen's mountain, which so often in Celtic lands dominates an entrance to the underworld.

St Herbot
Map 230, fold 19

Between **Huelgoat** and **Lannédern** on the D14, 7 km south-west of **Huelgoat** lies the village of **St Herbot,** watered by the Elez, river of Hell (see **Brennilis**). The church is well worth a visit as evidence of the continuation of a pre-Christian cult to the divine protector of horned beasts, to whom cows' tails and horsehair are still offered (cf. **Carnac**). Herbot also defeated a giant, Guevrel, or the Gawr (cf. **Huelgoat**), symbol of the old religion, like Gargantua, Cernunnos and Merlin the wild man.

Lannédern
Map 230, fold 19

Whatever you do while in this area do not miss the church of **Lannédern** on the D14. Edern has the same name, *Yder*, as two important characters in Chrétien de Troyes' first Arthurian romance – *Erec et Enide*. Here he is clearly a Merlin figure, riding a stag in several sculptures and paintings, both in the church and the graveyard.

St Edern has a sister, Genovefa, who stands in the same relationship to him as Gwenddydd does to Merlin – as his soul partner – although Genovefa has been 'Christianized' and possesses both saintly and malicious characteristics. The Welsh tale of Culhwch and Olwen actually mentions Edern as one of the sons of Nudd, the other being Gwynn, Lord of the Wild Hunt and the Underworld (cf. **Glastonbury**). So, if one wanted an image of a Christianized Merlin in Brittany, St Edern, the only character besides Merlin-Lailoken in Western literature to ride a stag and carry a book, is clearly that – an intermediary figure between the ages of Cernunnos and Christ.

Images of Ankou, the Breton personification of death, are all around, as is a splendid sculpture of Morgan at the side of the ossuary. On the calvary two angels bear the Holy Grail above St Edern and beneath the crucifixion (cf. **Edern**).

Brasparts
Map 230, fold 19

Continuing the circuit of Hell, a stop at **Brasparts** is indicated. In the churchyard, on the calvary, there is possibly the finest representation anywhere of the Celtic triple mother carrying the Christ away. They may also be the Matronae, the Norns, the Matres or the Fates, in Christian form. The details of this calvary repay close scrutiny. On the south portico can be seen one of the most impressive sculptures of Morgan, with the breasts of a woman, the horns of the Devil and the tail of a serpent (which ends in a man's head), holding an apple in her right hand.

Montagne St Michel de Brasparts
Map 230, fold 19

6½ km N. of **Brasparts** on D785 turn left up to the **Montagne St Michel**, at 380 m the highest peak of Armorica.

No other mountain in the Celtic world combines so dramatically the Merlinesque unity of the two worlds. The chapel is locked but the view over the lake of death below, surrounded by the black and tan swampland – the entrance to the underworld of *Yeun Elez* – is magnificent, especially on an evening of gales and rain.

Spain

France

Pyrenees

Ribadeo

La Coruña

Lugo
River Eo

St Juan de la Peña ●

● 9

4 ● 5 ● 1
2

● 6
● 3

Huesca ●

● Pontevedra

● 7

8 ●

Portugal

● Madrid

● Toledo

Valencia ●

10 ●

11 ●

N

↑

Scale: 1cm = 72km

1 Santiago de Compostela
2 Santa Eulalia de Bóveda
3 Pedrafita do Cebreiro
4 Finisterra
5 Noya
6 Padrón
7 Bayona
8 Santa Tecla (Guarda)
9 Merlí
10 Navahermosa
11 Ruidera
  Cave of Montesinos

Spain

Galicia

Michelin Map 990 and Salvora Mapa de Galicia

Mirroring its northern brothers of Brittany, Cornwall and Wales, this north-west peninsula of Spain, the ancient land of the Celtiberians, whose god Lug remains to this day in the city and province of **Lugo**, was repopulated by Celts from the north in the fifth and sixth centuries. The land is unmistakably Celtic – standing stones, petroglyphs, gorse, broom, moors and mist – and is the opening to the Otherworld of the western ocean, to whose coast strange travellers come and go.

Celtic is no longer spoken there but the place-names, the bagpipes, the drams drunk at breakfast, testify to its heritage. Bayona plays quite a significant part in Ariosto's *Orlando Innamorato* in which he also mentions a spring, created by Merlin in such a city. Is it the Bayona in Basque France or Galician Spain? No record exists to point the way to the fountain in either city, though there is an impressive aqueduct from the mountains, east of Bayona, to the fortress-Parador, where we stayed.

The major centre of interest for Merlin followers is, however, inland in the province of **Lugo**. It was here, on the border of León at Pedrafita Do Cebreiro that Sir Galahad achieved the vision of the Grail. The Grail was later kept in the monastery of St Juan de la Peña (**Map 42 fold 11**) and is now preserved in Valencia cathedral. A modern Galician writer, Cunqueiro, has written much about the presence of Merlin in this southernmost realm of Celtia. He places him in the mythical inn of Miranda on the river Eo to the north-east of **Lugo**; perhaps somewhere near the frontier with Asturias by the Peña do Lobo (wolf-stone) on the Rio Eo 24 km S.W. of Ribadeo on N640 to **Lugo**.

Whether Merlin's presence is imaginary or not, there are a dozen place-names in Galicia which bear testimony to it – the majority in the province of **Lugo**.

Santiago de Compostela

Map 990, fold 2 and Map 441, fold 2/3

Galicia is the goal of the greatest pilgrimage in the West, that of **Santiago de Compostela**. Writers, such as Charpentier, have suggested that it was already in pre-Christian times the road to the isles of the blessed which all souls must take at death. We will not concern ourselves here with the Christian legend of St James, rising from the Field of the Star to slay the Moors; more to our purpose is the story of a proto-Merlin, Priscillian, the first Christian to be executed for heresy in the West. He was a native of Padrón, a fishing village 20 km S.W. of **Santiago** on the N550, where St James is reputed to have landed on his journey from the Holy Land. This makes an immediate connection between the two patrons – one canonized and one a heretic – of **Galicia**. They are *alter egos*, somewhat in the manner of Merlin with Kentigern and Dubricius, and Sweeney with Moling. The place where the apostle's boat landed from Jaffa is still shown under the altar of the church by the bridge. Galicia's national poet, Rosalía de Castro, was also a native of Padrón and is celebrated in the park opposite by a larger-than-life statue.

Priscillian is of interest in that he combines aspects of the Gnostic religion – not dissimilar from druidism – with a deep interest in astrology, numerology, the role of women in religious practice and the cult of nature in temples not made with hands. In this context one should remember that one of the derivations of druid is *very wise*, e.g. Gnostic. Priscillian was executed at Trier in AD385 and was at once venerated as a martyr. His disciples brought his body home along the Milky Way, the route to **Compostela**, and some, including one Atienza, are of the belief that it may be his body, rather than that of St James the Greater that lies beneath the High Altar of the cathedral of **Santiago de Compostela**.

The only prominent defender of Priscillian was St Martin (see **Lake District** and **Land's End**), who himself had many magical and druidic qualities. He nearly killed himself testing the properties of hellebore on an island off the coast of Liguria, a land named for Lugh, and whenever he said Mass a globe of fire appeared above his head. The miraculous cure of the King of Galicia's son, by contact with relics of Martin, made him the most popular saint in the country, and many churches were dedicated to him.

The most mysterious church in **Santiago** is Santa María la Real del Sar, an architectural impossibility, like the tower of Pisa, built by the Sar which flows down to Padrón. If, however, you wish to honour Priscillian as a true saint of the era between two orthodoxies that Merlin also inhabited, you must go to **Santa Eulalia de Bóveda**.

Santa Eulalia de Bóveda

Map 990, fold 2 – 15 km S.W. of Lugo, by the Santiago-Orense road.

The church of Santa Eulalia is built on top of an earlier healing shrine, puzzling to archaeologists, and not excavated until 1924. You will notice to the right of the entrance a stone carving which appears to show a priestess guiding a pilgrim to the healing waters. The interior shows remnants of the once luminous green colour. The walls are

After 4 km bear right to Friol then left after 2 km and right after 7 km. Park the car in the small square opposite the church and ring the bell for admission.

decorated with a variety of birds and vines and in the centre there is the bath. Whether of baptism or healing, Christian or pagan, might have been of little significance at the time of its creation: this is a shrine where the body of Priscillian rested on his journey back to his homeland.

Noya
Map 990, fold 2 – 35 km W. of Santiago on the C543

Another site of interest is **Noya** just north of Padrón, where Noah landed in his ark. This is also a place where Christianity and Paganism meet in an unaccountable manner. **Noya**, called the key to **Galicia**, is famous for its extensive collection of tombstones, in the churchyard of San Francisco, which are astonishing and quite puzzling to archaeologists. They contain intricate carvings of craftsmen, depicting their particular trade, but do not make a mention of their name or date. Archaeologists are uncertain whether these 'tombstones' ever lay on top an actual body. Are these perhaps the initiation pieces of the apprentice who gives up his personal identity in this world to become the master builder? Tombstones are certainly relevant in **Noya**, the point of departure for Finisterre and the sunset world beyond (cf. **Pointe du Raz**, **Land's End** *et al.*).

According to a traditional Galician legend the whale, on which St Brendan and his sailors landed, thinking it was an island, bore them to a safe haven on the coast of Finisterre.

Other sites in Galicia

Galicians also claim that their ancestors, setting out from La Coruna, then the great port of the goddess Brigantia, discovered Ireland. They took with them the *Stone of Destiny* to Tara whence it was removed to Iona and Scone and finally to Westminster Abbey where it is still the coronation stone that confers the sovereignty of Britain. In Galicia we generally stayed in the excellent Paradors and ate at the best local seafood restaurants we could find. As in all Celtic countries, the bars are well worth visiting for their individual tapas and alcoholic specialities, above all in Pontevedra in the street that leads up from the Parador to the church of Santa María la Mayor.

There is a village called Merlin in the province of Pontevedra and a dozen other place-names suggestive of the enchanter in Galicia as a whole. The only other place-name we have found in Spain with a possible Merlin connection is Merlí in Huesca.

In the southernmost tip of the province of Pontevedra, near Guarda, is the best preserved Celtic village to be found anywhere, at Monte Santa Tecla. Santa Tecla was the self-ordained female priest and tireless pursuer of the misogynist St Paul. St Egeria, a disciple of Priscillian, brought her relics and cult back from Armenia, refuge of Gnostics and other heretics, to this Galician mountain where she maintained the traditional worship accorded to Celtic nature goddesses.

Other sites in Spain

Navahermosa, Merlin's bridge and spring
Map 990, fold 24 – 51 km S.W. of Toledo on the C401

This Templar stronghold had a now vanished castle of the two sisters near the present municipal cemetery on the banks of the *Arroyo Merlín*, Merlin's stream. Atienza (*Guía de la Espana Templaria*, p. 151) has no doubt of its connection with the magician. The bridge of Merlin, the first bridge after a petrol station and a new house as you enter the town, is quite an impressive old structure for what today, in summer at least, is so small a stream. It must once have been a trysting place for lovers.

Merlin's Bridge at Navahermosa.

The entrance to the Cave of Montesinos.

La Mancha – The Cave of Montesinos

Map 990, fold 26 and Map 445, fold 16 – 235 km S.E. of Madrid

Take the N IV to Ocaña, the 301 to Quintanar de la Orden, then to El Toboso and on to Pedro Muñoz, Tomelloso and from here take the C310 for a few miles until you come to a T-junction, turn left to Ruidera and go straight through the town to the **Cave of Montesinos**.

As recently as the early 1960s the lagoons of Ruidera were still remote from any large town, difficult of access and innocent of tourists. At that time one of the authors, while exploring La Mancha with a friend on the trail of Don Quixote, tried to find the **Cave of Montesinos**, the southernmost point in Europe directly associated with Merlin.

Cervantes' tale relates in brief how Don Quixote was lowered on a 150 ft. rope into the cavern about which he had heard many marvels. There, he met a group of people who had been enchanted and held captive by Merlin, 'the French wizard', the first being the Count of Montesinos himself, who acted as guide to his long-awaited visitor. After the massacre of Charlemagne's rearguard under Roland at Roncesvalles in AD778, Montesinos had cut out the heart of his friend Durandarte and carried it, as he had promised, to the Lady Belerma (cf. Bruce, whose heart was brought back from Spain to Melrose by Sir James Douglas). These two were also imprisoned in the cave along with Lancelot, Guinevere and the squire of Durandarte, Guadiana, whom Merlin transformed into the great river that bears his name (in fact, it is more likely to be the Wadi of the goddess Anu). Ruidera and her seven daughters were no longer there, having been turned into the lakes below the cave, where their tears feed the river daily as he flows the breadth of Spain to enter Portugal in great triumph and lose himself in the Atlantic. He is a melancholy river who journeys underground for much of his course, shunning the daylight which painfully reminds him of his earthly existence. His waters bring forth only coarse and tasteless fish.

On the earliest visit we stopped the car on a dusty track to ask a

Inside the cave, where Merlin turned the squire of Durandarte into the great river Guadiana, whose source is here.

peasant standing outside the only inhabited house the way to the cave. He asked us where we came from, and, when we said Oxford, told us that a very long time ago some people from Oxford had come on the same quest. Could this have been a distant folk memory of Inglis' expedition of 1823? As we spoke, and he agreed to be our guide, he plucked a passing horse-fly from the air, transfixed it with a sharp blade of dried grass and launched it on its way.

A quarter of a century later as we were recalling this detail at the same spot where the road made a sharp left turn, a horse-fly few into our car. We let this one fly off unscathed in honour of the synchronicity and the gadfly Merlin. This act of mercy was not repaid; on our return from the cave, swimming across the first cool, green lagoon, one of us was buzzed by yet another horse-fly and dropped a favourite pair of swimming trunks to the bottom, an offering to the naiads and the underground stream. No hand clothed in white samite restored them, but the Morgan connection is not without relevance. Usually it is she rather than Merlin who enchants and imprisons people in watery places. The fact that the seven daughters were also joined by Ruidera's two nieces evokes the many parallels in the literature where nine priestesses under a high druidess live in or by a lake.

The modern pilgrim, spared the steep walk of more than an hour, can drive straight up to the cave, which is signposted from the road. When we got out it felt as if nobody had been there for centuries; the air was perfectly still except for the buzzing flies, and again we felt that we had the whole area to ourselves. The cave did not look at all spectacular from the outside – a gaping wide hole in the side of the rockface. We walked down a couple of steps into the darkness and realized that we had left our torch behind. A dead snake was lying on one of the steps. We took another few steps until the darkness enveloped us completely and at any moment we might have plunged into the abyss. So we stood there, at the very edge of chaos or chasm and allowed the atmosphere to penetrate us. We tried to get some sense of what it must have been like for Don Quixote. He quite clearly had had a transpersonal experience in this cave. When he returned to the surface of the earth he thought that he had been away for three days and three nights, yet he had only been underground for one hour. He was most upset that his companions had hauled him back into the light of day for, as he said, 'you have robbed me of the sweetest existence and most delightful vision any human being ever enjoyed or beheld. Now, indeed, I positively know that the pleasures of life pass like a shadow and a dream, and wither like the flowers of the field . . .'

The main town of the area is Tomelloso which claims to be the largest producer of spirits in the world. Do not miss the experience of bathing in one of the lagoons near the cave. When we were there we had a whole lake to ourselves. There are a few restaurants in the area but you may prefer a picnic by an isolated lakeside. The Ruidera Hotel has the rare distinction of a Michelin red rocking-chair.

NB: **La Mancha** produces more wine than any other region in Spain and the quality has improved dramatically in recent years. The local Manchego cheese is famous throughout the world.

Glossary

This glossary is not intended to be comprehensive, but to offer an amplification of some characters not treated fully in the text.

Ahès Also known as **Dahud**. Breton name for a pan-Celtic figure symbolizing the pre-Christian religion and women's independence. As Ahès she is presented as the cruel and insatiable princess who dispatched her lovers nightly into the chasm of the River Argent (see **Huelgoat**). The town of **Carhaix** is named for her (Ker-Ahès). As Dahud ('good witch') she is the daughter of King Gradlon of Quimper. She built a city below sea-level and ruled there according to her own laws. In Christian legend this city of *Is* belonged to her father and was submerged when Dahud, in collusion with the Devil, let in the sea. Gradlon jettisons his daughter into the sea on the advice of St Corentin, whose feast day, 1st May, no doubt indicates that he took over the prerogatives of the goddess (cf. Morgan).

Alan The 'Man of the Woods' who went mad after a battle, whom Sweeney encounters in a great forest after flying from Ailsa Craig to Britain. He prophesies his own death – falling from a cliff into a waterfall – and his burial in the churchyard of a saint. This sounds like Merlin. The name Alan was unknown among the Britons until the Norman conquest, but Alan the Fat, the son of Joseph of Arimathea, was known as the *Rich Fisher*. He was the ancestor of the line of Fisher Kings including Pelles and the Grail Knight, Galahad.

Anaon In Breton tradition the wandering souls of the dead (see **Ankou**).

Ankou In Brittany, the personification of death, the first person in the year to die after Samhain (1st November) and captain of the night-boat of wandering souls, the Anaon. A vision of the Ankou presages a death. He is usually presented as a skeleton with a scythe.

Anu, Ana, Aine, Danu, Don Great mother of the Celtic peoples and their gods whose name can be found in many rivers from the Danube to the Don. She was the ancestress of the Tuatha De Danaan, the magical rulers of Ireland.

Arianrhod   Heroine of the Mabinogion whose name means *silver wheel* and whose celestial home is the Corona Borealis. She has two children by her brother Gwydion, Dylan and Llew (see **Caer Arianrhod**).

Bedivere, Bedevere, Bedwyr   Along with Kay, with whom he is closely associated, Bedwyr is one of Arthur's original companions, his butler or constable, whose magic spear and remarkable speed make him formidable in battle despite his being one-armed. Some see him as a lover of Guinevere before Lancelot. He is present when Arthur slays the giant of **Mont St Michel** and was created Duke of Normandy. The last survivor of Camlann, he remains with Arthur until the departure of the King for Avalon and reluctantly returns *Excalibur* to the lake whence it came.

Bohor, Bohort, Bors   King of a part of Brittany and cousin of Lancelot, he succeeds in the Grail Quest with Galahad and Perceval and alone survives to tell the tale. Later he helps Lancelot to avenge the death of Arthur and seems to have been the last of the Knights of the Round Table.

Brigit, Brighid, Brigid, Bride   'The exalted one' – the great Celtic goddess of fire, fertility and healing, daughter of the Dagda, inspirer of poets, bestower of wisdom, protectress of warriors, patroness of farmers and shepherds. She is also associated with gods of the arts and crafts. Her name survives in the names of towns, hills and rivers, from Bregenz to Brechin and the great tribe of the Brigantes were her people. She was easily Christianized into St Brigid, b. AD450, Mary of the Gael, foster-mother of Jesus and midwife of the Virgin, who took over the old feast of the goddess, Oimelc, 1st February, the start of the lambing season, and continued to tend the sacred fire at Kildare. She was the daughter of a druid and possibly a priestess of the goddess she succeeded.

Brons   The Fisher King, son-in-law of Joseph of Arimathea and grandfather of Perceval. He is often associated with Bran the Blessed.

Ceridwen, Cerridwen   Welsh mother goddess – whose animal is the sow – possessor of a magic cauldron in which she brewed a draught made from six herbs called the *greal* (see **Taliesin**).

Dagda   Druid-god and god of druids, All-Father, who is called *good*. He possesses an inexhaustible cauldron and a club which kills with one end and resuscitates with the other. He also has a harp that plays by itself and a black horse whose name is ocean. He is the Lord of New Grange and father of Brigit and Aengus Og.

Dahud   See **Ahès**.

Epona   Mare-goddess of the Gauls, usually depicted riding side-saddle and sometimes carrying the key to the underworld. Her Irish and Welsh equivalents are Macha and Rhiannon.

Faunus

Sometimes known as Silvanus, a woodland god connected with Pan, Mars in his pastoral form, the oak and the woodpecker. He presided over the February fertility festival of the Lupercalia.

Gargantua

An amiable and primitive giant from old French folklore. He has much in common with the Dagda (cf. **Mont St Michel**). Like Merlin he helps Arthur defeat the giants and is then taken away to the Otherworld by Mélusine or Morgan.

Gawain

Arthur's nephew and therefore potential heir. A great warrior, exponent of courtesy, solar hero and servant of ladies. It is he who finds Merlin after his enchantment by Vivian and is the last mortal to speak with him. His Welsh name, Gwalchmai, means *Hawk of May*.

Gildas

c. AD500–*c.* 570, St Gildas the Wise is a notable pan-Celtic figure and protagonist in the story of Merlin. Born in northern Strathclyde, possibly of Pictish descent, he became a student of St Illtud in South Wales. He visited Ireland where he had many disciples and founded the great Breton Abbey of St Gildas de Rhuys. He also lived as a hermit on Flatholm in the Bristol Channel for a number of years. In *c.* 540 he wrote the earliest history of the period, *De Excidio Britanniae* (On the Ruin of Britain).

He does not mention Arthur by name, possibly because his family were defeated by him in battle. Merlin-Lailoken conferred with Taliesin, who had just returned from Rhuys, where he had been studying with Gildas (see **Hartfell**).

Gwenddolau

Minor king, Merlin's patron, who died at the battle of **Arderydd**, his citadel. Merlin calls him his sovereign in his poem *Afellanau* (Apple-Trees). Carwinley, near the **Moat of Liddel**, preserves his name.

Gwyddno Garanhir

Long-legged prince of Cantref y Gwaelod, now sunken land beneath the waters of Cardigan Bay, he was the possessor of a magic inexhaustible cauldron or hamper, one of the Thirteen Treasures of Britain. His son, Elphin, rescued the infant Taliesin from the sea.

Hengist, Hengest

Saxon leader invited to Britain with a mercenary army by Vortigern, *c.* AD449, with his brother, Horsa, to help stem the Pictish invasion. Vortigern marries his daughter Rowena (Renwein), giving Kent in exchange. He massacres the chiefs of the Britons during a peace conference at Amesbury and is finally defeated and killed at **Conisbrough** by Aurelius Ambrosius with the assistance of Merlin.

Janus

Roman god of all doorways and beginnings, his two faces look in and out to the new year and the old, the coming day and the ending night. Like Kronos/Saturn he was the King of the Golden Age. He is linked to Diana, the goddess of the witches and some of his attributes were

Christianized in the two saints John whose feast days stand at the poles of the year, the winter and summer solstices.

Kay, Cei, Ke

Arthur's foster-brother and seneschal, he is an ambiguous figure – gallant knight, mocker, braggart, figure of fun, giant with supernatural powers and even saint, associated with stags (see **Pointe du Raz**).

Lludd, Lud

King of Britain, who, with his brother Llefelys, freed the land of three plagues and trapped two dragons at the centre of Britain, **Oxford**, transferring them to **Dinas Emrys**. London, *Caer Lud*, is named for him, as is Ludgate, the site of his tomb. Lludd is a corruption of the god Lugh/Nudd/Nuada/Nodens, whose temple was on the site of St Paul's Cathedral.

Llyr, Lir, Lear

Sea-god, father of Bran and Manannan, possible model of Shakespeare's King Lear.

Macha

Threefold goddess, also involved in a trinity with Babd and the Morrigan. Her properties include the horse, fertility, healing, war, death and the sovereignty of the land. Her city is Armagh, primatial see of Ireland (cf. Epona and Rhiannon).

Macsen Wledig, Magnus Maximus

Emperor of the West, AD383–388. According to the legend he dreamed of a beautiful unknown woman and sent messengers to seek her throughout the Empire. She was Elen of Wales, or Helen of **Caernarfon**, for whom many roads in Wales are still named. Macsen built the cities of **Caernarfon**, **Carmarthen** and **Caerleon** in her honour. Vortigern's claims to royal legitimacy rested on being his son-in-law through his first marriage.

Mark, Marc'h

Semi-legendary King of Cornwall, uncle or father of Tristan and husband of Iseult. He also had connections with Dumfries and Galloway (see **Mote of Mark**) and pursues Tristan and Iseult into the forest of Celyddon. The fact that he had horse's ears suggests his Otherworldly origin.

Mélusine

Water- and snake-goddess, whose centre was Poitou, she became the ancestress of the Lusignan Kings of Jerusalem and other royal families of Europe (see **Pontrieux**, **Huelgoat** and Introduction).

Melwas, Meleagraunce

Son of Bagdemagus, ruler of the Kingdom of Glass. He is a god of death and the underworld to which he abducts Guinevere. Gawain and Lancelot rescue her and the latter kills him (see **Glastonbury**).

Mylor, Melor

Titular saint of Amesbury Abbey and of Merther Mylo in Cornwall. He was threatened with death by his uncle as a prince of seven years old but was maimed instead. His amputated right hand was replaced by a silver one. At fourteen he was beheaded and buried at Amesbury. These legends and his various names connect him to Merlin, the Irish god Nuada of the Silver Hand, his Welsh equivalent, Nudd, King Lud of **London** and Nodens (see **Lydney**).

Pelles, Pellehan	The Fisher King and guardian of the Grail who dwells in the castle of Corbenic (see **Llangollen**), wounded in the thigh or genitals by Balin's *Dolorous Blow*.
Perceval, Parzival, Parsifal, Percival, Perlesvaux, Peredur	Naïve, perfect fool and Grail hero, grandson of the Rich Fisher King.
Rhiannon	'Great Queen' – heroine of the Mabinogion, Welsh mare-goddess and daughter of the Lord of the Underworld. Her birds send the living to sleep and awaken the dead (cf. Epona and Macha).
Rhydderch	Surnamed Hael (the generous), King of **Dumbarton** in the sixth century.
Taliesin	Sixth-century bard associated with three kings, Maelgwn, Urien and Gwyddno Garanhir. He is the most famous of the old Welsh poets and several of his poems have survived. As a mythical figure he had many incarnations, in one of which, as Gwion Bach, he tastes three drops from the goddess Ceridwen's cauldron of inspiration, destined for her ugly son, Afagddu (dark monster), also known as Morfran (great crow), who survived the battle of Camlann. Ceridwen, after a magical contest of shape-shifting, assumes the form of a black hen and swallows Gwion, now a grain of wheat. She gives birth to him in a new form at the feast of Beltaine and abandons him to the waves in a leather bag. Elphin, son of Gwyddno Garanhir, rescues him from the sea and names him Taliesin (*shining brow*). He is frequently identified with Merlin (see **Caerlaverock** and **Hartfell** *et al.*)
Taranis	One of a Celtic trinity of gods with Teutates and Esus. His name means thunder. Human burnt sacrifice was offered to him in a gigantic wickerwork idol. His symbol was the wheel and he was associated with Dispater, ancestor of the Gauls and god of the dead.
Tristan	Nephew or son of King Mark and lover of Iseult, he is the exemplar of a Celtic hero-warrior, poet, harpist, familiar with the language of birds, famous for his great leaps, at home in the natural world, model of courtesy, possessor of a magic sword and immune to wounds. He was also one of the great honoured swineherds of the Celts. The theme of tragic love leading to death enters European literature with him and Iseult. His original name, Droston, is Pictish.

Urien

King of Rheged, land of the Britons of the North between the Mersey and the Clyde in the sixth century. Husband of Morgan, father of Owain and patron of Taliesin.

Vivian, Nimuë, Niniane, Lady of the Lake

Merlin's paramour who receives the secrets of his magic and encloses him within an invisible castle (cf. Gwendydd, Merlin's sister and see **Comper** and **Barenton**). It is also the name of a river which flows through the heart of **Brocéliande (Michelin Map 230, fold 37).**

Bibliography

A Guide to Glastonbury's Temple of the Stars, London, 1935
AA Illustrated Road Book of England and Wales (4th ed.), London, 1966
AA Illustrated Road Book of Ireland (2nd ed.), London, 1966
AA Illustrated Road Book of Scotland (4th ed.), London, 1956
Alvarellos, L., *Las Leyendas Tradicionales Gallegas*, Madrid, 1977
Ariosto, *Orlando Furioso*, trans. Reynolds, B., Harmondsworth, 1975
Artus, *Brocéliande ou l'Obscur des Forêts*, La Gacilly, 1988
Ashe, G., *King Arthur's Avalon*, Glasgow, 1957
Ashe, G., *Avalonian Quest*, London, 1982
Ashe, G., *The Landscape of Arthur*, New York, 1988
Ashton, G., *The Realm of King Arthur*, Newport, IoW, 1974
Atienza, J., *Los Santos Imposibles*, Barcelona, 1977
Atienza, J., *Guía de los Heterodoxos Españoles*, Barcelona, 1985
Atienza, J., *Santoral Diabólico*, Barcelona, 1988
Attwater, D., *The Penguin Dictionary of Saints*, Harmondsworth, 1965
Avalon to Camelot, Vol. 2, No. 4, 1987
Barber, C., *Mysterious Wales*, London, 1982
Barber, C., *More Mysterious Wales*, Newton Abbot, 1986
Begg, E., 'Gnosis and the Single Vision', in M. Tuby (ed.), *In the Wake of Jung*, London, 1983
Begg, E., *Myth and Today's Consciousness*, London, 1984
Begg, E., *The Cult of the Black Virgin*, London, 1985
Bellamy, G., *La Forêt de Brocéliande*, 2 vols, Rennes, 1896, Paris, 1985
Boney, W., *How to Spend a Day or a Week in Tintagel*, Wadebridge, 1959
Bord, J. and C., *Ancient Mysteries of Britain*, London, 1986
Bradley, A. *et al.*, *A History of Marlborough College*, London, 1893, revised ed. 1927
Bradley, M., *The Mists of Avalon*, New York, 1982
Briant, T., *Le Testament de Merlin*, Paris, 1985

Butler, A. (ed. Kelly, B.), *The Lives of the Saints*, 5 vols, London, 1959

Caldecott, M., *Women in Celtic Myth*, London, 1988

Campbell, J., *The Hero with a Thousand Faces*, Princeton, 1949

Capt, E., *The Traditions of Glastonbury*, Thousand Oaks, Calif., 1983

Cervantes, *Don Quixote*, trans. Cohen, J., Harmondsworth, 1950

Chadwick, N., *Celtic Britain*, London, 1964

Charpentier, L., *Les Jacques et le Mystère de Compostelle*, Paris, 1971

Chrétien de Troyes, *Arthurian Romances*, trans. Owen, D., London, 1987

Clarke, C., *Everyman's Book of Saints*, London, 1914, 1956

Cunqueiro, A., *Merlín*, Vigo, 1955

Death of King Arthur, The, trans. Cable, J., Harmondsworth, 1971

Derveaux, D., *De la Côte d'Emeraude à Brocéliande*, St. Malo, 1960

Duxbury, B. and Williams, M., *King Arthur Country in Cornwall*, Bodmin, 1979

Ellis, P., *A Dictionary of Irish Mythology*, London, 1987

Farmer, D., *The Oxford Dictionary of Saints*, Oxford, 1978

Franz, M.-L. von, *C.G. Jung: His Myth in Our Time*, New York, 1975

Geoffrey of Monmouth, *History of the Kings of Britain, The*, trans. Thorpe, L., Harmondsworth, 1966

Gillard, H., *Oeuvres Complètes*, 20 vols, Tréhorenteuc (undated)

Giraldus Cambrensis, *The Itinerary Through Wales*, trans. Hoare, London, 1908

Goodrich, N., *King Arthur*, New, York, 1986

Goodrich, N., *Merlin*, New York, 1987

Graves, R., *The White Goddess*, London, 1961

Green, M., *The Gods of the Celts*, Totowa, N.J., 1986

Guerber, H., *Legends of the Middle Ages*, New York, 1896

Heaney, S., *Sweeney Astray*, Derry, 1983

Henderson, I., *The Picts*, London, 1967

High History of the Holy Grail, The, trans. Evans, S., Cambridge (undated)

Inner Keltia, No. 7 (undated)

John, C., *The Saints of Cornwall*, Redruth, 1981

Jowett, G., *The Drama of the Lost Disciples*, London, 1980

Jung, E. and von Franz, M.-L., *The Grail Legend*, Zürich, 1960

Lacy, N. (ed.), *The Arthurian Encyclopedia*, Woodbridge, 1988

Lancelot of the Lake, trans. Corley, C., Oxford, 1989

Langlais, X. de, *Le Roman du Roi Arthur*, Paris, 1982

Layard, J., *A Celtic Quest*, Zürich, 1975

Le Scouezec, G., *Guide de la Bretagne Mystérieuse*, Paris, 1979

Lecouteux, C., *Mélusine et le Chevalier au Cygne*, Paris, 1982

Mac Cana, P., *Celtic Mythology*, Feltham, 1968

McNeill, F., *The Silver Bough*, Edinburgh, 1956, 1989

Malory, T., *Le Morte Darthur*, London, 1911

Markale, J., *Women of the Celts*, Rochester, Vermont, 1986

Markale, J., *Histoire Secrète de la Bretagne*, Paris, 1977

Markale, J., *Merlin l'Enchanteur*, Paris, 1981

Markale, J., *Petit Dictionnaire de Mythologie Celtique*, Paris, 1986

Markale, J., *Brocéliande et l'Enigme du Graal*, Paris, 1989

Markale, J., *Huelgoat*, Rennes (undated)

Matthews, C., *Mabon and the Mysteries of Britain*, London, 1987

Matthews, C., *Arthur and the Sovereignty of Britain*, London, 1989

Matthews, C., *The Elements of the Celtic Tradition*, Shaftesbury, 1989

Matthews, C. and J., *The Aquarian Guide to British and Irish Mythology*, Wellingborough, 1988

Matthews, J., *The Grail: Quest for the Eternal*, London, 1981

Matthews, J. (ed.), *At the Table of the Grail*, London, 1984

Matthews, J., *Gawain, Knight of the Goddess*, Wellingborough, 1990

Michelin Guide: Bretagne, Clermont-Ferrand, 1984

Michelin Guide: Scotland, Clermont-Ferrand, 1985

Michelin Guide: Spain, Clermont-Ferrand, 1985

Moody, T. and Martin, F-X., *The Course of Irish History*, Cork, 1967

Moore, A., *The Folk-Lore of the Isle of Man*, Isle of Man, 1891

Morris, J., *The Age of Arthur*, London, 1973

Nutt, A., *Studies in the Legend of the Holy Grail*, London, 1888

Nye, R., *Merlin*, London, 1973

O'Keeffe, J., *Buile Suibhne*, London, 1913

Ó'Riordáin, S., *Tara: The Monument on the Hill*, Dundalk, 1972

Rabelais, F., *Oeuvres*, 2 vols, Paris, 1912

Rio, M., *Merlin*, Paris, 1989

Robertson, I., *Blue Guide: Ireland*, London, 1987

Rolt-Wheeler, F., *Mystic Gleams from the Holy Grail*, London (undated)

Room, A., *A Dictionary of Irish Place-Names*, Belfast, 1986

Ross, A., *A Traveller's Guide to Celtic Britain*, London, 1985

Rutherford, W., *The Druids*, Wellingborough, 1978

Salway, P., *Roman Britain*, Oxford, 1981

Scott, W., *Poetical Works*, Edinburgh, 1871

Shakespeare, W. and Rowley, W. (attributed to), *The Birth of Merlin*, Shaftesbury, 1989

Sharkey, J., *Celtic Mysteries*, London, 1975

Sir Gawain and the Green Knight, trans. Stone, P., Harmondsworth, 1959

Skinner, M., *The Return of Arthur*, London, 1955

Smith, D., *A Guide to Irish Mythology*, Blackrock, Co. Dublin, 1988

Stenton, F., *Anglo-Saxon England*, Oxford, 1971

Stewart, M., *The Crystal Cave*, London, 1970

Stewart, M., *The Hollow Hills*, London, 1973

Stewart, M., *The Last Enchantment*, London, 1979

Stewart, M., *The Wicked Lady*, London, 1983

Stewart, R., *The Mystic Life of Merlin*, London, 1986

Stewart, R., *The Prophetic Vision of Merlin*, London, 1986

Stewart, R. (ed.), *The Book of Merlin*, Poole, 1987

Stewart, R. (ed.), *Merlin and Woman*, London, 1988

Sutcliffe, R., *Sword at Sunset*, London, 1963

Tennyson, A., *Collected Works*, London, 1891

Tolstoy, N., *The Quest for Merlin*, London, 1985

Tolstoy, N., *The Coming of the King: The First Book of Merlin*, London, 1988

Toulson, S., *The Celtic Alternative*, London, 1987

Villemarqué, H. de la, *Myrdhin, ou l'Enchanteur Merlin*, Paris, 1862, 1989

Voragine, The Blessed James of, *La Leyenda Dorada*, Madrid, 1982

Wace, R. and Layamon, *Arthurian Chronicles*, trans. Mason, E., London, 1962

Walker, B., *The Women's Encyclopedia of Myths and Secrets*, New York, 1983

Wentz, W.Y. Evans, *The Fairy Faith in Celtic Countries*, Oxford, 1911

Weston, J., *From Ritual to Romance*, New York, 1957

Westwood, J., *Albion: A Guide to Legendary Britain*, London, 1985

White, T., *The Sword in the Stone*, London, 1939

Whitlock, R., *In Search of Lost Gods*, Oxford, 1979

Wilson, C., *The Occult*, London, 1971

Wolfram von Eschenbach, *Parzival*, trans. Hatto, A., Harmondsworth, 1980

Yates, F., *Giordano Bruno and the Hermetic Tradition*, London, 1964

Yates, F., *The Occult Philosophy in the Elizabethan Age*, London, 1969

Zimmer, H., *The King and the Corpse*, Washington, 1948

Index

Aberystwyth 88
Abreuvoir de Merlin 174
Afon Pib 82
Alderley Edge 69-71
Alleluia Stone 73
Alnwick 65
Altar Stone 152
Alternan 129-30
Ambleside 68-9
Anglesey 19, 34, 92
apple-trees 13, 14, 15, 95, 115
Arderydd 66
    battle of 15, 19, 134, 148, 149, 155
Arthur
    and Avalon 48-9, 85, 166-7, 168
    and battles 35, 45, 49, 89, 181
    birth of 16, 148
    and Brittany 159, 168, 169
    and Caerleon 75-6
    and Camelot 50, 53, 55, 62
    conception of 12, 34, 59
    and Excalibur 16, 54-6, 68, 81, 85
    and Guinevere 16-17, 34, 47, 92
    and Holy Grail 18, 28
    as King of Scotland 157-8
    and Round Table 17, 65, 92, 157
    tomb of 166, 177
    and underworld 47, 141
Arthur's Camp 185
Arthur's Cave 185
Arthur's O'On 157
Avalon 13, 17, 22, 35, 47, 48-9, 50, 85, 89, 136, 166-7, 168, 182

Badbury Rings 45-6
Baie des Trépassés 27, 130, 182, 184
Ballasalla 114
Bamburgh Castle 63-5
Barbury 43
Bardsey Island 89-90, 130
Barenton 21, 27, 28-9, 168-9
    fountain of 14, 29, 164, 172-5
Bath 31, 46

beasts and Merlin 30-32
Belen 21, 161
Ben-Bulben 131
Birdoswald 66
Blaise 17, 31, 63
Blue Lough 136
Bosherton 85
Bossiney Mound 61
Bran 22-3, 39, 48, 73-5
Brasparts 187
Brennilis 186
Brittany
    and Arthur 159, 168, 169
    Merlin saints in 27-8
Brocéliande 21, 26, 27, 35, 61, 72, 126, 163, 165, 172-5
    forest of 16-17, 28-9, 176-7, 180
    fountain of 36
Buile Suibhne 19, 115, 122
Burnswark 147

Cadair Idris 88-9
Caer Arianrhod 91
Caerlaverock Castle 25, 148
Caerleon 29, 50, 75-6
Caernarfon 91-2
Caerwent 75
Camboglanna 66
Camelot 50, 53, 54, 55, 62, 155
Camlann 89
Camp du Tournoi 174
Cap Fréhel 164
Carhaix 34, 55, 92, 184
Carlisle 66, 144
Carmarthen 11, 15, 21, 31-2, 45, 82-3, 93
Carmel Head 34, 92
Carmelide 33-4
Carnac 20, 25, 27, 181
Castle Dore 54-5
Castle Rushen 113
Castletown 113
caves, Merlin's 40-41, 43, 61, 81, 82, 144
Cernunnos 20-21, 32
Champ-Dolent 162-3
Chaos du Moulin 185
Chênes de Kernéan, Les 181
Chepstow 65

Castle 75
Chislehurst 40-41
Clochmabenstane 149
Comper 158, 175-7
Conisbrough 71, 72
Craig-y-Ddinas 80-81
Croix de Merlin 165

Dee, Dr John 30
Derwent Water 68
Devil's Highway 40
Didot-Perceval 18-19
Dinard 163
Dinas Bran 22, 73
Dinas Emrys 33, 38, 39, 53, 73, 82, 93-4
Dingle Peninsula 118, 123
Dol 26, 146, 162-3
Don Quixote 36, 193
Dozmary Pool 54, 56
dragons 11, 38, 39, 46, 93, 95, 164, 168, 171, 184
    return of 36-8
druids 19-20, 24, 40, 48, 61, 83, 92, 137, 141, 149, 151, 161, 172, 177
Drumelzier 151-2, 154
Dumbarton 25, 155-6
Dumfries 146
Dundrum 135
Dunmore East 121
Dunragit 144
Dunseverick Castle 139
Dunseverick Head 117
Dunstanburgh Castle 65
Dynevor 81-2

Edern 91
Edinburgh 157-8
    and National Museum of Antiquities 145
Eildon Hills 30, 153-5
eisteddfod 83
Eon de l'Etoile 28-9
Eorann 35
Estoire de Merlin 16-17
Excalibur 16, 17-18, 41, 48-9, 54, 55-6, 68, 81, 85

Fast Castle 155

Fews 117, 137-8
forest and Merlin 20-21, 24-5
Fountain Dale 71-2

Gaël 181
Galava 68-9
Galicia 26, 189-91
Galway 125
Ganieda *see* Gwenddydd
Ganllwyd 89
Gawain, Sir 17, 76, 85, 113
Geoffrey of Monmouth 16, 27, 34-5, 40, 48, 50, 61, 75, 79, 82, 87
  History of the Kings of Britain 11-12, 29, 39, 44
  Vita Merlini 12, 15, 23, 35, 47
Giant's Dance 44, 87, 115, 126
Glasgow 25, 153
  Cathedral 155
Glastonbury 28, 46-50, 75, 133
  Tor 48, 53
Gleann na nGealt 117, 123-5
Glendalough 141
Glenelly 133
gods, old 19-23
Godstow Priory 39
Grasmere 68
Great Orme's Head 92-3
Greenan Castle 50, 155
Grotte du Diable 186
Guendoloena 35
Guinevere 16, 27, 34, 35, 47, 92
Gwenddydd 12-13, 15, 25, 27, 32, 35, 156

Hart Fell 49, 150-51, 152
Heaney, Seamus, *Sweeney Astray* 19, 115, 139
Helvellyn 68
Historia Regum Britanniae 11-12, 29, 39, 44
Hoddom 26, 147
Holy Grail 11, 17, 18, 28, 34, 38, 47-8, 88, 133, 189
  as inner quest 9, 36-7
Hôtié de Viviane 180
Huelgoat 185-6
Huth Merlin 17-18

Ile Aval 166-7
Ile de Sein 182
Inishmurray 131
Ireland
  Northern 133-41
  Republic of 118-33
Iseult 55

Ile de Cèzembre 163
Isle of Man 92, 95-114

Jardin aux Moines 171-2
Joseph of Arimathea 28, 48-9

Kerduel 166
Keswick 67
Kilkieran 121-2
Killaney 117, 118, 134
Killibury Castle 59, 62
Kilrean 131-3
King Arthur's Cave 77
Knocklayd 139-40

La Mancha 193-5
Lady of the Lake, *see* Vivian
Lake District 26, 67-9
Land's End 26, 58-9
Lannédern 27, 187
Layde Church 140
Liddington Castle 41
Lisardowlin 128
Little Doward 77
Llangollen 62, 73-5
Llyn y Fan Fach 81
Loch Arthur 145, 145-6
Loch Lomond 156
Lochmaben 22, 24, 26, 79, 146
Locronan 31, 183-4
Loe Pool 54, 55-6
London 22, 39
Lorge, Forêt de 165
Lough Derg 141
Lough Erne 133
Lugh/Lug 21-2, 83, 128, 151, 189
Lugo 191
Lydney 22, 23, 24, 78-9

Mabon 24, 59, 61, 70, 79, 146, 149
Madley 26, 31, 47, 76-7
Madman's Stone 124
Madman's Well 118-19
madness
  of Merlin 12, 149, 151, 155-6, 181
  of Sweeney 117-18, 149, 183
Magh Rath 117
  Battle of 130, 132, 133-4, 138
magicians and Merlin 28-30
Major Oak 72
Manannan 95
Marazion 56-7
Marlborough 43-4
megaliths 20, 177, 180
Melerius 29-30

Melkin 28, 49-50
Mélusine 34
menhirs 167
Merlin
  as astrologer 37-8
  and beasts 30-32
  as a boy 11, 16, 33, 43, 93
  and caves 40-41, 43, 61, 81, 82, 144
  death of 13, 22, 151
  and different accounts of life 11-14
  and forests 20-21, 24-5
  and magicians 28-30
  and parallels with Sweeney 19, 115, 117
  as prophet 37-8
  and religion 19-28
  and the saints 23-8
  and women 33-6
Merlin's Bridge 86-7
Merlin's Cave 40-41, 43, 61
Merlin's Cross 86
Merlin's Grave 151
Merlin's Hill 83-5
Merlin's Tomb 43, 61, 79, 177-9
Merlyn's Rock 57-8
Meslin 164
Moat of Liddel 149-50
Moira 117, 133-4, 149
Mold 73, 114
Mona 92
Monmouth 79
Mont Dol 161-2, 163
Mont St Michel 58, 159-61, 162
Montagne St Michel de Brasparts 54, 187
Montesinos, Cave of 193-5
Morgan le Fay 17, 34-5, 39, 48-9, 59, 113, 144, 154, 159, 163, 169-70, 171
Mote of Mark 145
Mount Killaraus 12
Mountains of Mourne 135
Mousehole 57-8
Moylinney 138
Mynnydd Merddin 79
Myrddin 15
Myrddin's Quoit 85

Navahermosa 192
Nefyn 91
New Grange 141
Nimuë *see* Vivian
Nivienne 18
  see also Vivian
North Berwick 158
Notre Dame de Lorette 164
Noya 191

Old Sarum 45

Oxford 39-40

Peel 114
Pendragon, Uther *see* Uther
  Pendragon
Pendragon Castle 66, 67
Penrith 66
Pentre Ifan 88
pigs 15, 31-2, 46, 47, 76, 95
pilgrimage 9-10
Pointe du Raz 182
Pont du Secret 32, 179
Ponthus 174-5
Pontrieux 165
Preseli (Prescelly) Mountains
  44-5, 84, 87-8

Quintin, forest of 27, 165

Rasharkin 115-17, 123, 138-9
Rathmore 138
religion and Merlin 19-28
Richmond 65
  Castle 75
Robin Hood 21, 71-2, 173
Rocher de Morgan 183
Rocher Merlin 164
Rock of the False Lovers 171
Romans 16, 19, 23-4, 66, 78,
  147
Round Table 17, 34, 36, 65, 66,
  76, 92, 156-7, 166
  Glastonbury 49
  Manx 95
Rushen Abbey 114
Rydal Water 68

St Blazey 55
St Brendan 26-7
St Cado 25, 181
St Cadoc 24-5
St Columba 24-5
St David's 76, 87
St Dubricius 26
St Efflam 168
St Gildas 49
St Govan's Head 85-6, 113
St Herbot 187

St John 114
St Kentigern 25-6
St Kieran's 117
St Malo 163
St Martin 26
St Michael's Mount 56-7
St Molings/Mullins 22, 31, 117,
  118-20
  Holy Well 120
St Mylor 27-8
St Nectan's Glen 61-2
St Ninian's Cave 144
St Patrick's Isle 114
saints and Merlin 23-8
Santiago de Compostela
  190-91
Segontium 78, 91-2
Sewingshields 65-6
Sherwood Forest 71-2
Silchester 40, 75
Skreen 129-30
Slaughter Bridge 54, 62
Slemish 138
Slieve Gullion 136-7
Slieve League 131-2
Solsbury Hill 46
sources, literary 11-19
South Barrule 95
South Cadbury 50-53
Spanish Head 113
Spenser, Edmund, *Faerie
  Queene, The* 30, 81
stags 16, 21, 32, 68, 115, 179
Stewart, Mary 47, 53, 68, 78,
  83-4, 91, 181
Stirling 50, 156-7
Stobo, 147, 157
  Kirk 26, 152-3
Stonehenge 12, 16, 20, 21, 28,
  44-5, 50, 87, 115, 126, 127,
  171
Strangford 134-5
Sweeney 19, 35, 95, 115-41
  and madness 117-18, 149,
    183
  and parallels with Merlin 19,
    115, 117
Sweetheart Abbey 145

Tara, Hill of 141
Teltown 22, 128
Tintagel 16, 34, 52, 55, 59-61,
  62, 145, 148
Tolkien, J.R.R., *Lord of the Rings,
  The* 87, 157
Tolstoy, Nikolai 19, 21, 87, 117,
  151
  Coming of the King, The 28,
    41, 114
  Quest for Merlin, The 15, 149,
    150
Tombeau de Merlin 177-9
Tombelaine 159-61
tourism 9-10
Tréhorenteuc 169
Tristan 31, 55
Tristan Stone 54-5, 145
Tynwald 114

Uffington Castle 41
Ushnagh 44, 87, 115, 126-8
Uther Pendragon 11-12, 16, 37,
  39, 46, 59, 62, 87, 159

Val-sans-Retour 35, 169-71, 180
Vita Merlini 12-14, 15, 23, 35, 47
Vivian 16-17, 18, 27, 32, 35-6,
  37, 54, 56, 81, 87, 154, 158,
  168-9, 172, 175-7, 180, 184
Vortigern, King of the British
  11-12, 16, 77, 93-4, 159

watercress 117, 119-20, 121-2,
  130
Wayland's Smithy 41
Welsh Marches 73-9
Welsh texts, medieval 15-16
Winchester 46, 50
  Castle 49
wolves 12, 30-31, 55, 115
women and Merlin 33-6

Yeun Elez 54, 186
Ygraine 12, 34, 39, 59

Zennor 59